Gaon Guide to Jewish Morocco

JEWS under MOROCCAN SKIES
Two Thousand Years of Jewish Life

Raphael David Elmaleh and George Ricketts

JEWS under MOROCCAN SKIES
Two Thousand Years of Jewish Life

Gaon Books
www.gaonbooks.com
Jews under Moroccan Skies: Two Thousand Years of Jewish Life.

For permissions, group pricing, and other information contact
Gaon Books, P.O. Box 23924, Santa Fe, NM 87502 or write
(gaonbooks@gmail.com).
        Manufactured in the United States of America.
The paper used in this publication is acid free and meets
all ANSI (American National Standards for Information
Sciences) standards for archival quality paper. All wood product
components used in this book are Sustainable Forest Initiative
(SFI) certified.

Library of Congress Cataloging-in-Publication Data

Elmaleh, Raphael.
Jews under Moroccan Skies: Two Thousand Years of Jewish Life /
Raphael David Elmaleh and George Ricketts. -- 1st ed.
        p. cm.
  Includes bibliographical references.
  ISBN 978-1-35604-47-1 (Cloth: alk.paper) -- ISBN 978-1-
935604-24-2 (pbk. : alk. paper) -- ISBN 978-1-935604-34-1
(ebook)
  1. Jews--Morocco--History. 2. Judaism--Morocco--History. 3.
Jews--Morocco--Social life and customs. 4. Morocco--Ethnic
relations. 5. Morocco--Description and travel. I. Ricketts,
George. II. Title.
                DS135.M8E55 2012
                964'.004924--dc23

                        2012001863

Table of Contents

Prologue

Of all the Islamic countries, Morocco is the most tolerant and respectful when it comes to people of different religions.

Moroccans, in general, are warm, friendly and very rarely judgmental about Western eccentricities. Most have an easy-going manner and a sense of humor. The people in the south of the country, Berbers mainly, are noted for their steadfast honesty and genuine hospitality. But, there are many contradictions in every day living, which results in a complex mosaic of life unique to Morocco.

The country's natural and geographical diversity caters for all tastes: sandy beaches, many completely isolated and deserted, miles of rugged mountain scenery, attracting trekkers, and, in some areas, the possibility of skiing in the winter.

Most foreign visitors want at least a glimpse of the desert and the experience of strolling through one or two villages set in tranquil desert oases.

The geographical diversity also calls for variety in the way people live, particularly in the rural and mountainous regions, where some towns and villages have kept many of their centuries-old traditions.

The major towns and cities, on the other hand, are making great strides to move with the times. One obvious sign is the increasing number of young women who are shunning the traditional *djallaba* for the latest figure-hugging Western fashions. The late King Hassan II summed it up accurately when he said, "Morocco is a tree with its roots in Africa and its branches in Europe".

It is a country that has inspired and attracted artists and photographers, who, no matter how often they return, never run out of material to inspire their work.

The historical richness of Jewish Morocco prompted the elders of Casablanca's Jewish community to form the Foundation for the History and Culture of Moroccan Jews and a Jewish Museum under the leadership of the late Simon Levy. Its task is to preserve Morocco's Jewish heritage, and it is housed in a former Jewish orphanage in the Oasis suburb of Casablanca. This is the Arab world's only Jewish museum. It was opened in 1995.

As one of the authors, I, Raphael Elmaleh, was also one of those who helped in the collection and transportation of artifacts and furniture from many Jewish sites around the country to the Museum. In the years immediately following the Museum's opening, the Foundation carried out a program of restoration of synagogues, and I had an instrumental role in supervising the work done on synagogues in the south of the country. This project keeps alive the memory of former Jewish communities for visitors from abroad, and it keeps that memory alive in the hearts and minds of the Jews of Morocco. Jewish tourists and visitors are often surprised at the richness of the Moroccan Jewish heritage and the involvement and interest of Muslims in preserving that heritage.

Raphael David Elmaleh
George Ricketts
Casablanca

Section One:

Brief History of Morocco

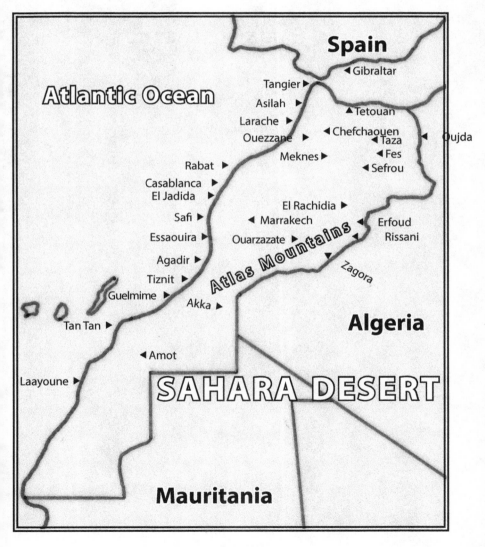

Map of Morocco

1

EARLY HISTORY

Romans up to 429 C.E.

Umayyad Arabs (690 to 786)

Idrisid Dynasty (786 to 985)

The Berber Dynasties:

Almoravid Dynasty (1040 to 1147)

Almohad Dynasty (1147 to 1244)

Merenid Dynasty (1244 to 1465)

Wattasid Dynasty (1465 to 1554)

Saadian Dynasty (1521 to 1659)

🌼Early Moroccan history begins with the Berber residents of the land, later joined by the Jews and Arabs. This unique braiding of tradition, religion, and ethnicity combined with its location as the contact point between North Africa and Europe makes Morocco a special place. The history and culture of Moroccan Jews can only be understood in the larger context of Moroccan life. Jews and non-Jews have had symbiotic relationships for centuries, if not millenia. Before the arrival of Islam, Jews had close relationships with the indigenous Berbers, that have continued into modern times, and similar ties were also developed with the Arab groups after they arrived.

The First Jewish Footprints

Jews have been in Morocco for two thousand years, and some think they came with Phoenician traders before the common era. Historical documents indicate Jews leaving Jerusalem after the destruction of the second Temple, and some of those Jews seem to have settled in Morocco.

The first Jewish traders initially settled in the coastal areas of the Mediterranean around Tangier and Tetouan, in the north, and Rabat, Essaouira (formally known as Mogador), and Salé, further down on the Atlantic coast, where they built synagogues and set up trading posts and workshops.

Later, other Jews migrated westward along the North African coast from Libya and Egypt, establishing settlements in strategic places along the caravan routes of Tunisia, Algeria and Morocco. And, with the march of time, trading posts and commercial contacts were established all the way to Senegal, Niger, Mali, Sudan and Mauritania

From early in the human experience, people have migrated, either to start a new life, to search for economic improvement, or to flee the horrors of violence and political repression. The recurring motives are political or religious persecution. All of these categories are relevant to Moroccan Jews and their history.

Many of the Jews who came to Morocco settled in the southern oases around the regions of Tafilalt and the Anti-Atlas Mountains. Both regions were once situated at the convergence of the ancient caravan routes between the northern frontier of the Sahara and Morocco. There were rich opportunities in the handling of gold and various other highly sought after commodities, passing through from sub-Saharan Africa. Other Jews chose to settle within the mountains of the interior but made sure to stay close to their lifeline, the caravan routes.

Some Berber tribes, the indigenous inhabitants of Morocco, converted to Judaism and became known as Berber Jews, a major force in the country before and after the arrival of the Arabs. In addition to conversion, marriage between Jewish traders and Berbers was common, and the Jewish community multiplied.

There is clear evidence (Hebrew inscriptions on tomb stones in the Rabat Museum) of Jews having lived prior to the Romans at Volubilis, the Roman settlement near Meknes.

The Romans were also known to have transported hundreds of Jewish slaves to Morocco, and a good number stayed on after the decline of the Roman Empire.

Jewish farmers were successful in cultivating the rich fertile land in the region around Volubilis and became wealthy from growing wheat and the production of olives and olive oil.

Islam arrives in Morocco

In the seventh century, the Umayyad Arabs brought Islam to North Africa. Their reputation spread like wild fire as they marched westwards, taking control wherever they went.

Thousands of Jews then living in Algeria and Tunisia fled to Morocco, where the influence and power of the Muslim invaders had not taken hold. Several travelled south to join their co-religionists in oases settlements in the Deep South.

In the late 600s a Jewish woman, Damia al-Kahina, a Berber queen or priestess, united the Berber tribes and led the resistance against the Arabs in Algeria and Morocco. A generation long struggle ended with Kahina being killed during a fierce battle in 690 and many of her followers converting to Islam. The newly converted Jews and Berbers joined forces with the Arabs in the invasion of Spain in 711.

By the end of the eighth century, the Muslims of the Maghreb (Morocco and Algeria) and Spain were building civilization centers that would compete with those of the Middle East, and Jews played an integral role in this process.

Around 786 C.E., Idriss ibn Abdallah, grandson of the Prophet Mohammed, settled in Volubilis (known to Moroccans as Oualili (Waleelee). The regional inhabitants acknowledged his lineage, and Idriss was proclaimed sultan. As Idriss I, he made Volubilis his capital and, on his orders, Jews were forced to contribute to his coffers, and some converted to Islam. Shortly before his death, he moved his capital to a site located in the present day quarter of *el-Andalus* in Fes, starting a small settlement that was to grow into one of Morocco's most important cities.

Idriss I died at a young age, said to have been poisoned by representatives of the Abbasid caliphate in Baghdad, who resented his moves to break away from under their direct control.

Idriss II (791-828), respecting the wishes of his father, completed the creation of the city of Fes (Fes el-Bali), said to be on a site that had once been inhabited by a Jewish tribe. Idriss encouraged thousands of Jews, in particular those who had fled from the tumultuous conditions in Spain, to come and work in his new city. So many heeded the call that Fes became known as the City of Jews.

Although the Jews and Muslims lived in close proximity, Idriss placed restraints on the Jews, citing *Sharia* or Islamic Law. Under various interpretations of the Pact of Omar, Jews, and other non-Muslims, were classed as *Dhimmis–ahl al-Dhimma* (People of the Book), required to pay a special head tax (*dhimma*), live in separate areas and wear identifying clothing. These rules were often altered, depending on the policy of the Muslim ruler and the political or economic conditions of the time.

In addition, they were expected to follow strict guidelines: no sexual relations or marriage with a Muslim. It was forbidden to speak ill of any aspect of Islam, especially, the Prophet Mohammed and the Koran. There was to be no involvement in the conversion of a Muslim to another religion, nor the use of arms against a Muslim. Breach of any of the restrictions could result in harsh punishment. Despite the strict rules, Idriss allowed the Jewish culture to develop, and traders and businesses prospered.

Throughout Morocco's past, Muslim rulers varied in their relationships with the Jews. Some applied harsh restrictions on the Jews, but others gave preferential treatment and protection. Some levied the payment of high taxes. Certain rulers even went as far as entrusting and appointing Jews as diplomats, ministers, counsellors and financial advisors. Moulay Ismail (1672-1727), for one, surrounded himself with Jewish intellectuals and advisors, who influenced him in matters of governance. Several sultans, it has been said, had beautiful young Jewish women in their harems.

In contrast, one Almohad sultan, Yacoub al-Mansour, i.e. the Victorious, (1184-1199) forced Jews to go barefoot and wear the *shikla*, a special identifying sign, as a punishment for pretending to embrace Islam. This policy caused many Jews to be physically abused.

The Almohads, a Berber tribe from the region of the High Atlas Mountains, ruled Morocco and Muslim Spain during the twelfth and thirteenth centuries. Their mistreatment of the Jews was infamous: forced conversions, Jewish martyrdom and the routing of Jews from many areas of the country, resulting in hundreds of Jews fleeing from Morocco or choosing to settle in areas out of reach of Almohad influences.

Under the Merenid dynasty (the latter part of the thirteenth century), Jews were treated well. At one point in 1275, when a riotous mob attacked a group of Jews, the sultan took it upon himself to intervene. The Merenid rulers valued having Jews among their intimate courtiers. They entrusted their own personal finances and that of the country to Jewish advisers.

The Sephardic Jews

In 1492, the Muslims lost their grip on Spain to the Catholic Monarchy. One consequence was that over 165,000 Spanish Jews were given an ultimatum by Christian King Ferdinand and Queen Isabella: convert to Catholicism or leave the country. Several thousand came to Morocco. These were referred to as Sephardic Jews (meaning from Spain in Hebrew) or as *Megorashim* (the banished) by the already established or settled Moroccan Jews, *Toshavim*. Others, not convinced Morocco was a safe haven, chose to travel to the Ottoman Empire or European Christian countries that accepted Jews.

In Morocco the established Jews were resentful of the newcomers, whose commercial and technical knowledge was superior. They brought skills in arts and crafts, such as weaving, thread making, dyeing, metal work and printing. The newcomers had knowledge of various European languages, which benefited them when working with traders from those countries.

Financial success, for some, came rapidly. They were recognized as playing a central role in the nation's economy and development, and some were duly rewarded with special rights and privileges. Others became government officials.

Megorashim very quickly rose to dominate the communities where they lived. Fes became their spiritual center, and Jewish laws on marriage, divorce and inheritance in Morocco came to be based on Judeo-Spanish traditions. The Spanish Jews saw the *Toshavim* as being backward culturally and less intellectual. There were also differences in the way they practiced religion, from the way they presented the *Ketouba*, wedding contract, to the ritual slaughter of animals. In many instances, *Megorashim* and *Toshavim* were forbidden to intermarry. As a consequence, both segments of the Jewish community are said to have lived a separate way of life for more than four centuries. Inevitably, the separation and differences caused tensions that sometimes led to feuding and bad relationships between the communities.

The Jewish and Muslim refugees from Spain in 1492 were responsible for introducing Andalucian music to Morocco. It was the music of Al-Andalus, Muslim Spain, and Jewish musicians were among those who performed in the royal courts of Cordoba and Granada. The custom was later repeated in the royal households in Morocco after 1492.

The Portuguese Occupy Morocco

The Portuguese became interested in establishing trading posts at strategic points along the Atlantic and Mediterranean coasts of Morocco in the second half of the fifteenth century. By the sixteenth century the Portuguese occupied several coastal towns: Mogador, now called Essaouira, Asilah, Tangier, Safi, and Mazagon, known as El Jadida today, Anfa, later becoming Casablanca and Tetouan among others.

Before long, they had constructed a series of fortress towns, surrounded by fortified walls and bastions, most of which can still be seen today. Jewish merchants, intermediaries and translators, especially those with Spanish origins, worked hand in hand with the Portuguese, who were frequently Jewish *conversos* or *anusim*.

The Portuguese brought the cultivation of sugar cane back from sub-Saharan Africa and introduced it to Morocco. It became a major cash crop with exports to Europe, and Jews played a significant role in the new industry. Within decades it would be taken to the Caribbean, transforming the face of the Americas.

The Portuguese were defeated in 1578 at the Battle of the Three Kings, fought near Ksar El Kebir, south of Asilah. Later in 1769, the Moroccans won back El Jadida. The Portuguese presence in Morocco ebbed as the Alouite kings established control over the country.

17

Portuguese Cistern in El Jadida
Photo by Vanessa Paloma Elbaz

2

Alaouite Dynasty

* Al-Rashid (1666–1672)
* Moulay Ismail Ibn Sharif (1672–1727)
* Abu'l Abbas Ahmad II (1727–1729)
* Abdallah (1729–1736)
* Mohammed II (1736–1738)
* Al-Mostadi (1738–1743)
* Abdallah (1743–1757) (again)
* Mohammed III (1757–1790)
* Yazid (1790–1792)
* Slimane of Morocco (1792–1822)
* Abderrahmane (1822–1859)
* Mohammed IV (1859–1873)
* Hassan I (1873–1894)
* Abdelaziz (1894–1908)
* Abdelhafid (1908–1912)

Under French Protectorate (1912–1956):
* Yusef (1912–1927)
* King Mohammed V (1927–1961), changed title of ruler from Sultan to King in 1957. Deposed and exiled to Corsica and Madagascar (1953–1955)
* Mohammed Ben Aarafa, Imposed by the French (1953–1955)

Independence (1956 to present):
* King Mohammed V (1955–1961)
* King Hassan II (1961–1999)
* King Mohammed VI (1999–Present)

In 1660 the first of the Alaouite rulers, Moulay er-Rachid, became king. The Alaouites are originally from the Middle East and are descendents of the Prophet Mohammed. After arriving in Morocco, they settled in the southern oasis town of Rissani. There are suggestions that Jews living in Taza (near Fes) gave financial assistance to support Moulay er-Rachid's bid to become ruler of the kingdom.

When Moulay Ismail, a later Alaouite sultan, decided to make his capital in Meknes, the Jews asked for and were given protection. They also requested a piece of land where they could live in relative peace. The Sultan designated an area of land for them near the royal palace and the storage depot where he kept his stockpile of the precious commodity of salt, which he owned and entrusted to them to sell and manage. They built a Jewish quarter, *mellah*, which included the salt depot, and, for reasons of security, surrounded it with a high wall, together with a gate.

During the reign of Moulay Mohammed ben Abdallah (1759–1790), grandson of Moulay Ismail, the Jews gained influence, both economically and politically. Mogador (known today as Essaouira) was established as a principal trading and fishing port, with the Jewish community outnumbering the Muslims.

Between 1790-1792, resentment toward the Jews grew, and after the death of Moulay Mohammed, many *mellahs* were attacked and looted, resulting in a number of fatalities and hundreds of injured among the Jewish inhabitants. The real culprit, though, was Moulay Mohammed's son, Moulay al-Yazid.

While waiting in the wings for his turn to rule, he had asked Jewish businessmen of Tetouan for a loan, which they had refused. On taking power, al-Yazid inflicted revenge on them, sending in the military, to attack the Jewish community, both killing and raping. These attacks spread to other towns and cities across Morocco. The prominent Jews who had served his father were rounded up and hung upside down outside the walls of Meknes.

Many of the Muslim elite gave sanctuary to the Jews by concealing them in their homes. This act of defiance inflamed Sultan al-Yazid. To extract revenge, thousands of Muslims were called together to the Great Mosque for prayer, and once inside he had them killed.

In the nineteenth century successive Alaouite sultans permitted Jews to improve their living conditions, as well as places of work and worship but always within the *mellahs*. Jewish life returned to a degree of normality, and Jews actually thrived in some cases.

Hassan II Mosque
One of the World's Largest Mosques
and the World's Tallest Minaret
Casablanca
Photo by Ron Hart

3

France and Spain
in Morocco

1860 -- Spain occupies Tetouan

1907 -- France occupies Casablanca

1912 -- Treaty of Fes
(Making Morocco a French Protectorate)

1956 -- Moroccan Independence
from France and Spain

In 1860 Morocco's neighbor, Spain, invaded the north, and took control of the town of Tetouan. The Jewish community developed good political and business relations with the Spanish occupiers, but two years later, Tetouan was back under the control of the Moroccan king, who eventually expanded control over most of the northern part of the country, including the Rif Mountains.

With every change in government, Jews felt vulnerable and feared reprisals by the Muslims. European consulates urged the king to protect Jews, and some intervened by issuing foreign passports to Jews they considered to be important to their policies. The Europeans had a clear understanding of the important role the Jews could play in their goal of establishing economic and political influence in Morocco.

A *Dahir* (a royal decree) was made by the king, Sidi Mohammed, in 1864, giving Jews equal rights and protection under the law. It made the mistreatment of a member of the Jewish community a criminal offense. Some prosecutions were carried out, but there were instances in which the decree was not respected by corrupt governors and other government representatives.

Morocco as a French Protectorate

French military forces occupied Casablanca in 1907, and the Treaty of Fes was signed in 1912, proclaiming Morocco a French Protectorate. Troops loyal to the King revolted in Fes, leading to two decades of resistance to the French.

Fierce opposition to the French control of Morocco continued for years, and it was not until the 1930s, with the assistance of a few politically ambitious southern tribal chiefs, that the entire country was completely subjugated. Following pacification, the French began improving the infrastructure. New roads, a rail network and the expansion and development of major ports were given top priority. The French also constructed several new towns and created new industries.

Hostility to the French colonists intensified, particularly during and after World War II. The Moroccan resistance groups, now much better organized, carried out attacks on isolated and poorly protected French communities. Mohammed V, king at the time, called for the independence of his country and its citizens. Under pressure from Morocco's main allies, the United States and others, the French eventually relinquished control, and Morocco gained its independence in 1956.

French Colonialism and the Moroccan Jews

In the early 1900s, Jewish business families tended to align with the newly dominant European powers (France and Spain), speaking French and Spanish and wearing European-style clothes. Some even went as far as to abandon or disregard their Jewish traditions. The majority, though, remained loyal to their religious practice. Many of the better-off Jews abandoned the *mellahs* around the country and set up homes in the nearby new towns constructed by the French.

The *Alliance Israélite Universelle (AIU)*, a Jewish educational organization based in Paris, had already set up schools in various Moroccan cities and towns, the first in Tetouan in1862. They were regarded as prestigious by most parents, who went to great lengths to have their children enrolled.

However, the mainly secular curriculum and attempt to Europeanize the children created conflict and frustration with some rabbis in the south, who advised parents not to enrol their children in the schools lest they lose Jewish traditions. Rabbis might have resented loosing their role and income as educators within the religious schools, but they recognized that the AIU would lead to a secularization of Jewish life.

The goal of the AIU was to "civilize" Moroccan Judaism, which, from the AIU's and French government's point of view, was steeped in superstition. The Alliance saw its duty as taking Moroccan Judaism out of the past and preparing it for the modern world. The French Government paid subsidies of up to 60 percent to the AIU. In 1960, the AIU schools were nationalized and came under the control of the Moroccan government.

Through the services of the French subsidized *Alliance Israelite Universelle*, Jews were offered free education and an opportunity for equality. The schools encouraged the Jews to learn French and drop their Arab and Berber names for French ones. They were also instructed to refrain from using the Arabic language.

A new elite group of Europeanized Jews began to separate themselves from the wider Jewish community. They dressed in European-style clothes, refused to speak Arabic and even abandoned their Jewish traditions. Worse still, this created a divide between Jews and the Muslim masses and led to resentment by the latter.

Their new found status, however, did not lessen the anti-Semitic feelings among the French colonists, who eventually took over much of the commerce, which had been the exclusive domain of the Jews. Unemployment became rampant among Jews.

When the French administration became unpopular among the general Muslim population, the colonial occupiers found ways to create divisions between the Muslim and Jewish communities to protect themselves by employing the colonial tactic of divide and rule. The same strategy was used to cause divisions between the Berbers and Arabs.

Throughout the 1930s *mellahs* were repeatedly attacked by Muslim rioters who saw themselves as scapegoats for the policies of the French. For example, the Muslims found it intolerable that the majority of minor administrative posts were given to

Jews, leaving qualified young Muslims unable to find work. Yet another even more unacceptable policy, in the opinion of the Muslims, was the promotion of Jews to officer status within the military.

Jewish Morocco,
the Rapid Decline (1947-1967)

From 1947 to 1948, the first Arab-Israel War caused tensions in Morocco. Violence broke out and Jews were systematically attacked in some towns in the north, resulting in Jews being killed or injured. As a consequence, emigration to Israel increased rapidly.

As the year 1948 ended, 270,000 Jews remained throughout Morocco, but the exodus gained momentum, leading to thousands of Jews having to be placed in tented transit camps until matters of transportation and documentation were settled. Food was distributed free, and nobody was allowed to work.

The policy of selective immigration by Israel and its agents was put into effect in 1951: restrictions were placed on those who were unable to pay their own travel expenses. Families accompanied by a mature breadwinner (aged 18 to 45) and in good health were placed on the priority list. If one member of a family was disabled or had a serious medical condition, every member of the family was rejected.

Two principal reasons were given for the restrictions. Firstly, the recently formed State of Israel was experiencing an economic crisis, while the huge influx of desperate immigrants from elsewhere was becoming unmanageable.

Secondly, it was decided that the Moroccan Jews, as a whole, were not in any imminent danger and, therefore, did not merit the same priority as Jews living in other Arab lands or those who had survived the horrors of the European Holocaust.

Morocco and Independence

Morocco became independent in 1956, and with it Jews were given equality with Muslims. A small number of Jews filled important ministerial posts within the administration, and some held managerial positions in industry. Nevertheless, for the majority of Jews, the old fears and feelings of vulnerability and uncertainty became even stronger. When Morocco joined the Arab League, aligning itself with Arab nations antagonistic to Israel, and by implication antagonistic to Jews, it contributed to that fear.

The Moroccan economy was in a critical state and unemployment and deprivation among the Jews was endemic. The pressure by the Zionist movement to move to Israel, coupled with the prospects of living in a Jewish state, fuelled the desire to emigrate.

Emigration, however, was limited by controls imposed by the newly formed Moroccan government. The party of the *Istiqlal* was in power and opposed any Jewish emigration that would strengthen Israel's hand to the detriment of their Arab brothers in Palestine. In 1956, applications by Moroccan Jews for the issue of a passport were mostly rejected, and the ban on Jewish emigration stood until the death of Mohammed V in 1961.

In response, a secret organization was set up by Israel's intelligence arm, *Mossad*, to overcome the obstacles of the restrictions. 35,000 Jews were secretly taken out of the country, and the majority went to Israel.

Following the Six Day War (1967), many of the more affluent and middle-class Jews concluded that there was no real future either for themselves or their children in Morocco as an Islamic country. Then, as the instability in the Middle East grew, people increasingly chose to emigrate to France or Canada rather than go to Israel.

The late King Hassan II gave a speech encouraging the Jews to stay and be an integral part of the Moroccan nation, and he continued to appoint Jews to positions in government. In 1991, André Azoulay, a Moroccan Jew and ex-banker at PARIBAS, a French bank, was appointed as one of King Hassan II's advisors, a position still held under the present king, Mohammed VI.

28

Mohammed V with Jewish Leaders
in Meknes
Photo courtesy of
Mordekhai Perez and Isaac Ohayon

Encounter of Cultures
Medina in Fes
Photo by Gloria Abella Ballen

4
Moroccan Diaspora

Why did almost the entire Jewish community abandon Morocco between the 1950s and the 1970s, a country where they had lived in large numbers for 2,000 years? In the late 1940s, the Jewish population was 300,000. However, by the early 1970s, that figure had decreased to an estimated 35,000. Presently, the official figure quoted is around 5,000, the majority living in Casablanca.

The question most asked by baffled Jewish visitors to Morocco is what extraordinary circumstances compelled such a vast number of people to sacrifice everything and leave the land of their ancestors and the land of their own birth within a period of twenty years?

To begin with, it is impossible to give one precise and satisfactory answer to this question. Furthermore, the range of reasons is so wide and varied that it would take almost a separate book to explain the subject in detail. But, it is possible to summarize a few of the principal causes.

Although mass emigration began with the formation of the state of Israel in 1948, the seeds of insecurity, real or imagined, among the majority of Moroccan Jews had been planted some years before. The European powers began destabilizing the centuries-old symbiotic relationship between Morocco's Muslims and Jews around the middle of the nineteenth century. Their efforts to take complete control of the country and the ongoing resistance to colonization left the sultans in a position where they could no longer guarantee protection for the Jewish population.

When the King's troops revolted in Fes in 1912 after the signing of the Treaty of Fes, which essentially surrendered the country to the French, they were unable to take revenge on the Europeans in their protected quarter, so they attacked the *mellah*, the Jewish quarter, instead. In turn, French troops bombarded the *mellah*, in their counterattack on the loyalist troops. Three days of fighting resulted in the death or wounding of 125 Jews and 900 Muslims. A third of the *mellah* was left uninhabitable, and 12,000 Jewish residents were left homeless. With the French military control of Morocco, the feeling grew among Jews that the king could no longer protect them. The bond between the Jewish and Muslim communities was breaking, and Jews began to feel mistrust toward the Muslims, which would later serve the objectives of the Zionist movement to encourage emigration to Israel.

Angry protests by international Jewish organizations about the attacks on the Fez community led to the French taking control of the administration of all Jewish affairs, further undermining the authority of the king. Although Jews were granted French citizenship in French colonial Algeria next door, Moroccan Jews were not.

A trickle of emigration to Palestine began in 1919, mainly from Casablanca and Marrakech. The port of Casablanca was the point of departure, with Marseille, France, the intermediary port on the way to Israel. For some emigrants, the motivation was the promise made by Zionist groups for a better life. While others left because of their religious beliefs, convinced that if they were buried in the sacred soil of Jerusalem, their bodies would not decompose after death but would remain intact until the arrival of the future Messiah.

Some 340 Jews, mainly families from Fes, left for Jerusalem during 1923. No doubt, many more would have left if it had not been for the French authorities imposing a requirement of 1,000 francs as a guarantee for each emigrant, so they could pay for their own repatriation should they wish to return to Morocco at some point. The large amount of money required was widely seen as a deliberate policy to prevent mass emigration.

August 1941-1942, the Nazi-controlled, French Vichy government passed laws discriminating against the Moroccan Jews: those living in the French quarters of the towns and cities were forced to move back into the *mellahs*. Jewish school children and students were expelled from French-run schools. Jews also lost their jobs with the French administration, and in many cases Jewish businessmen were not allowed to trade with the French residents in Morocco. Acting on behalf of the Germans, the French also registered property owned by Jews and conducted a census of the Jewish population.

King Mohammed V (1927–1961) protested the French policies and took quick action to protect the Jews, declaring that Moroccan Jews were his subjects and, therefore, under his protection. Also, as a sign of defiance, the King invited all the rabbis of Morocco to the 1941 Throne Day celebrations. Mohammed V refused the German demand that Moroccan Jews wear a yellow star, and he prevented the planned deportation of Moroccan Jews to Europe. While 200,000 French Jews died in Nazi concentration camps, Mohammed V saved his 300,000 Jewish subjects.

Mohammed V was responsible for the decree which is still in force today: the Jewish calendar or date was to be printed on the front page of the Muslim owned newspapers, in addition to the Muslim date. To this day, Mohammed V is greatly respected and remembered as the saviour of the Moroccan Jews.

In 1941-1942, the Nazi-controlled Vichy government of France enacted decrees discriminating against Jews in all of France's colonies, including Morocco. Quotas were established for the number of practicing Jewish professionals, doctors and lawyers etc, Jewish students were expelled from French-run schools and Jewish residents in European quarters were ordered to relocate to the *mellahs*.

Rumors abounded that increasing presence of German military officers and governmental officials in the country. Panic stricken, many Jews went into hiding or moved to areas that they thought were safe.

Although Mohammed V attempted to ease the harshness of the decrees, he was pressured to formally concede to some of the German imposed Vichy policies. However, he made it clear that the Moroccan Jews, under his country's laws, were equal to his Muslim subjects, with the right to his protection. Because of the king's strong stance and the pragmatic judgment of the then Resident General, the Vichy-controlled administration did not execute the discriminatory laws vigorously.

American forces landed in Morocco in 1942 and ousted the Vichy administration from the control of the country. However, the laws discriminating against the Jews remained in place for a further year, until pressure to remove them was brought to bear by the Jewish lobby in Washington.

Jews came to the conclusion that although the king had saved them from the tyranny of the Nazis and the European Holocaust, he had little power to protect them from anti-Semitic attitudes.

Poverty and lack of economic opportunity were high on the list of causes contributing to emigration. Early in the years of the French Protectorate, thousands of Jews lived and survived in the rural towns and villages in the southern part of the country among the Berber population, especially the Anti-Atlas, the Souss region and the Draa Valley. Berber Jews frequently had knowledge of agriculture, whereas others earned a living as craftsmen, artisans and small merchants.

Jews lost their traditional economic roles as French colonists pushed them aside and soon dominated the Protectorate's economy. Given the changes, thousands of young Jews living in the rural areas chose to move to the larger urban towns and cities in the north in search of work, in particular, Casablanca, Marrakech and Rabat. The subsequent migration caused chronic overcrowding within the urban *mellahs*, and the previous expectations of finding work failed to materialize. As an example, in 1950, more than 10 percent of Marrakech's Jewish population lived in deprivation, and the elders of the local community found great difficulty in satisfying even their basic needs.

By 1960, Casablanca's *mellah* had become the main destination for rural to urban Jewish immigrants. Only 39 percent of Jews between the ages of 16 and 65 were born in the city at that point. The more affluent among the local Jewish community organized assistance by raising taxes from certain foodstuffs, such as kosher meat, wine and *mahiya*, a distilled alcoholic drink made from figs and anise. The Jewish charitable organization, the American Jewish Joint Distribution Committee (JDC), also played a part in bringing relief.

Sanitation and hygiene became a top priority as the overcrowded conditions led to the rapid deterioration in the health of the inhabitants. Child mortality and trachoma, a contagious eye disease, hit the Jewish community badly.

When the State of Israel came into being in 1948 and the surrounding Arab nations vowed to defeat it, Morocco's Mohammed V declared support for the efforts of the Middle East Arabs. The war came as a blessing to the Moroccan nationalists, giving them a suitable cause around which they could unite the Moroccan people, without the French realizing they were the real common enemy and that Moroccan independence was the ultimate aim of the nationalists.

Tensions associated with the Arab-Israeli conflict sparked an anti-Semitic backlash, and the King had to step in and warn his Muslim subjects not to harm the Moroccan Jews, who had always been a protected community in the country and had always shown allegiance to the sovereign. Jews, in turn, were warned not to give support to the Zionist movement, which was gathering strength within Morocco.

Further tensions attributed to Israel's war of independence are said to have been responsible for the attacks in the northeastern towns of Oujda and Djerrada in the summer of 1948. The outcome of the pogroms was more than 500 wounded, 8 fatalities and up to 900 homes destroyed or made uninhabitable.

The lack of any appearance by the security services raises the question whether the French authorities supported the attacks although it is more than likely the French simply stayed in their barracks to avoid the conflict. The fear created in the Jewish community from these attacks encouraged many people to emigrate to Israel. These attacks confirmed that the French would not and the king could not always give Jews the protection they needed to function as a community.

In 1947 and 1948, the French ban on emigration to Israel forced the Israelis to operate a clandestine emigration network by way of Algeria and Marseilles, France. However, following the 1948 attacks in the northeastern region of Morocco, the French agreed to allow the Jewish Agency to set up a transit camp close to Casablanca, where formal preparations were made for emigration to Israel.

The Zionist movement was quick to take advantage of the fear and vulnerability of the Jewish community by reminding them of the Fes riots of 1912 and the recent attacks in the north of the country. Zionist leaders knew the fears of the Moroccan community and organized the 92,000 Jews who embarked for Israel in advance of Morocco's independence in 1956.

The Treaty of Fes was officially abolished in 1956, making Morocco an independent country. The new constitution guaranteed equality for all citizens, Jews and Muslims alike. Jews replaced the French in important administrative posts and in the management of major industries. Parliament had four elected Jews, and a Jew was given a ministerial post as Minister of Posts and Telegraphs.

In 1956, the *Istiqlal*, a right wing party, succeeded in winning the national elections, and among their demands was the immediate severing of all communications with Israel and an end to Jewish emigration, claiming it would benefit Israel and weaken the

Palestinian Arabs. They also called for the prohibition of Zionist organizations. The Government subsequently met all demands.

The transit camp in Casablanca was closed down, leaving up to 9,000 people trapped inside and stuck in limbo. The Presidents of the United States and France strongly condemned that action in a letter to King Mohammed V. The Moroccan government subsequently decided to delay the closure of the camp by three months. That was embarrassing to some Moroccans, so the Jews in the transit camp were quietly moved out and sent on their way to Israel under cover of darkness.

37

In the late summer of 1956, Mohammed V signed a decree preventing any Moroccan Jew travelling to Israel to return to Morocco. Even more serious, Jews were banned from receiving passports, which caused alarm throughout the Jewish community. Families already separated between Israel and Morocco were now completely cut off.

The Israeli secret service, *Mossad*, increased its clandestine network to support emigration by issuing false passports and paying bribes to corrupt government officials. This falsified emigration process was aided by sympathetic Spanish authorities. Although the ban on emigration to Israel stood until the death of Mohammed V in February 1961, Jews, like Muslims, expressed sorrow and grief at the passing of their king.

The month previous to the death of Mohammed V, an overloaded boat with forty-two Jews capsized off the Mediterranean coast, leaving no survivors. As part of their campaign to lift the ban on legal emigration of Moroccan Jews, the international Jewish organizations held the Moroccan government responsible. The resulting international outcry and negative publicity forced Morocco to reconsider its emigration policy toward Jews.

Mossad and American Jewish organizations held negotiations with the highest level of the government for an easing of Jewish quotas for immigration. On conclusion of the negotiations, Israel paid $50-250 per person for more than 100,000 emigrants in the years 1961 to 1964. It is claimed the money was deposited into a Swiss bank account.

Passports were soon issued, but the fact that Israel was the destination was falsified. Eventually, whole populations of *mellahs* were transported to Israel by air. Thousands of leaflets were distributed, declaring that Jews no longer had a stake in independent Morocco and Zionists who wished to go to Israel should not be kept against their will. Evidence was produced about young politically active Jews being arrested and tortured, and even dying, while in detention.

The resulting international outcry forced the new king, Hassan II, to begin talks with *Mossad* and the American-Jewish organizations about reopening channels for legal emigration. To save a backlash from internal opposition, it was announced that Israel was not the final destination. The total emigration of Jews between 1948 and 1967 totalled 237,813 people.

On arrival in Israel, Moroccan Jews faced discrimination. Considered to be inferior by the more educated European Jews, they were often refused employment. The new arrivals were described as "poor human material" and "the dregs of the *mellahs*". European Jews openly insulted Moroccan Jews, calling them monkeys, human scum and uneducated savages. "We didn't want them, but the new state needed to populate the land," said an Israeli politician.

In effect, they were treated like second-class citizens in the "Promised Land." In years to come many would completely abandon their North African origins and change their names to more acceptable European ones in order to succeed in the professions and business.

After 1964, the number of Moroccan Jews taking up the option of emigrating to Israel began to decrease; discouraging news had filtered back relating to the dire state of the economy in Israel and the discriminating treatment of Moroccan Jews as worse than second-class citizens. Bad housing and obstructions in entering certain fields of employment, especially the professions, were just some of the complaints.

A few of the more affluent Moroccan Jews chose to remain in Morocco and take advantage of the stability and the fairly buoyant economic climate. Fears about restrictions on freedom of movement had long subsided. They also took into consideration the difficulties in transferring their assets out of the country.

The Israeli-Arab Six-Day War (1967), however, changed everything. The Moroccan Muslims expressed their support for the Palestinians and the Arab countries in the Middle East. There was also talk of boycotting Moroccan Jewish companies and small businesses.

The Moroccan political establishment voiced their opposition to Zionist groups and their simultaneous support for Moroccan Jews. Tensions on the streets in and around Jewish quarters intensified, and Jewish schools felt the need to ask for protection by the police. King Hassan II went to great lengths to reassure the Jews that their security was being given the utmost priority.

That said, the old fears and insecurities, permanent and deeply embedded in the psyche of most Moroccan Jews, caused thousands to emigrate over the following four years. Between 1967 and 1971, the number of Jews fell by almost half from 60,000 to 35,000.

The majority of the less well off Moroccan Jews and those at the bottom of the economic ladder had by the mid-sixties already emigrated to Israel. Those Jews that had remained were living in relatively comfortable circumstances and were much better educated and informed. They understood the difficulties of the Israeli economy and were aware of the discriminating behavior shown toward Moroccan Jews in Israel.

Having been educated by the French-supported *Alliance Israélite Universelle* schools and exposed to French culture, many Moroccan Jews felt it more prudent and practical to emigrate to France and Canada.

The Jews in the north of Morocco, who had lived alongside the Spanish and knew their ways and culture, decided on emigrating to Spain and South America. In fact, the 1970s saw more Moroccan Jews choosing to resettle in Europe, Canada, South America and the United States, rather than risk going to Israel.

Currently, the Moroccan Jewish community consists of mainly upper and middle class families, who are doing well in modern day Morocco. This number includes a few poor and elderly Jews, who are monitored and supported by the social services run by the Jewish community. There are Jewish schools, clubs, and retirement homes in addition to synagogues. Casablanca has a full complement of Jewish services from kosher restaurants to bakers, doctors, lawyers, *shohets*, and *mohels*, as well as a Jewish Museum and a Jewish library.

Exclusive Jewish quarters or *mellahs* are a thing of the past. Jewish schools and synagogues (thirty-seven in Casablanca alone) still receive financial assistance from the Moroccan Government, and the Jewish community is given strong support from King Mohammed VI. Most Moroccan Jews today speak French, Hebrew and Arabic, and many of the younger generation have studied in European universities. Like most Moroccans, they look toward Europe for international trends.

The mass emigration to Israel was based on the climate of fear created by the unique set of circumstances in colonial and post-colonial Morocco combined with recruiting by Zionist organizations and the promises of better employment prospects in Israel. The latter assurances appealed to the economically marginalized Jews in the south, the Berber Jews.

These less educated people were influenced by the Jewish leadership, the Moroccan hierarchy, and Zionist groups representing Israel. The Zionists relied on the historical messianic sentiments of the rural classes to persuade them that the time to inherit the "Promised Land" had come.

In spite of the statements made by Zionists that they were responsible for saving the lives of Moroccan Jews, those who stayed on in Morocco have continued to maintain their culture, religious life and communities and have maintained a thriving smaller community. The more affluent and educated Jews, who chose to emigrate to France and Canada in the 1960s, have largely prospered in those countries.

41

Finally, one very important fact rarely mentioned is that Moroccan Muslims also emigrated in large numbers to find a better life outside of their homeland during this same time period. From the 1960s to the present, more than three million Moroccan Muslims have emigrated. Their main reasons, in some respects, are similar to that of the Moroccan Jews: the lack of employment prospects and (until the ascension of Mohammed VI to the throne in 1999) the political situation.

Group of Jews in Marrakech before the Diaspora
Photo Courtesy of
Mordekhai Perez and Isaac Ohayon

5

Contemporary Jewish Morocco

Contemporary Jewish Morocco
Urban, professional and international
Photo by Gloria Abella Ballen

Many of the Jewish families, who made the decision to stay in Morocco, live comfortable lives with successful businesses, mainly in international commerce, but occasionally there can be problems.

In May, 2003, suicide bombers made an unprovoked attack on four Jewish establishments in Casablanca. Since it was *Shabbat*, when most Jews remain close to home, no Jews were killed, but innocent Muslims died.

Soon after, the Moroccan Muslims organized a rally, and marching side by side with Jews, they demonstrated their support for the Jewish community and their disapproval of the culprits who had committed un-Islamic acts against fellow Moroccans.

The current king, Mohammed VI, appeared on national television and re-affirmed the monarchy's traditional protection of Morocco's Jews. Following the king's speech, government officials and the security services put in place a plan to give more protection to the Jewish community.

Jewish law is still very much respected and upheld. The government has a Jewish judge on its payroll to deal with cases related to members of the Jewish community. Each year on the day of *Yom Kippur*, the governors of the main cities visit the principal synagogues to read a personal letter from the Moroccan king, wishing the Jewish community well. In the Muslim holy month of Ramadan members of Morocco's Jewish community donate their blood to the national blood bank, as Muslims are fasting and not seen as suitable donors.

In 1995 the only Jewish museum in an Arab country was opened, and it houses a collection of Moroccan Jewish artifacts spanning several centuries. The museum is visited by Jews and Muslims, as well as people of other religions. The curriculum in state schools calls for every Muslim child to be taught about the country's Jewish history and about the Holocaust. As a result, groups of school children frequently tour the museum.

Visitors to Morocco can find kosher restaurants in Casablanca, Fes, Rabat and Marrakech. The restaurant in Marrakech is situated within a hotel complex some distance from the city center, but it does include its own synagogue. It is also possible for the visitor to enjoy the experience of eating in the home of a Moroccan Jewish family.

"Every cloud has a silver lining" is the expression of an optimist, and optimism is on the minds of many Jewish families that are returning to the land they left so many years ago. The improvements in the economy and changes in the regulatory practices that favor foreign investment are actually encouraging Jewish companies from abroad to invest, particularly in agriculture and services that will bolster tourism, which the Moroccan government is keen to develop.

For example, Israeli agricultural companies have long been established in the deep south of the country, growing crops for exportation back to Israel. This benefits Morocco's economy and provides gainful employment for local Muslims. Several tourist complexes have also been developed with significant Jewish investment.

In recent years Morocco has witnessed a substantial growth in the number of Jewish tourists visiting from the United States, Canada, and Israel. An estimated 30,000 and 40,000 Jewish tourists visit Morocco every year. Many have commented on how astonished they are to be greeted by Muslims with *Shabbat Shalom* while making their way to the synagogue for *Shabbat* services. What's more, Muslims have taken the initiative to sell palm branches on the streets to Jews preparing for the feast of *Sukkot* (Festival of the Tabernacle), another small, but significant detail that surprises Jewish tourists.

Many people, including a large number of Jews, who themselves or their families originated from Morocco, are buying into the market for holiday homes. If they cannot return on a permanent basis, at least they have the satisfaction of staying for a few weeks, or even months, in the year.

Another group not to be overlooked are the former residents who now return on an annual basis to honor their dead ancestors and venerated *tzadiks* buried in cemeteries all over the country. An elderly lady when asked why she came so often replied, "How can I face my deceased parents in the next life if I ignore them in this one?" Casablanca has seen at least three hundred new, high fashion retail units open in recent years, many owned by Moroccan Jewish families returning from France. The Morocco Mall in Casablanca has beautiful architecture and includes Parisian and other upscale international stores. It has been called the "most spectacular" modern shopping experience in Africa.

Due to the upsurge in anti-Semitism in France, the high living costs in many European countries and the negative effects of the European climate, a small trickle of former Moroccan Jews are returning to spend their retirement years in the country of their birth. One elderly gentleman is said to have confessed on his return that he had held on to the very shoes he had worn on his departure from Morocco forty-five years before. He was also heard to say "They carry the soil of the place of my birth." Could it be that these returnees have finally come to realize that their hearts beat with an African rhythm, and not the one they tried with great effort to adopt while living all those years abroad?

Moroccan security is stringent and entry points to the country are thoroughly controlled. The presence of the security services, such as the national police force, is visible wherever you go. Private security firms have had an increase in their manpower, with security guards posted at all public buildings, shopping malls, large stores and, just to reassure tourists and foreign visitors, hotels and tourist venues.

Jewish tourists and visitors to Morocco will find that the majority of Moroccans are law-abiding and extremely tolerant of other religions, especially since they have lived side by side with Moroccan Jews for two thousand years. Jewish tourists can engage an officially registered guide, who is on call twenty-four hours a day. Larger organized tour groups can request a security escort in the major towns and cities. The security arrangements are low-key and unobtrusive, and a request is never refused.

Author Raphael Elmaleh with Torah
Photo by Yehuda and Nurit Patt

Bima
Jewish Museum in Casablanca
Photo by Vanessa Paloma Elbaz

6

The Moroccan Jewish Museum:
Guardian of Jewish Heritage

The Moroccan Jewish Museum
(Musée du Judaïsme Marocain)
81, Rue Chasseur Jules Gros, Oasis,
Casablanca
Telephone – (212) 22 99 49 40
Fax – (212) 22 99 49 41
Email–fondationmusée@yahoo.fr
Web site – casajewishmuseum.com
Hours – Monday-Friday, 10am – 6pm
(Sundays by appointment)

A short taxi ride from the center of Casablanca to the quiet suburb of Oasis brings the visitor to the Moroccan Jewish Museum, the only Jewish museum in an Arab country. The building was built in 1948 to house orphaned Jewish children. When emigration to Israel grew to a rapid pace, there was no further need for the orphanage, so, the building was closed and the remaining children sent to Israel. At the end of the 1970s, the building was reopened and functioned as a *yeshiva*, a religious school, until its closure in 1985. It then remained empty for a number of years.

Confronted by the fact that so many Jewish sites were being lost as people migrated out of the country, community leaders decided that the Jewish heritage had to be preserved. Serge Berdugo, Boris Toledano and others formed the "Foundation for the History and Culture of Moroccan Jews". Simon Levy, a history professor and former political activist, was appointed as its first Secretary-General.

The former orphanage was chosen as the site to create a permanent home for the identification and collection of Jewish artifacts. On completion of alterations and modernization, under the supervision of a Moroccan Jewish architect, the museum opened to the general public in 1995. The exhibits give an interesting and educational insight into the history, religion, customs and daily life of Jews in the context of Moroccan society.

For instance, two rooms are given over to displaying the complete contents of two synagogues. One, which was originally located in the *mellah* of Meknes, *Slat-L-Khadra* (The Green Synagogue), dates from the eighteenth century. The other, the 1930s *Synagogue Pariene*, was brought from the town of Larache, north of Rabat.

To date, the museum has collected 1,000 ethnographic pieces such as everyday religious and domestic objects: Torahs, work tools, a *mahiya* brewing still, Moroccan Hanukkah lamps, exquisitely made brooches and clasps, clothing and furniture. The oldest object, a tombstone, dates from the fifteenth or sixteenth century. Prior to the French Protectorate, the Jews were responsible for minting the country's coinage, and the museum owns a small collection. On the walls of the hallway hang exhibits of photographs and paintings depicting daily life and Jewish leaders.

Restoration and research play an integral and ongoing part of the Foundation's work. Since its conception, restoration work has been carried out on synagogues in Fes, Meknes, Tangier and Tetouan, not forgetting those in former settlements and small villages in the south of the country, home to the Berber Jews. Some forty crates of documents collected from unused synagogues sit in storage at the museum, awaiting study and analysis, but a lack of funds has hampered bringing an expert to study and classify them.

The administration of the museum relies on financial assistance from business people in the local Jewish community and admission receipts at the door. Financing its operation has been an ongoing issue. The heritage of the Moroccan Jewish community is important to save and preserve, and the heritage that has been kept alive for centuries is now preserved in this unique museum.

The museum also caters to scholars of Jewish history, and there is easy access to a document library, a video library and a photographic library. The Curator and staff are always on hand to give a warm welcome and provide guided tours. Also on offer are sponsored seminars and conferences on Moroccan Jewish history and culture. Group visits can be arranged and conducted in Arabic, French, English and Spanish.

Witnesses to the Past:
Memory and Jewish Heritage[1]

Solica

Solica, an elderly Moroccan Jewish woman, who was not quite
sure of how old she really was, kindly agreed to be interviewed   51
at her home in Agadir in 1995. It is vital for scholars and other
interested parties to have this record about how Moroccan Jews
conducted their daily lives in the past from informants who lived
the experience.

Originally a resident of the *mellah* in Taroudant, as were the
previous generations of her family, Solica recounted how well the
relations were between the Jewish and Muslim inhabitants of the
town. (The Muslims were mostly Berber, as were the Jews). The
Jewish population was around 10,000 until the time of the French
Protectorate. Poverty was common for the majority of Jews. The
American Jewish Joint Distribution Committee (JDC) distributed
food and medicines to the elderly and the poorest of the poor.

It was normal to exchange visits for the various religious
feasts; the Jews shared their food with their Muslim guests,
and Muslims attended Jewish events, especially weddings, in
which the better-off families could afford elaborate costumes.
In contrast, Jews were unable to eat at Muslim feasts because
of the rules governing non-kosher food. It was the custom, for
marriage ceremonies to last seven days, in contrast to today's
"quickie" ceremonies, which only last three days.

If a Jew or Muslim got sick, there was an assortment of
remedies used: herbal treatments, faith cures and the belief in the
healing powers of the water from certain underground springs,
called *aïn* or "spring" in Hebrew. Both groups also used the
facilities of the town's clinic and hospital. In the case of Jews, more
serious illnesses required a special blessing from the local rabbi.

---

1   Taped copies of the interviews reported in this book are
available at the Jewish Museum in Casablanca.

Under the French Protectorate, relations between the Jewish and Muslim communities remained good, unlike the difficulties faced by the Jewish communities in the north of the country. During the 1960s, there was a lot of talk among Jewish families about moving to Israel. By 1967, practically all of the Jewish community had left Taroudant.

The elderly lady told how she had discussed the move with her then husband. However, because her five young children, three boys and two girls, were attending one of the two *Alliance Israélite Universelle* schools, she was reluctant to disrupt their education. Her husband tried to convince her to go with him to Israel but without success.

Later, when the two schools had to close due to the low number of attendance, the family moved to Agadir. In order to support the family, her husband went back and forth to Taroudant, where he had agricultural land. He, sadly, died a few years later. Finally, once the children had finished their education, the boys went to live and work in France while the girls stayed in Morocco.

Assaraf

The Assaraf family lived in Inezgane, formerly a small trading post, but now a busy commercial town between Agadir and Tiznit. The interviewee was a Jewish man sixty-six years old. He had a long white beard and his facial characteristics and dark complexion defined him as being of Berber origin. He was born in 1929 and brought up in the oasis town of Akka, which lies on the edge of the Sahara Desert, southwest of Tata. He had no formal education and did not learn Hebrew, but, as a child, attended readings of the Torah given by the local rabbi. The *Alliance Israélite Universelle* opened a school in the 1930s, solely for the education of the local Jewish children. Akka's first state-run school did not come about until 1974, long after the exodus of most of the Jews.

The man's mother was strictly observant and fasted frequently. She always said she was preparing for the next life and claimed she was only passing through this world. His father and uncle arranged his marriage when he was sixteen to a young girl of fourteen. And, in line with the customs of the day, there was no contact between the couple until the day of the wedding ceremony.

His wife subsequently gave birth to five children, three boys and two girls. He supported his family with a business that grounded wheat into flour and also by brewing and selling *mahiya*, the alcoholic drink distilled from figs and anise. Later, he sold textiles.

Like so many other Jewish children, his sons migrated to France after finishing their education. One daughter got married and lives in Casablanca. At the time of the interview, the other daughter was engaged to be married and was preparing to join her future husband in France.

There were two synagogues in Akka, one large and one small, the latter constructed by his uncle. As the larger synagogue was more established and had a larger attendance, the man said he continued to be part of the congregation. The poorer members of the community received assistance from the wealthier people, partly in the form of bread and eggs that were regularly distributed. Meals were shared on *shabbat* and other religious occasions and feasts.

Two hundred and fifty Jewish families, all Berber, lived in close harmony with their Muslim neighbors, and the differences in culture and religion were respected by the two communities. Several Jewish men worked as tailors, shoemakers and saddle makers. Akka was also renowned for its expertise in designing jewelry and its manufacture. People travelled for days from far away places to bring their gold and silver to be made into objects of beauty.

The wealthier Jews owned land, which was bought from the Muslims, but rarely worked it themselves. In some instances, the land was rented to the Muslims, who cultivated it, and later gave a percentage of the harvest to the Jewish landowner. Other Jews rented or "borrowed" land from the Muslims. To "borrow" the land, (the interviewee's expression), they would pay a large sum of money in advance, employ Muslims to cultivate it, then, at a later date, the land would be returned to its rightful owner. Another example of the enterprising skills of the Jews was when a Jew rented a cow to a Muslim. There was an agreement that the Jew would take possession of the first calf.

He told of a rabbi who came from Israel to Akka a few hundred years ago to collect money. The story is told that he hit a stone with a stick, after which water came gushing from the ground. One day the rabbi instructed his followers to build a compound around their settlement, in reality, creating a walled *mellah*. The rabbi later died and was buried in Akka, and he was later pronounced a *tzadik*.

To this day, Jewish and Muslim pilgrims come to drink from the spring, the *aïn* in Hebrew. Others ask for improvements to their financial circumstances. Young women with fertility problems also visit the site; others come with requests for assistance in finding a good husband. There are reports that an American Jewish woman who visited the rabbi's grave was cured of a long, debilitating illness.

The community shrank drastically when the majority left for Israel in the 1960s. The desire to live in a Jewish state was given as the main reason for leaving, even though, most had everything they needed in Akka. Reluctant to leave Morocco, the interviewee moved to Inezgane with some members of his family, built a new home, and set up a business in textiles. There were already some Jewish families in Inezgane.

At the time of the interview, the elderly man still had ownership of land in Akka, which he rented to Muslims and received a percentage of the harvest. The way it had been done for hundreds of years. He talked about the frequent visits to family in Israel, where he felt more comfortable being a Jew. The long conflict between the Israelis and the Palestinians, however, prevented him from realizing his dream of living permanently in Israel.

He also mentioned regular visits to a brother, who was still living in Guelmime, often referred to as the gateway to the Sahara. His brother had a license to sell alcohol in his small shop. Alcohol licenses are only issued to Jews and Christians. Despite this fact, Muslims get around the regulations by buying the license from a non-Muslim license holder.

Sarah

Sarah was born in the predominately Berber town of Tiznit, which is south of Agadir, and has lived there for most of her life. Her father came to Tiznit from Essauoira. Her mother and grandmother originated from a small village in the region of Tiznit, which had some Jewish inhabitants. Both Sarah's mother and grandmother later moved to Tiznit. Sarah's mother got married while still a young girl. It seems the grandmother had a large influence on the way Sarah was brought up, including not permitting her to attend the local school.

According to Sarah, there were around 20,000 Jews living in Tiznit before the call came for them to move to Israel. Most Jews lived in one of two *mellahs*, namely Ouezzane and Äit Oufrane. Relations between the two *mellahs* were good, and the rich and poor lived side by side. The principal source of employment came from working with gold and silver to make jewelry. Sarah also said the Jews bought land from the Muslims to build their houses.

She remembered the weddings when everyone was welcome to partake in the festivities. The gifts included trays made of gold and silver, displayed on long tables. Many guests brought large coned-shaped blocks of sugar, indicating future prosperity.

"Leave your father's wealth here, and take the wealth of your husband." Sarah said she had heard these words so often that they were now inscribed on her brain.

Sarah was married at the tender age of eleven to a man old enough to be her grandfather. He was forty-six years old and had a business selling fabric wholesale. She brought eleven children into the world, but alas, only seven survived. All were breast-fed. Her children went to a Jewish school in the *mellah*, where Hebrew and French were among the subjects taught. Although many Jewish schools included Muslim students, this one did not.

If the children got ill, she never thought to take them to a doctor. Instead, she would use herbal cures. Other times she would resort to local belief practices. For example, when a baby had an upset stomach, she would first take a mouthful of *mahiya* and cumin and then spit it on to the baby's stomach. She claimed that shortly after, the problem was resolved.

When the time came to move to Israel, the Jews sold their property to Muslims. Sarah was upset to see her Jewish neighbors leave. However, her children were at school, so she decided to stay. Her husband wanted to go, but due to a series of illnesses, including diabetes, he was unable to make the move. He passed away not long afterwards.

Once they had finished their formal education, all her children departed for Holland and France. At one point, she joined the members of her family living in France. However, unable to adapt, she returned to Morocco with one of her sons, who suffered from mood swings. The son later commuted daily from Tiznit to Agadir where he was employed as a kosher butcher.

During the interview, Sarah said she had never encountered problems with her Muslim neighbors, who are fully aware she is Jewish. On one occasion when she was ill, a Muslim neighbor transported her to the local hospital.

A Note on Jewish Sites in Morocco

For those who make the effort, a visit to a Moroccan Jewish site can be both an emotional and spiritually uplifting experience. Many synagogues are still in use; others have been carefully restored;

cemeteries have shrines to miracle working rabbi *tzadiks*; and, there are traces of former settlements and, of course, the *mellahs*.

The four imperial cities, Fes, Rabat, Marrakech and Meknes have their *mellahs* close to the royal palaces, confirming the close link between the Jewish community and the rulers. A trip to the coastal towns of El Jadida, Casablanca and Essaouira (some Jews still use the old name of Mogador) will reveal just how much the Jewish traders and their institutions contributed to these cities.

On the Mediterranean coast in places such as Tangier, Tetouan and the Spanish enclaves of Melilla and Ceuta (conquered from Morocco) there is clear evidence of the closeness between Moroccan Jews and Spain going back 500 years. Further to the east, close to the Algerian border lies the town of Oujda. Being a border town, it would be inevitable that some enterprising Jews had decided on making a living from cross-border trading. Here, the *mellah* is still standing, though, now inhabited by Muslims.

Exploring the south of the country is a must for any visitor to Morocco, for this was the land of the Berber Jews. Most Jewish sites are in stunning locations, and all roads leading to them pass through breathtaking scenery: high mountain passes, semi-arid deserts and lush green oases. The local Berber people are exceptionally hospitable and friendly, like most Moroccans. Centuries of close association with Moroccan Jews with whom they shared similar languages and traditions have created a culture of tolerance and understanding.

As the visitor tours the country, the knowledge and experience gained about Morocco's Jews will be a gift to be cherished for many years to come.

A Note on Sites of General and Historical Interest in Morocco

Although of great interest and importance, Morocco has much to offer in addition to Jewish sites. The country is rich in historical buildings, as can be seen when visiting the imperial cities. Starting with the imperial city of Fes, which is the most ancient, the visitor can see the long historical and cultural association Moroccan Jews and Muslims.

It has the greatest collection of ancient royal palaces and riad-style houses, grand mosques (not open to non-Muslims) and extravagantly decorated *madrasas*, Koranic schools, which, for the most part, can be visited by all interested parties.

The city is divided into three distinct parts: Fes el-Bali (Old Fes), Fes el-Jdid (New Fes) and the French built *Ville Nouvelle*. Fes el-Bali calls for incredible navigational skills as you wind your way through the maze of narrow alleyways, some leading seemly to nowhere. The main thoroughfares are abuzz with the inhabitants going about their daily business as they have done for hundreds of years.

Around the country medieval-type kasbahs still exist. These are fifteenth and sixteenth century fortified towns, and many of them are worth visiting if only for their unique location, architectural charm and relaxed pace. Some are set in fertile valleys or on top of hills with views that will definitely take your breath away. Others are next to the open sea. Morocco is fortunate to have many kilometers of superb golden beaches. Several are isolated and most of the time completely deserted. The country can certainly claim it has some of the finest mountain scenery in all of North Africa.

The people of Morocco are what really makes the country memorable, people who welcome foreigners with genuine hospitality. There are few places in this world where a person will stop you in a remote region and invite you to take tea or even share a meal, regardless of their financial situation. Form a friendship with a Berber, and you have a friend for life.

Section Two

Jewish Morocco by Region

Presentation at the Jewish Club in Casablanca with portrait of
King Mohammed VI
Photo by Gloria Abella Ballen

7

Mediterranean Coast

Tangier
Tetouan
Ceuta
Melilla

❀ From the closest point, the distance between Morocco's Mediterranean coast and Europe is a mere fourteen kilometers (nine miles). Historically, the short distance across the Strait of Gibraltar allowed relatively easy access to foreign invaders from Europe, who in many ways have left their mark on the towns and cities along this expanse of rugged and, in certain places, beautiful coastline.

61

Moroccans also took advantage of the narrow crossing at Gibraltar to invade Spain and conquer it in 711 C.E., where they successfully remained until 1492, leaving a cultural legacy in the language, architecture, and life of Spain. Morocco's Mediterranean coast sees an invasion of a different kind these days, as thousands of foreign tourists arrive in Tangier weekly to discover Morocco and seek adventure in a country with so much to offer.

Tangier

To most foreigners, it is known as Tangier, but to the majority of Moroccans, when expressing their fondness, it is *Tanja*. In ancient times, it was called *Tingi*. Located at the entrance to the Straits of Gibraltar, the city, from the earliest of times, has been an important link between Europe and Africa.

The Jews can trace their association with Tangier going back thousands of years; the Phoenicians built a settlement and port at this location and worked alongside Jews, who were said to come from lands further east along the North African coast. Some archaeological evidence, small pieces of ceramics with *menorahs* dating back to the time of the Carthaginians, place Jews in Tangier following the destruction of the first Temple in 572 B.C.E.

The Romans later made Tingi part of their empire in the first century B.C.E., which also included the inland settlement of Volubilis, north of Meknes. Jewish traders were employed in the shipments to Rome of wheat, wine, olive oil, salted fish and fish oil. Large quantities of olive oil came from the region of Volubilis, where Jews owned olive groves.

Around 429 C.E., the Vandals crossed the Straits and occupied the town. It then came under Visigoths rule. At this point, the town's history becomes blurred for the next few centuries.

The town's strategic position, directly across the narrow strip of water from Spain, did not go unnoticed with the arrival of the Arab leader, Moussa ibn Noceir in 705. After capturing Tangier, he set up alliances with local Berber tribes. The indigenous Riffian Berbers, as they are called, have a long and proven reputation for being tough, fearless and staunchly rebellious. A large army was formed under the command of Tariq, also a Riffian Berber. It embarked from nearby Ceuta on the conquest of Andalusia in 711.

There followed a period when the town changed hands between various Arab rulers, who had to contend with the independent nature of Tangier's inhabitants.

In 1075, the Almoravids, a dynasty originating from the Atlantic region of the Sahara, took control. Under them trade links between Morocco and Andalusia grew to an unprecedented pace, and Tangier's Jewish traders shared in the resulting prosperity. Jewish traders and scholars also travelled without hindrance to and fro across the Straits. The country benefited from the economic and cultural exchanges, so much so that the period was dubbed, the "Golden Age".

The Almohads, Islamic fundamentalists with roots in the High Atlas Mountains, came to power around 1145. They expressed their contempt for the Jews of Tangier by obliterating the bulk of the Jewish establishments: synagogues and Talmud schools. It was a time of forced conversions in which Jews all over the country were forced to seek refuge wherever they could. Several fled through the Mediterranean ports to Christian Spain.

Ironically, thousands more came to Morocco to escape similar anti-Semitic violence being perpetrated in Muslim Spain.

Good fortune, however, returned to Tangier in 1274, after the Almohads had been ousted by the Merinids, a tribe from deep within the Sahara. The change in regime saw a host of Jews flocking back to the town.

Under the Merinids, the Jews were given preferential treatment; all commercial activities were entrusted to the Jewish traders. Tangier developed trade links with other ports in Italy, France and Catalonia, and exported goods such as wool, sugar, carpets and animal skins were exchanged for spices, textiles and various metals.

Following two battles, the Portuguese succeeded in occupying the town in 1471. Tangier then became part of the Portuguese chain of trading-posts up and down the Moroccan coastline. The Portuguese, together with the Jews, made the town and its port a great success. However, it was the Jews who travelled into the interior of Morocco in the role of intermediaries, organizing and seeking out requested commodities, later to be transported to the port in Tangier.

Thousands of Jews, who had refused to convert to Christianity, moved to Morocco from Spain and Portugal in 1492, and Tangier received a sizeable portion of the refugees. The event is remembered in the name of a local river west of the city, Oued L'Yehoud (River of the Jews), which comes to an end at a bay with the same name. It is the location where many Sephardic Jews came ashore.

In 1580, Portugal fell into the hands of the Spanish crown and Tangier was then ruled from Spain for the next sixty years. When Portugal regained its independence in 1640, Tangier came under its control once again. Some twenty years later, the town was given as a dowry by the *Portuguese Infanta*, Catherine of Braganza to King Charles II of England.

To show they were there for the long term, the British constructed a military garrison and produced a written statement or charter, which declared that the town had the same legal and political status as any other English town. The British presence subsequently attracted a good number of Jews to the town.

The Moroccan sultan, Moulay Ismail, an Alaouite ruler, tried to take possession of the town in 1679, but initially failed. Nevertheless, with persistence and his tactic of laying siege to all landward accesses, he eventually won the day.

The English were compelled to leave, but not before completely destroying the town and wrecking the port. Though Moulay Ismail could claim success in taking control of the town, the long siege had caused untold damage to its economy. In addition, the majority of Jews had left.

Nonetheless, Moulay Ismail managed to carry out some reconstruction; for example, the Dar el-Makhzen, Royal Palace. The town's economy improved further after 1725 when the sultan asked his treasurer, Moses Maman, a Jew, to assist in encouraging the return of the Jews. One of the incentives was the exemption from taxes, and, although some Jews later prospered, the greater part of the community remained in abject poverty. After Moulay Ismail's death in 1727, Tangier's economy declined catastrophically.

The Americans entered the scene in 1787. Two influential Jews were given the responsibility of negotiating and signing a treaty between the United States and Morocco. Under the treaty, Morocco was paid to protect American commercial shipping interests in the Mediterranean.

In 1821, Sultan Moulay Suliman gave the United States the American Legation Building to be used as the consulate. Morocco was the first country to recognize the declaration of the United States as an independent state. The original small building was later badly damaged during an off-shore bombardment in 1844 by the French. Evidently, they were upset at the Moroccan sultan's support for the rebels fighting against their forces in Algeria. The present larger building was constructed at a later

date and was in use by the diplomatic service until the beginning
of the 1960s. It now houses a museum.

From the outset, American consuls issued passports and
other documents to prominent Jews who cooperated with
American interests, placing them beyond the reach of Moroccan
laws. Also, as they were classified as *protégés*, they no longer had
to pay taxes in the country.

Toward the end of the nineteenth century and the beginning
of the twentieth century, Tangier was at the center of European
political and commercial rivalry within Morocco. Added to that,
the sultan's position was extremely tenuous and the country close
to bankruptcy. International espionage and smuggling were also
rife. The French expressed an interest in Tangier, which upset Kaiser
Wilhelm II of Germany, whose hostile reaction almost caused a war.

As the French and the Spanish carved up Morocco between
themselves in the early twentieth century, the Spanish occupied
the northern towns and the region of the Rif. The Europeans
settled their differences by creating Tangier as an international
zone, jointly administered by a Commission made up of twenty-
seven members, with seats held by Britain, France, Spain,
Italy, and America among others. The authority also included
Moroccan nationals, three Jews and six Muslims. However,
Morocco ostensibly retained its sovereignty by installing a *Naib*,
a representative of the sultan. The Jewish community at this
juncture was around 10,000. The *Alliance Israélite Universelle*
was already running two schools, first established in 1863.

Throughout World War II, the generosity of the Jewish
community was put to the test when they were asked to give
refuge to thousands of European co-religionists. The American
Legation also played a role in processing Jewish refugees fleeing
the Nazis and certain death in war-torn Europe.

In 1948, on the creation of the state of Israel, many Jews took
the offer to emigrate. The majority were poor with no prospects
of seeing a change in their circumstances in Morocco. Unlike
some other large towns and cities around the country, Tangier's

Jewish quarter was open and unprotected; in fact, similar to all the other districts or suburbs of the town.

Prior to the exodus, the town's gold and silver market provided untold wealth for a good number of Jewish traders. Many others were involved in the manufacture of jewelry, with rich and eminent foreigners among their best clients. Most import and export companies were run by Jewish businessmen. Jews also owned the warehouses dealing in herbs and spices, textiles and wines and liquor from all corners of the globe.

Tangier was finally handed back to Morocco when it became an independent state in 1956. The loss of the Europeans and the insecurities brought on by the demonstrations of Arab nationalism on the streets throughout the Arab world, caused fear among Morocco's Jewish communities. Emigration gained rapid momentum, and by the early1960s, the majority of Tangier's Jewish community had departed, mainly to Israel.

Between the 1950s and the late 1960s, Tangier attracted several of the world's rich and famous: wealthy eccentrics, Hollywood stars and starlets, writers, artists, rock musicians and unsavoury types with shady pasts. The city had a reputation as a place where every human vice could be satisfied. The Moroccan government purged the city toward the end of the 1960s by closing down the brothels and gay establishments, and by rounding up the "usual suspects" involved in the illicit drug trade and other spheres of international crime.

In 2007, the total number of Jews in Tangier stood at around 170. People in the local Jewish community socialize at the El Casino Community Center, which includes a restaurant, card playing tables, and areas to socialize. The community center is located in the *Ville Nouvelle* (New Town), on Rue de la Liberté, and has on display a copy of the *Dahir*, a royal decree signed by the sultan, Sidi Mohammed, (1864), granting Jews equality and protection under the law.

Tangier originally had twelve working synagogues in the Jewish quarter of the Medina, which included a Rue des

Synagogues. All are now closed. However, the Assyag and the Akiva synagogues have their entire contents intact. *La Sinagoga Nahon* (Nahon Synagogue), dating from 1570 was constructed by followers of Rabbi Nahon, who led his people to Tangier from Spain. The building has been lovingly restored by a generous Jewish family, with roots in Tangier, but now residing in Canada. The Sha'ar Raphael synagogue, out in the *Ville Nouvelle*, on Boulevard Pasteur, is the only synagogue in active use today.

67

Tangier has two Jewish cemeteries. The old Jewish cemetery is located on Rue du Portugal, opposite the American Legation Museum. Although there is a small team of caretakers, apparently, government employees, it appears that not much attention is paid to its maintenance; the site is overgrown with weeds, sometimes waterlogged, and some gravestones have toppled with time.

A number of gravestones possibly date from the fifteenth or sixteenth century. Gravestones were cut in flat slabs, with those graves belonging to a female carved with breasts and males left plain. This concept follows the custom of the Sephardic Jews (*Megorashim*), who originally came from Spain. Other graves are surrounded by a low metal fence and inscribed in English and Hebrew, a style more common to Europe. Several burials seem to have taken place in the 1950s. The modern Jewish cemetery is located on Rue Moulay Abdel Aziz, out in the suburbs southeast of the *Ville Nouvelle*. Finally, the elderly and frail are cared for by the Hospital Benchimol.

Tetouan

Looking back in history, the Phoenicians, Romans, Greeks, the Barbary Corsairs (pirates), the Portuguese and, ultimately, the Spanish have taken advantage of Tetouan's strategic position close to Morocco's Mediterranean coastline. More than two thousand years ago, Jews migrated along the North African coast to eventually settle in the area that is today Tetouan.

Over the next few centuries, they became skilled in the field of international trade, particularly in salt and ore of precious metals. What is more, they had the ability to speak multiple languages, a skill that was profitable.

Tetouan's existence can be traced back to the third century B.C.E. when it was known as *Tamuda*. The Romans built a fortified settlement there in second century B.C.E. and stayed for several hundred years. Tetouan became an important place in modern Morocco when Merenid ruler, Sultan Abou Thabit, built a palace in the town at the beginning of the fourteenth century.

An increase in trade with Muslim-ruled Spain and ports around the Mediterranean made the town prosperous, and some Jewish traders were successful in this trade. A few constructed grand houses with servants, employed from the poorer Jewish classes.

As Muslim and Christian powers competed for control of the Mediterranean Sea in the fourteenth and fifteenth centuries, Morocco's Merinid princes commissioned a fleet of ships and manned them with pirates, who for the next few years terrorized and robbed European commercial shipping. Their bold and audacious actions enraged the Spanish king to the point that, in 1399, the Spanish attacked Tetouan and razed much of it. Scores of occupants were massacred. At the other end of the Mediterranean, the Turks also used freebooters, who were sometimes Jewish, to harass Christian shipping. The English later used the same tactic against their competitors.

The Portuguese gained control during the fifteenth and sixteenth centuries. In order to protect their prize, they surrounded the town with defensive walls. The number of Jewish inhabitants swelled dramatically following the expulsion of Jews from Spain in the latter part of the fifteenth century. Good working relations between the Portuguese and Jewish traders brought wealth to the town.

In the seventeenth century, under Sultan Moulay Ismail, trade with Europe increased substantially. Tetouan's Jewish merchants were largely responsible for setting up trade agreements. Jewish influence reached an even higher level during the reign of Moulay Mohammed, and Jews were considered fundamental to economic and political life. European powers appointed selected members of Tetouan's Jewish community as consuls to look after their economic interests.

As described earlier (pages 19 and 20), life for Tetouan's Jews took a turn for the worse during the short rule of Moulay el-Yazid (1790-1792). The next sultan, Moulay Suleiman, (1792-1822) took steps to curtail the expanding European influence.

69

His successors, however, came under great pressure from the Europeans to step up economic activity. The Europeans also gave their Jewish consuls added protection by issuing diplomatic passports and declaring them their *protégés*, exempt from paying tax and immune from prosecution. This move allowed the foreign powers to interfere in the internal affairs of Morocco.

Spain was the first to react when one of its consular agents was executed, seemingly on false charges. Under the pretext of protecting its citizens, it sent an army 35,000 strong to invade Tetouan in 1860. While the Spanish were at the gates, local Muslims and the Moroccan military, accusing the Jews of collaboration with the enemy, attacked and looted the *mellah*. As a result, several Jews fled to Oran in Algeria and also to Gibraltar.

The Spanish developed good political and commercial relations with the remaining Jewish community. During the nineteenth century, many of Tetouan's Jewish intelligentsia of rabbis, writers, legal experts and scholars held a positive attitude toward secular education for the Jewish population. Prior to this period, most education had been Talmudic, with only the children of the very wealthy receiving secular education.

Financial assistance was given to the Paris-based *Alliance Israélite Universelle* in establishing its first school in Tetouan in 1862. Throughout the 1880s there was a major migration of young Jewish men from Tetouan to South America, predominately to Brazil and Venezuela. At that time the South American economies were growing, and by all accounts many Jewish immigrants found success there.

In 1912 the Treaty of Fes gave the Spanish complete control of Tetouan and the region of the Rif Mountains, and they made Tetouan the regional capital. The Spanish allowed the Jews complete freedom in all aspects of their religious, traditional and daily life. Freedom of movement permitted several businessmen to be involved in the smuggling of contraband goods.

General Franco had his headquarters in Tetouan, prior to the Spanish Civil War of 1936. It was in Tetouan that he recruited several Riffian tribesmen into his army in readiness for his planned campaign to take control of the Spanish mainland. In 1956, the Moroccan's finally won their long struggle for independence and the Spanish reluctantly had to cede Tetouan back to Morocco.

Forty-odd years of Spanish occupation have certainly left influences on the town of Tetouan. The locals prefer to speak Spanish as a second language rather than the French now taught in local schools and found in the rest of the country. A leisurely stroll through the town confirms the former Spanish presence: white-washed houses with protruding balconies, palatial homes embellished with Hispano-Moorish elegance. A smattering of pseudo-Spanish art deco is also still present. Order a coffee with milk (*café con leche*) in one of the many cafes and watch as the waiter pours in the milk from a jug as they do in Spain.

The *Mellah*. Tetouan's *mellah* was created in 1808 by Sultan Moulay Suleiman. The streets and narrow lanes, which more or less exist in their original form today, were constructed in a grid formation, rather similar to that of Essaouira, and most of the architecture has Portuguese and Spanish influences. UNESCO has added the *mellah* to its long list of World Heritage sites.

The Jews of Tetouan were known for their masterly skills and expertise in producing every variety of gold and silver jewelry and associated crafts. The original retail outlets and workshops, tiny boxes in comparison to today's high street shops and malls, are now owned by local Muslims, the majority Rif Berbers.

The *mellah* has one restored synagogue (not in use), Ben Gualid, from the first half of the nineteenth century. The synagogue is named after Rabbi Itzhak Ben Gualid, known to have been a forward-thinking modernist. He is credited with giving his approval to Tetouan having the first *Alliance Israélite Universelle* school to be set up in Morocco in 1862.

71

Rabbi Itzhak Ben Gualid Synagogue Tetouan

Photo by Gloria Abella Ballen

The Beth El synagogue, on Calle Luneta in the more modern part of town, is closed and no longer holds services. The cemetery, which is large and maintained by Spanish Jews from Ceuta, is located in the area of Monte Dersa, on the outskirts of town. Several tombstones are laid out on terraced ground, and in accordance with *Megorashim* traditions, those of women are engraved with breasts while those of men are plain and unmarked. Other tombstones have names engraved.

The total sum of today's (2008) Jewish community is estimated to be forty-five, mostly elderly. The good news is that the local Jewish social club is still in operation and many of the regular guests are local Muslims.

Spanish Controlled Cities

Ceuta and Melilla have a unique status in that they were not surrendered by the Spanish at the time of Moroccan Independence in 1956. The two cities are still controlled by Spain.

Ceuta (Sebta)

A strategically placed peninsula at the closest point to Europe, the peninsula of Ceuta, or Sebta as Moroccans call it, is a valued Mediterranean port. In ancient times, the Romans added the peninsula to their vast empire and gave it the name Septum. Septum later fell into the hands of the Vandals, who, in turn, were defeated by the Byzantines.

In 705 C.E. the Arabs, under the leadership of Moussa ibn Nocier, made an unsuccessful attack on the fortified town. However, by joining forces with Berbers from the Rif, success came a few years later, and the name of the town was changed to the more Arabic sounding Sebta. The Arabs next turned their attention to Spain, considered a much more significant prize, only a short distance across the narrow straits.

An imposing army, consisting mainly of Riffian Berbers, crossed the straits in 711 C.E. and landed close to Mount Calpe, later named Jebel Tariq (now Gibraltar) in honor of the army's leader, Tariq, who defeated the Andalusian princes near the coastal town of Tarifa. With Muslim rule now entrenched in Andalusia and in North Africa, Sebta became ever more important, particularly in commerce and trade. Specific information on how Jewish merchants fared at this time is limited.

From the ninth century to the beginning of the fifteenth century, the town remained under the control of Moroccan sultans, except for the period between 931 and 1010, when the Muslim Umayyad rulers of Cordoba in Spain seized it from the Idrisid dynasty based in Fes; 1010 marked the end of Umayyad rule in Cordoba. Under the Almoravids, who took contol of the town in 1083, ties with the Muslim princes in Spain were strengthened and Sebta prospered more than ever.

Several Jewish scholars from Andalusia passed through the port en route to Marrakech and Fes, and Jewish traders used the port on their frequent business trips to and from Spain. Morocco's economy was on such a high level that the period came to be known as the "Golden Age". Life, however, turned sour for the Jews of Morocco under Almohad rule in the twelfth century; forced conversions and stories of brutal behavior led to widespread fear, causing a large number of Jews to flee the country. Sebta became a much used exit point for the many Jews who had the means to escape to Christian Spain. Ironically, at the same time, several Jews came to Morocco to escape the anti-Semitic purges of the Almohad rulers in Andalusia.

As he had done elsewhere, the Almohad sultan, El Mansour, added some development to the town by constructing an arsenal and much needed shipbuilding yards.

The Merinids, after seizing power from the Almohads, took control of the town in 1273. Despite the years of continual bickering between certain princes over the right to govern the town, prosperity reached an unprecedented high. This success was due to the numerous merchant vessels from Italy and France and Catholic Spain making use of the port. The Merinids even managed to carry out a program of constructing mosques and madrasas. Jewish traders were given preferential treatment and encouraged to invest by paying low taxes.

The situation changed drastically in the fifteenth century when Muslim rule was challenged by the Catholic rulers in Spain. Taking advantage of the upheaval that followed, Portugal captured the town in 1415. Toward the end of the fifteenth century, Queen Isabella of Spain issued the *Edict of Expulsion*; Spanish Jews were given the option to convert to Catholicism or leave the country. A large number of Spanish Jews migrated to Ceuta, and most of the Jews in the town today trace their ancestry to that migration.

74   During a period of Portuguese dominance in this region during the seventeenth century, Portugal controlled Ceuta, later ceding it to Spain in 1668. During that transition, Moulay Ismail, the Alaouite sultan, laid siege to the town for twenty-seven-years (1674–1701), but failed to bring it back under Moroccan control.

Spain had long considered Ceuta as its sovereign territory and refused to cede it to Morocco in 1956, when it handed back the territories in the north acquired under the Treaty of Fes in 1912. They cited that Ceuta was never part of the Spanish Protectorate.

Spain's refusal to cede Ceuta to Morocco was accepted by the predominantly Spanish Jews of Ceuta, who were reluctant to relinquish their Spanish citizenship and potentially their way of life. During the late 1950s and the early1960s, when an independent Morocco restricted the emigration of Jews, Ceuta's Jewish community was instrumental in assisting Moroccan Jews to leave clandestinely.

In 2002 Moroccan troops occupied the small island of Perejil, a short distance from Ceuta, but were soon removed by the threat of Spanish gun ships, and the diplomatic intervention of the United States. The town's Jews fear a future escalation could lead to the outbreak of conflict with the Muslim community, mostly Berbers with Spanish citizenship, who make up much of the population.

Certain compromises and agreements to bring calm to the situation have been made between the two governments; many Moroccans living close to Ceuta have special dispensation to work in the town, such as housemaids and unskilled laborers.

Many others have been issued passes that entitle freedom of movement across the frontier. Most take advantage of such freedoms by purchasing large quantities of lower-priced items or tax-exempt goods, later sold at a profit after crossing back into Morocco.

Until fairly recently, Ceuta was administered from the province of Cadiz. Now it is officially known as *Ciudad Autónoma de Ceuta* (Autonomous City of Ceuta), with powers to collect certain local taxes and to take decisions on matters directly connected with the town's inhabitants.

Ceuta, presently, has a small Jewish community, mostly elderly. The majority of the young tend to complete their studies and take up employment on the mainland in the larger cities like Barcelona and Madrid, and rarely return to Ceuta. As a consequence, the Jewish population is dwindling, less than 300 in 2002 compared to 800 in the early 1970s.

Shabbat services are held at the town's large and modern Beth El synagogue. The Jewish cemetery is located to the east of the town in the direction of Monte Hacho and faces an islet known as Santa Catalina.

Melilla

Often referred to as Ceuta's smaller sister, **Melilla,** also a Spanish enclave, is situated on a peninsula much further to the east, jutting out on Morocco's Mediterranean coastline. Originally known in ancient times as Russaddir, the town began as a small trading-post run by the Phoenicians and then the Romans, who actually upgraded it to a Roman colony governed by elected local officials.

At the beginning of the eighth century, Moussa ibn Nocier led an Arab invasion which completely destroyed the town. The site then remained almost forgotten for the next two centuries until it was taken over by the Umayyad caliph, Abd er Rahman II, of Cordoba. The last vestiges of the Idrisid dynasty took an interest in the town around 1067, but were soon replaced by the Almoravids. Under them links to Sijilmassa, the then capital of the Tafilalt, and the caravan routes were quickly developed and expanded. The port, too, became an important gateway between Morocco and Andalusia, in Southern Spain. It was a period of prosperity for the town's Jewish community, who played a central role in its success.

The Almohads captured the town in 1142, during the country-wide conquests led by the sultan, Abd el-Moumin. The Almohad's reputation for the maltreatment of the Jews caused Melilla's Jewish community to leave, and many sought refuge in the interior of the nearby Rif Mountains.

After numerous attempts, in 1272 the Beni Meri, a southern tribe, managed to dislodge the Almohads from the town, a defeat which later led to the founding of the Merinid dynasty. Under the Merinids the Jews returned, and the port took on a new dimension with expanded commercial ties between various countries around the Mediterranean.

However, the turmoil following the fall of Granada, the last Muslim kingdom in Spain, to the Christian forces in 1492, badly affected Melilla's commerce, and the town went through a period of steep decline and became almost desolate. The Spanish, after very little resistance, occupied the town in 1497, and built a fortress town, Medina Sidonia, named after a duke reported to have been of Jewish origin, known as Juan Alonso Pérez de Guzmán. Spain has held possession of Melilla to this day.

The Jewish community moved into a small section of the fortress called *Barrio del Poligono*, and worked harmoniously alongside the new rulers, mainly as intermediaries, translators and commercial traders.

Successive Moroccan sultans, over the next few centuries, lay long-term sieges and blockades in an effort to remove the Spanish occupiers. The Alaouite sultan, Moulay Ismail, tried, but failed in the seventeenth century. The greatest effort was made by another Alaouite sultan, Moulay ben Abdallah, in 1774, with an army numbering up to 40,000 troops, but he also failed.

In the second half of the nineteenth century, the Spanish felt secure enough to start the development of the "new" town and also encouraged trade by declaring Melilla a free port, which benefitted Jewish merchants.

The Rif Berbers have made more than one attempt to seize control of Melilla. In 1893, they besieged the town. On this occasion, Spain only kept possession by sending 25,000 troops from the mainland. Troubles arose again in 1909, but this time the Spanish were better prepared. The rebels surrendered within a year.

The biggest threat came during the Rif War in 1921, when Abd el-Krim, leader of the Rif's rebels came very close to capturing the town. The war and hostilities ended when Abd el-Krim, with help from the French, was finally captured in 1926.

Further expansion of the town and port took place during the years of the Spanish Protectorate in Northern Morocco. With the exportation of such commodities as goatskins, beeswax and eggs and the importation of tea, sugar and cotton goods, business was brisk. Later, the port played an integral part in shipping lead and iron from the Rif mining industry. In 1936, General Franco made use of the port as one of his staging points to launch his rebellion against the government in Madrid.

A new class of *nouveau riche*, which included Jews, expressed their enriched status by building large homes in the modernist style of architecture, a style inspired by the work of the Catalan architect, Enrique Nieto. It continued in Melilla after going out of vogue elsewhere. As in Ceuta, Melilla has played a role historically as a place of sanctuary for Jews experiencing anti-Semitic persecution.

The ancestors of some of today's inhabitants came as a result of the expulsions from Spain in 1492. In 1535, another 1,500 Jews, fleeing an outbreak of anti-Semitism, arrived from Debdou, in the north east of Morocco. During the years of Nazi tyranny against the Jews in Europe, Jewish refugees were issued with Spanish passports and allowed safe passage through mainland Spain, and onto Melilla.

Hitler had planned to eliminate the entire Jewish population of North Africa, but General Franco refused to go along with his plans, as did Mohammed V in Morocco. It is one of history's ironies that a Muslim king and a Fascist dictator blocked the nefarious plans of a Christian tyrant and saved many Jewish lives.

78   An elderly Jewish woman, long settled in Melilla, spoke of the days when Franco was in power. His regime, with a reputation for being repressive and unpredictable, caused some wealthy Jews to move temporarily to Tetouan and Oujda in Morocco when they heard he was to pay an official visit to the enclave.

The woman's father owned two large boats and had a successful business importing tea from China. In World War II he feared the policies of the Vichy government that controlled the central and southern regions of Morocco. He especially feared the confiscation of businesses and property. In response her father signed over his business to a friendly Spaniard for safe keeping until he returned after the war.

The total number of Jews in Melilla was around 20 percent of the town's population. However, after the end of World War II, the size of the community began to shrink drastically as more and more Jews left for the Spanish mainland, and a few to Israel.

Venezuela had been a popular destination for local Jewish men before World War II. Several of them later returned to Melilla after making their fortunes and married local women. Some built synagogues, and one man donated the entire cost of constructing the town's Jewish Center, including a nursery school. Another man commissioned the construction of a road through the mountains in Morocco to make access easier to the tomb of a local *tzadik*.

Years of Melilla's tax breaks have made some of today's Jewish community wealthy. Several own second homes on the Spanish mainland in such places as the Costa del Sol, Madrid and Barcelona. In recent years, the Jewish population has stabilized and stands at around 600. Some young couples have made a commitment to stay on, with the result that the Jewish school has around eighty pupils.

There are twelve functioning synagogues, built and attended by extended families. One of the oldest and finest, the Yamin Benarroch, was built in 1921, based on a design by the Catalan architect, Enrique Nieto. The town has two Jewish cemeteries. The oldest is located just outside the walls of the Medina Sidonia. It dates from the time when the Jews lived within the old town; some graves go back as far as 1565.

The more recent Jewish cemetery is on a hill that looks over into Morocco. The land is shared by the Catholic cemetery. The graves are laid out on terraced ground and the tombstones are simple, with inscriptions in Hebrew and Spanish.

Melilla was once considered part of the province of Malaga, on the Spanish mainland. In 1995, it became an autonomous city with the title, Ciudad Autónoma de Melilla. Its population is made up of Christians, Jews, Muslims, for the most part Rif Berbers, and a small minority of Hindus. Most locals seem to agree that relations between the different religious groups are cordial and extremely tolerant. Though Spanish is the official language, Arabic and Taghifit (*Tirrifit*) are also in use.

As in the case of Ceuta, certain trade agreements between Spain and Morocco allow Moroccan citizens with the relevant passes to cross into the enclave to work and to do shopping. It appears very little is actually done to control the daily trade in contraband goods. Since unemployment rates are high in northern Morocco, the buying and selling of contraband merchandise from Ceuta is an important occupation for many local Moroccan families.

8
Rif Mountains

Chefchaouen
Ouezzane

❀T he region of the Rif Mountains, in the north of
Morocco, extends from around Tangier in the west to Melilla
(Spanish enclave) in the east, and from the Mediterranean coast
in the north to the Ouargha Valley at the southern end.

The indigenous inhabitants are Berbers, known as Riffians.
They speak Arabic and Taghifit (*Tirrifit*), a dialect of Tamazight,
the principal language of Morocco's Berbers. The towns and cities
in the coastal region are inhabited predominately by Berbers,
with a large section of Arabs. In the Jewish communities of the
north, *Haketía* (Judeo-Spanish) was spoken. It was a fusion of
Castillian, Arabic and Hebrew.

Since the Berbers and Arabs have integrated over the
centuries, it is sometimes impossible to judge by their physical
appearance which is which. However, thousands of Berbers live
and work in culturally specific social and language groups.

Jews came 2,000 years ago and settled along the coastline of
the Rif and have a long history of trading with the Riffians. The
Arabs arrived from the eighth century onwards, but never really
managed to fully subdue the tough and staunchly independent
Riffians living deep within the mountains of the *Bled es-Siba*.

Thousands of Sephardic Jews arrived in the region after the
1492 expulsions from Catholic Spain. Some chose to make a
new life in the small towns such as Chefchaouen and Ouezzane,
hidden deep within the folds of the mountains, where they
remained for generations until the 1960s.

Under the 1912 Treaty of Fes, the region became part of
the Spanish Protectorate. The Riffians, angered by the thought
of being dominated by an infidel Christian power, stood behind
their leader, Abdel Krim el-Khattabi, when he declared the
region as the independent, Republic of the Rif. He also called on
the people to take up arms against the occupying Spanish army.

Known as the Rif War (1921–1926), it was a war they might have won had it not been for the massive support the French troops gave to their fellow Europeans, the Spaniards.

When Morocco gained independence in 1956, the Riffians' stubborn resistance to full integration into the *Bled el-Makhzen* caused alarm in the Moroccan capital, Rabat. In 1958, the sultan, Mohammed V, sent the crown prince, Moulay Hassan, as Commander-in-Chief of the Army, to quell the unrest around the region. Several deaths and arrests occurred among the population. Although, physically restrained, Riffians still have a reputation for being independent. After the death of Mohammed V, Rabat took further revenge by holding back on investment in the region's infrastructure. The consequences for the inhabitants were catastrophic with massive unemployment.

The present king, Mohammed VI, ascended to the throne in 1999, and since then he has striven to reverse much of the region's past neglect. Investment in new infrastructure amounts to millions of dollars, particularly on the coast, where positive steps have been taken to bolster both tourism and commercial industries. Added to this, most towns and cities have undergone some restoration and beautification. Even so, the severe shortage of water resources within some areas of the mountains leaves a substantial part of the Rif as one of the least economically developed areas of the country.

Chefchaouen

Secluded deep within the peaks of the Rif Mountains, the small town of Chefchaouen, also known as Chaouen, is unquestionably one of the most picturesque and relaxed places on Morocco's tourist circuit. The name Chaouen, when translated from the local Berber dialect, means "the horns", and refers to the two mountain peaks looming high behind the town. Added together, Chef and Chaouen means "Look at the Horns".

Chefchaouen was founded in 1471 by Moulay Ali ben Rachid, not a sultan but an Alamiine, follower of a local holy man, known as the "Master of the Jebel Alam". The town's seclusion served him well as a base from where he carried out frequent attacks on the Portuguese occupying Ceuta and Ksar es-Seghir on the Mediterranean coast.

The town's economy increased significantly after the influx of Jewish and Muslim refugees who settled in the town, following the expulsions from Christian Spain in 1492. The Jews moved into the area southwest of the *kasbah*, where the main *souks* are situated today. Muslims and Jews built the town in a reconstruction of a typical Andalusian village: narrow lanes and alleyways, tiled roofs, small interior courtyards and bolt-studded wooden doors. Land ownership for cultivation, sheep farming, weavers and wool merchants were the main occupations taken up by Jews.

The Saadian dynasty took an interest in the town around 1561, after which the production of wool for exportation was increased. The local Jewish merchants and farmers controlled the majority of transactions. Moulay Ismail (1672–1727), in order to assert his authority on the troublesome local Berber tribes, reinforced the *kasbah*, originally built by Moulay Ali ben Rachid. He also constructed the Dar el-Makhzen within the *kasbah* and manned it with a garrison, under the command of his representative.

For the next few centuries, the region and town of Chefchaouen with its many *marabouts* (buildings holding tombs of Muslim holy men), were considered sacred places of pilgrimage, closed off to Christians. Charles Foucauld, a well-travelled French chronicler, risked everything by entering the town disguised as a Jew in the late nineteenth century. He was soon followed by Walter Harris, resident correspondent for a British newspaper, whose nagging curiosity almost cost him his life.

In those early days, it was quite common for foreigners, particularly Christians, to pass themselves off as Jews, when travelling through the interior. The disguise afforded them some protection as they went from area to area.

In October 1920, the Spanish entered Chefchaouen and claimed it as part of the Spanish Protectorate. They also changed the spelling of the town's name to *Xauen*. Much to their astonishment, they discovered the Jewish inhabitants still conversing in the local Judeo-Spanish language which sounded like Spanish from four centuries earlier.

The similarity in language very quickly assisted in cementing good relations between the Jews and the Spanish, which initially caused some friction with the Muslim inhabitants. Later in the decade, during the Rif War, the Spanish temporarily lost control of the town to the rebel leader, Abdel Krim el-Khattabi.

During this time Jews were accused of aligning with the Spanish, and in response several left Chefchaouen to avoid retribution. They did, however, return once the town was back in the hands of the Spanish under whom the Jewish community thrived. Religious and traditional rights were respected. Even though they were under the day-to-day control of the Spanish, Jews of Chefchaouen considered themselves to be subjects of the Moroccan sultan.

The Spanish, being sticklers for cleanliness, encouraged the Jewish community to whitewash the exterior of their houses. Doors and windows were painted blue, it is thought, to mislead insects into believing they were flying into water and, therefore, remain outside the house. This strategy then made it much easier for the Spanish to persuade the Muslim inhabitants to follow suit. The distinctive pale-blue colouring seen today is said to have been created by a Spanish artist who spent some time in the town many decades ago.

Another source claims that a local enterprising Jewish business man, returning from a trip to Spain, put the idea of whitewashing the houses to the local administration officer, a Spaniard, who then made an official order to the town's people to whitewash the exterior of their homes. The result was that both men shared the proceeds from the huge quantities of whitewash sold.

In 1956, Chefchaouen was returned to Morocco at independence. However, the Rif Berbers were less than keen to be ruled from Rabat after centuries of being part of the *Bled es-Siba*.

The 1960s saw the departure of the last remnants of the Jewish community. It also brought to an end the high standard of silver jewelry and leather goods the town was renowned for producing. A local Muslim man, wittily given the nickname El -Yehoudi, was entrusted to sell the land and property of the Jews, after they had emigrated to Israel. Today the local production of jewelry and leather goods does not have the same quality as before.

The Jewish quarter had always been in the area of the *souks* within the medina. The Jewish cemetery, restored in recent years by the Jewish Museum in Casablanca, is on the hillside to the north of the town. The town's former synagogues no longer exist.

Ouezzane

Positioned on the edge of the southern slopes of the Rif region, Ouezzane once marked the boundary between the ancient *Bled el-Makhzen*, the territories controlled by the sultans, and the *Bled es-Siba*, those territories refusing to accept the authority of the sultans. The region around Ouezzane was under the control of tribal sheikhs, known as the *Ouezzanis*.

The Ouezzanis kept their hold on power by aligning themselves to a religious fraternity or *zaouia*, in this case, the Taabia brotherhood. These were *charifs* (sherefs), descendents of the Prophet, through a direct line to the Idrissids, the first Moroccan dynasty of sultans.

It is said the sheiks did everything to encourage Jewish and Muslim refugees to the town, following the expulsions from Christian Spain, in the fifteenth and sixteenth centuries. The construction of today's old town, Andalusian in style and layout, bears witness to their influences. The Jewish community very quickly settled in and began to dominate the commercial interests in the town, mainly associated with the wool industry.

The town gained political and religious influence when, in 1727, the *charif,* Moulay Abdallah, created a *zaouia* in the nearby *Deshra Jebel er-Rhan* (Village of the Mountain of Myrtles). The religious fraternity then went on to found religious centers all over the country, and later extended its sphere of influence well beyond Morocco's borders.

Moulay Ali, an eighteenth century *charif,* called on Jews to move to the town to improve its prosperity, which up to that point had been floundering. In the older part of town stand the Moulay Ali mosque and the *zaouia,* with its octagonal minaret. In the same area are the former dwellings of the charifs of Ouezzane, easily identified by their elaborate glazed tiling (*zellij)* and heavily decorated doors.

Ouezzane was in the French administered zone during the years of the French Protectorate. Although one Muslim witness said that the Jews were given preferential treatment, the fact is that many Jews lived in poverty and occupied bad housing. The streets of the *mellah* were often strewn with garbage.

Jews worked in the usual trades as blacksmiths, metalworkers, shoemakers, tailors who made western-style suits and *djallabas,* and the makers of leather containers for carrying water. Some Jewish women owned treadle sewing machines and made clothes and *djallabas.* However, opportunities for stable employment were so scarce that Jewish men of the poorer class were prepared to do jobs that Muslims considered menial and degrading, such as being a water carrier.

Dealers in gold and silver moved around the countryside to repair, buy or trade for broken jewelry. Some customers, it is said, were duped into exchanging broken gold and silver for less valuable metal items. Other Jewish families lived on small farms outside the town, produced handicrafts and fruit and vegetables, to be sold at the weekly *souk.*

One man who was the son of an Imam in Ouezzane in the 1960s talked about Jews in the town. He said that not all Jews lived in the *mellah*, and there was a Jewish family living next door to his family, and he often played with one of their sons. The Jewish community consisted of mixed classes: rich, middle class and extremely poor.

The children attended the local *Alliance Israélite Universelle* school and later left to continue further education in France, never to return. The Jews were much better educated than the Muslims and many, especially the young, spoke French and Arabic. Although the AIU school building closed in the late 1960s, it is still there. It also includes a synagogue, which is also closed.

Mixed marriages between Jews and Muslims were quite common, often done with financial and social gains in mind. This is an indication that relations between the two communities were cordial and respectful. By the end of the 1960s, there were no Jews left in Ouezzane.

Mention Ouezzane to any Moroccan Jew, or his or her descendents, and you are bound to hear the name, Rabbi Amram Ben Diwan, the most revered and venerated of Morocco's Jewish *tzadiks*. He is said to have come to Morocco from Hebron and settled in Ouezzane, where his reputation as a miracle worker grew among the Jewish community all over the country. After his death in 1782, he was buried in the Jewish cemetery in the hamlet of Azjen, nine kilometers northwest of Ouezzane.

Many miracles have been accredited to this rabbi *tzadik* and his shrine receives the most pilgrims of all the *tzadiks* of Morocco. Mothers come to pray for a marriage partner for their son or daughter; young men and women pray for a spouse; and, the sick pray for a cure for ailments.

One miracle attributed to this *tzadik* occurred when a large marble slab was placed over his tomb, and the next morning it was found shattered into tiny pieces. This was interpreted as a sign he wanted his grave covered in simple stones only. Another is the phenomenon of the tree that overhangs the grave. Although during the pilgrimages hundreds of candles are lit under the tree, it never catches fire.

A rabbi and his two sons flew in from New York a few years ago for a two-day visit to pray at the graveside. The rabbi was a diamond merchant hoping to seal a deal worth one-half million dollars. Hours of prayer and chanting were offered to the *tzadik*. On their return to New York, the deal not only went through successfully, but it was increased to one million dollars.

It is possible to visit the rabbi's grave at any time during the year. However, there are two very well attended annual pilgrimages; one during *Lag Baomer* and the other in September, marking the *tzadik's* birthday. In 2007, more than 5,000 pilgrims from Israel, Canada, France and the United States visited the site.

The cemetery is enclosed within a high wall with a secure gate, manned by a guardian, who is a Muslim. It is looked after by members of the Jewish community in Casablanca. The complex includes recently built accommodations for pilgrims at the shrine.

David Elbaz placing a candle at the shrine of the *tzadik*
Rabbi Amram Ben Diwan in Ouezzane
Photo by Ron Hart

9

North Atlantic Coast

Asilah
Larache

❀T he Phoenicians and the Carthaginians sailed in the waters of the region, setting up trading posts up and down the coast of Morocco, and Jewish traders were with them. The Romans also occupied the immediate environs southwest of Tangier. Remains of settlements and fish factories are in abundance as far south as Asilah and Larache.

The fish factories produced *garum*, a sauce made from anchovies. They were also involved in the processes of drying and preserving fish. The Romans were keen agriculturists, especially in the cultivation of olives and cereals, evidenced by the discovery of the remains of ancient oil-works and farmhouses.

The Idrissids (eighth and ninth centuries C.E.) brought in Arab settlers into the region. The Portuguese took Tangier in 1460 and Asilah in 1471 from the Merenid sultans, as they expanded their presence along the coast. After 1492, Jews expelled from Spain and Portugal arrived, adding to the ethnic and religious mixture of the population. The Portuguese were defeated by the subsequent dynasty, the Saadians, in the Battle of Ksar El Kebir in 1578. For the next three centuries the region remained under the control the next Moroccan dynasty, the Alaouites.

In 1911 to 1912, with the signing of the Treaty of Fes, the region became part of the Spanish Protectorate. The Spanish Expulsion Edict against the Jews was no longer being enforced, and Jews were permitted to live in Spanish controlled lands. The Jews were given full rights and were left alone to practice their religion and conduct their traditional rabbinical courts and other institutions. The Spanish, unlike the French, kept few records on the Jewish community, so information on Jewish life in this period is limited.

Taking the southbound autoroute from Tangier, the first place of any real interest is the beautiful walled town of Asilah, less than an hour's drive. It is located on the Atlantic Ocean.

Asilah

Deciding it was a good site, the Carthaginians established a small trading post and gave it the name, Zelli. Like-minded Jewish traders accompanying them also settled there. It later came under the control of the Mauritanians, who had the Jews mint a regional coinage with the Punic script.

At the time of the Punic Wars the inhabitants gave their support to Bogud, the Mauritanian king, who sided with the North Africans. However, it was Rome that won, and as victors the Romans had the town's population transported to Spain and replaced them with their own citizens from Iberia. The town was designated a Roman colony with semi-autonomous privileges such as the right to run its own financial and legal affairs, controlled by an elected body.

In the eighth century, the Arabs arrived and the town was taken over by the Idrissid dynasty, which it is claimed changed the name to Arzilla. Constant attacks by the Normans left the town in ruins until it was rebuilt by El Hakim, the Umayyad caliph of Cordoba. A twelfth century chronicler mentions that under the years of the Almohads, the town was small and insignificant with very little commercial activity. This could be as a result of the Jewish community having fled from the anti-Semitic persecutions and forced conversions carried out during the reign of the Almohads.

When the Merinid dynasty had control of the town in the fourteenth century, commercial vessels were calling at the port from European cities, such as Genoa, Venice, Pisa and Marseilles, and the ports of Northern Spain. Agricultural produce and timber were exported.

The Merinids' realized that Jewish commercial contacts and expertise were the key to the country's success and granted them the monopoly on international trade.

When the power of the Merinid dynasty was at its weakest, the Portuguese sent a fleet of naval vessels and an army of more than 28,000 men. After taking possession of the town in 1471, they fortified it with a sturdy defensive wall, still in existence today.

With the presence of the Portuguese, some of the Jewish community acted as intermediaries and translators. Others covered the region negotiating and purchasing merchandise for export through the port. Later at the end of the fifteenth century, a small influx of Jews (*Megorashim*) arrived from the Iberian Peninsula after the Spanish expulsion.

In 1547 the Inquisition set up a mission in Tangier, where members of the Franciscan brothers arrested a Jewish notable visiting from Asilah (Arzilla). He was accused of encouraging former Jews, newly converted to Christianity, to re-convert to Judaism by promising marriage to beautiful young women and by offering enticements of wealth.

On hearing the disturbing news, the Portuguese commander of Asilah, quickly intervened, knowing the accused man's brother was influential and had the ear of the sultan in Fes. The Portuguese had already lost some of their trading posts along the Atlantic coast of Morocco, and the Jews would not take kindly to one of their own being held by Christians.

Another mitigating factor was that the Jews had a monopoly on the manufacturing, buying and selling of arms. The Portuguese feared that they might supply arms free of charge to the sultan, who was their vowed protector, if it meant they were to be used against the Portuguese. The accused was quickly set free and returned to Asilah.

In 1578 is a date that marks an important point in Morocco's history. King Dom Sebastion of Portugal, with more than 20,000 well-armed troops, disembarked at Asilah and nearby Larache, to join forces with the deposed Saadian sultan, Moulay Mohammed, against Abd el-Malek, another Saadian, who had displaced him. The ensuing bloody battle took place close to the nearby town of Ksar el-Kebir, and resulted in the death of the three leaders. The historical event became known as The Battle of the Three Kings.

The Spanish quickly claimed all Portuguese territories and subsequently took control of Asilah, but later, in 1589, ceded the town to the Saadian sultan, Moulay Ahmad el-Mansour. With the help of the Jewish merchants, he made the port commercially viable once again.

While the Saadian dynasty's grip on the country went into decline during the seventeenth century, the Spanish recaptured Asilah for a short period.

Moulay Ismail, the second Alaouite sultan, and an excellent war strategist, seized the town for Morocco in 1691. He resettled the town with Riffians and constructed a series of buildings, including mosques and a *madrasa* (Koranic school).

Regardless of his efforts, the town never returned to its former success; foreign vessels had already opted to use other Atlantic ports, and a number of Jewish traders followed suit.

The Jews of Asilah were among the communities singled out for special treatment by Moulay al-Yazid, The Abuser (1790-1792). Filled with resentment and hatred for Jews and their allies, he set local thugs and the military loose in the town to carry out atrocities on the Jews. Houses and businesses were ransacked; Jewish men were beaten or killed and women raped. It was the darkest period for the Jews since the time of the Almohads.

Mercifully, Yazid's reign only lasted two years. He died after being fatally wounded in a skirmish on the outskirts of Marrakech.

In the nineteenth century, the inhabitants of Asilah had a reputation for lawlessness and piracy against European commercial shipping on the high seas. The Austrian navy retaliated by bombarding the town in 1829. Because of attacks on its shipping, Spain sent naval vessels to shell Asilah in 1860, the same year they attacked Tetouan with the intention of occupying it and making it a Spanish colony.

The Scottish author and traveller, R.B. Cunninghame Graham, visited the town in the latter part of the nineteenth century. In his book, *Mogreb-El-Acksa*, originally published in 1898, he remarked that the town had fallen into decay and ruin, with heaps of garbage everywhere. Many buildings, though in use, were unsuitable for human habitation.

The fact that the Jewish inhabitants outnumbered the Muslims was also noted. The most notable Jew in the town served as consul to seven different countries, and other Jews dominated the market and cultivation of the locally grown oranges.

According to the same author, the local Jews spoke a dialect of old Spanish from the sixteenth century. At the time of his writing, the dialect was known as Toledan and was widely spoken by the Jews living in the towns in the northwest region of Morocco, which, coincidently, later became part of the Spanish Protectorate. He was referring to the language called Haketía today.

In 1906, a band of outlaws rode into town, western-style, and took it over. They were led by Moulay Ahmed Raisouli, a Rifi, who began his career as a small-time brigand in the Rif Mountains but eventually became a major figure. Through kidnapping well-to-do foreigners and cunning maneuvers, he amassed a fortune, some of which went toward building a palace in Asilah overlooking the ocean.

His reputation as a ruthless killer had the people of the Rif region, and beyond, terrorized, and his political astuteness forced the sultans to promote him to the position of Pasha (Governor) of Asilah, and, afterwards, Tangier.

In the early days of the Spanish Protectorate, the Spaniards paid him handsomely, after he had convinced them he had assisted in keeping the rebellious Riffians in check. However, old habits die hard; living an honest and uncontroversial life was not something Raisouli could be satisfied with. He continued to play every advantage in the pursuit of wealth and at one time gave support to the Germans, who had designs on conquering the Rif much to the annoyance of the Spanish. The latter grew tired of his skulduggery and forced him out of Asilah. He returned to his roots in the Rif Mountains, where he died shortly after.

Asilah was returned to the Moroccan kingdom when it achieved its independence in 1956. The Jews of Asilah, by now very few in number, left at the end of the 1960s, some to Israel and a few resettled in Casablanca.

Asilah's main activity today is tourism. Strolling around this picturesque white-washed town with colourfully painted doorways, it becomes apparent why there has been an increase in foreigners and wealthy Moroccans buying up the old houses within the medina. After some interior modifications, they are turned into beautiful holiday homes.

The medina has a heart-warming charm and an air of relaxation not found in any other location in the country. The maze of narrow lanes, and the slow pace of life contribute to its appeal.

Larache

Almost ignored by tourism (most likely because there is no town beach), Larache is a prime example of a Spanish-Moroccan town, whitewashed houses with blue-painted doors and window frames, and a main square with attractive Spanish architecture.

In 2008, work was in progress to give the town a facelift; walkways were being paved with decorative tiles and palm trees planted along the main streets. The cafes, of which there are many, near to and along the seafront, attract customers, who sip coffee and find relief in the constant fresh sea breezes.

The Phoenicians are said to have occupied the site on the south bank of the Oued Loukkos Estuary, which was the main port of exit for merchandise coming from the fertile regions in the interior. Jewish traders were present with the Phoenicians although it is thought their numbers would have been small.

The town was expanded during the Arab invasions in the eighth century and given the name, *Al Araich Beni Arous.* Today, most Moroccans call it simply *El Araich.*

The Arabs often had problems with the population of nearby Lixus, which refused to accept Islam. Several ancient temples have been uncovered on the Lixus site, though, it is not clear what religion was practiced at the time of the Arab invasions. In any case, by the tenth century, Lixus had long been deserted.

The Portuguese first took an interest in the unfortified town of Larache around 1471, and over the next few years constructed fortifications. However, they were forced to abandon the area in 1479 due to the constant attacks by the armies of the Merinid sultan, Mohammedes Said ech-Sheikh. The danger and destruction during the hostilities had caused the inhabitants to flee, including the Jewish community.

Once the town was back under Moroccan control, the Merinid sultan, es-Said ech-Sheikh, immediately repopulated the town with Arabs and set about the construction of mosques, emphasizing the town belonged to Muslims and not Christian infidels.

His brother, Moulay en-Nasser, later, in 1491, fortified the town and also built a *kasbah*-like fortress to guard the access to the river. Feeling much more secure, the Jews returned to take up where they had left off. It was reported that the port became one of the country's busiest. The exported commodities included agricultural produce, wool, cork and timber.

In the early sixteenth century, the port was a stronghold for Moroccan, Algerian and Turkish corsairs, whose piracy angered the Portuguese based in Asilah. As a consequence, they attacked the port, torched a few vessels and confiscated others.

In 1578, forces of King Dom Sebastion of Portugal disembarked at the port on their way to take part in The Battle of the Three Kings, fought close to the nearby town of Ksar el-Kebir, in which the king was killed.

Larache later became a center for boat building with ships being commissioned by pirates and with the full knowledge and approval of the sultans. This was part of a strategy of plundering European merchant shipping around the Mediterranean and as far away as the Canary Islands. Despite the activity of pirates, the port continued to function, and Jewish traders still made good livelihoods.

In 1610 the town was gifted to King Philip III of Spain by the Saadian sultan, Moulay ech-Sheikh el-Mamoun, in gratitude for his assistance in ousting the previous sultan, Moulay Zidan. Other sources claim the town was actually sold.

The Spanish further reinforced the walls with ramparts and also began exporting local produce to the Iberian Peninsula. Rather than venturing too far inland, the Spanish relied on Jewish traders to bring the goods to the port. The shopping lists were made up with orders for such fruits as lemons, oranges and grapes, the likes of which Morocco still produces for export today.

Larache returned to Moroccan control in 1689, when the Alaouite sultan, Moulay Ismail, with great determination, set out to free the country of all foreign occupation. Under his rule and with his full consent, piracy from the town's port continued, but on a grander scale, with the inclusion of other ports up and down the Atlantic coast. Bombardments from off-shore European battleships were so frequent that a later Alaouite sultan, Moulay Mohammed ben Abdallah (1757–1790), was compelled to strengthen the defensive installations around the port.

It was also around this time that hundreds of Christian prisoners were captured during a failed assault on the town. Among them was Théodore Cornut, an architect, whose skills were later used in the planning of the new Essaouira. The years of instability drove several Jewish traders to live elsewhere. Some chose to move south to Essaouira, where the sultan, Moulay Mohammed, had begun establishing a port in 1760.

With the decline of the importance of Larache in favor of Essaouira, ship building became the town's main industry during the eighteenth and nineteenth centuries. The largest orders came from the sea pirates based in Salé and Rabat. The exportation of agricultural goods from the port also continued.

Before 1806, Larache's Jewish community was estimated to be around 2,000, and several were involved in the trading of animal hides, wax and wool. A minority also served as agents for commercial companies based in Tetouan.

Sultan Moulay Hassan ruled during the latter part of the nineteenth century. His representative in Larache expelled a number of Jews from the town, accused of selling alcohol, *mahiya*, to Muslim sailors, who were later involved in a street brawl and the death of three people. Spain finally took possession of the town as part of the Treaty of Fes (1912).

During an interview conducted in 2008, an elderly Moroccan Jewish woman, originally from Larache, but who had moved to Casablanca in the 1960s, gave an insight into the relations between the Spanish and the residents of the town.

She said that under the Spanish Protectorate, there was no reference to *mellahs*. The Jewish community originally occupied a street called *Calle Real*, quite close to the Medina. Today, it is known as *Rue d'Espagne*. However, over time, the community dispersed to the Spanish-built new town and lived side by side with Muslims and Spanish Catholics.

Evidently, relations between the three religious communities were excellent; invitations to weddings and other celebrations were reciprocal. The Jews made their own wine for Passover and often shared it with their guests from the other religions. Neighborliness was underscored by the fact that doors were open to all, regardless of their religion.

Jews and Spaniards maintained a cordial relationship, not found between their counterparts on the Iberian Peninsula. Everyone spoke Spanish and listened to and danced to Spanish and Arabic music. There were never any questions as to what religion a person practiced when they entered the Jewish-owned social club, *Casino Israelita*.

Prior to Moroccan independence, the Jewish community numbered around 3,000. Men worked at various businesses, while women maintained homes and families like other Spanish and Muslim residents. The Jewish children, about 500, attended the local *Alliance Israelite Universelle* (AIU) school.

The town once had five synagogues; one on *Calle Real*, and the others were situated in the new town. Long after its closure, the furniture and lighting of the Synagogue Pariene, built in the 1930s, were taken to the Jewish Museum in Casablanca, where they are now on permanent display.

Larache has two Jewish cemeteries, perhaps, giving an indication of how long and how many Jews originally lived in the town. The oldest can be found north of the town and the other, created during the Spanish Protectorate, is to the southeast, at some distance from the town. The local *tzadik* is Rabbi Youssef Bagalalili.

The majority of the Jewish community left for Israel between the 1950s and 1965, including the kosher butchers. Any of the small community who stayed behind had to travel to Tangier to purchase kosher meat.

According to the elderly woman interviewed, Larache was an extremely beautiful, lively and scrupulously clean town during the days of the Spanish Protectorate. However, after the town was returned to Morocco in 1956, wanton neglect caused it to lose much of its appeal. This was the main reason her father moved the family to Casablanca.

Asilah, Modern and Traditional
Photo by Ron Hart

10

Central Atlantic Coast

Rabat
Salé

Rabat and Salé

Archaeological excavations have confirmed there was human habitation on this site in the fifth century B.C.E. The Phoenicians have been credited with developing this section of the Atlantic coastline by establishing a series of prosperous trading-posts. Similar evidence verifies that Jewish traders were present at the same time. There are stories about large shipments of gold from the sub-Sahara being transported from the port of Sala or Chella, near Salé, and they mention the presence of Jewish traders travelling with the caravan trains. Around the end of the first century C.E., the Romans had a settlement here, Sala Colonia, from where they sent wheat, wine, olives and olive oil to all parts of their empire.

Some time during the eighth century, a Berber tribe, the *Berghouata*, declared the area an independent kingdom and their chief, besides proclaiming himself a prophet, produced a set of religious codes in the Berber language, inspired by the Koran but with alterations compatible with Berber culture and social conventions. That infuriated the Arab tribes in other regions, who not only saw it as an act of heresy but also as a defiant challenge and a threat to the orthodoxy of Islam.

To eliminate the threat, a *ribat*, a fortified monastery from which the name Rabat is derived, was constructed, supposedly on the sight of the present Oudaia Kasbah, overlooking the River Bou Regreg, as it is known today. It was from here the Muslim armies set out to fight against the *Berghouata* heretics in an effort to conquer the independent state for Islam. The *ribat* was abandoned after the establishment of the newly built town of Salé on the opposite bank of the River Bou Regreg in the eleventh century.

In the middle of the twelfth century, the Almohad sultan, Abd el-Moumen took control of the town of Salé without much resistance and commandeered the former *ribat*. However, it took several attempts before defeating the rebellious *Berghouata* tribe. In order to impose his authority, Abd el-Moumen had a *kasbah* complete with a palace and a great mosque built on the site of the *ribat*, later used as a launching pad for campaigns into Southern Spain, which successfully brought Andalusia back under Islamic domination. Abd el-Moumen died in Rabat in 1163. The Almohads policies of persecution, forced conversions and multiple massacres led the majority of Rabat's Jews to flee to Christian Spain and to the more remote areas of Morocco.

In the twelfth century, Yacoub al-Mansour (the Victorious), made Rabat his capital, which then became known as *Ribat el-Fath* (Ribat of Victory). He oversaw major reconstruction of the defensive walls, gates and bastions and had witnessed the start of his grand plan, which was to build the largest and grandest mosque in the Islamic world. Unfortunately, he died from wounds sustained in a battle, and apart from the minaret, a number of supporting columns and some roofing, all work on the project came to a halt a few years later. The massive earthquake of 1755 destroyed much of the mosque, leaving only the minaret to survive.

The minaret of the mosque, given the name the Hassan Tower, as it stands today, commemorates the memory of one of Morocco's most courageous and glorious sultans.

At the time of Merenid rule (thirteenth century), Rabat suffered economically and lost its prominence when Fes became the new capital. It then took on the status of a small provincial town with very few inhabitants for centuries to come. Although, the Merenids reportedly treated the Jews well, not much is known about Rabat's Jewish community at the time. The Portuguese in the early sixteenth century failed to capture the well-defended *kasbah* during the period under Saadian rule.

In the fifteenth and sixteenth centuries Rabat and Salé became a sanctuary for pirates of European and Turkish origins, who plundered European shipping. As the power of the Saadian dynasty fell into decline, the pirates felt confident enough to declare their own state of the Republic of Bou Regreg.

France and Britain on several occasions made what turned out to be futile attempts at curtailing their illegal activities by bombarding the *kasbah* from the river estuary, but most of their ships were too large to navigate the shallow waters in the river. Added to that, the *kasbah* was well fortified and well supplied with cannon and other munitions. Ironically, both sides in the conflicts purchased their weapons from the same source, Jewish arms dealers, who dominated the weapons market at that time.

After the demise of the Saadians, the Alaouite dynasty came to the fore. The first sultan, Moulay er-Rachid, managed to take control of the Bou Regreg estuary, which was later followed up by Moulay Ismail, who succeeded in imposing his authority by appointing a royal representative and making both Rabat and Salé part of the Moroccan kingdom.

Nevertheless, rather than rein in the pirates, he set up a system where he benefited financially from their activities and where all captured prisoners were held until a ransom was paid. In the event of non-payment, the prisoners, many of whom were Christians, ended up as slaves working on Ismail's massive building projects around the country. The pirates were able to continue using the port of Rabat until 1829 when treaties were signed with various European powers.

Rabat became one of Morocco's imperial cities in the final stages of the nineteenth century. Then in 1912, the French, who found it strategically difficult to defend Fes in the interior, opted to make Rabat on the Atlantic coast the administrative capital. The French construction of the *Ville Nouvelle* helped in the expansion of Rabat, giving it a particularly modern look.

Under the French, Rabat's Jewish community, like thousands of Jews in other parts of the country, was badly affected by the 1941 anti-Semitic policies of the Nazi-controlled, Vichy government in France. The middle class lost social status and jobs as they were dismissed from departments of the French administration and prohibited from running certain businesses. Rampant unemployment among the poorer classes caused many to suffer great hardship.

When Morocco gained its independence in March, 1956, King Mohammed V made the decision to keep his capital in Rabat. It was from here that he had previously defied French attempts to deport all Moroccan Jews to the concentration camps in Eastern Europe by declaring, "There are no Jews in Morocco, only Moroccans."

Today, the city still has the distinction of being the official residence of the country's monarch and the seat of government, with all the foreign embassies based there too. As for the city's Jewish community, the 1960s saw a mass exodus of 16,000 Jews to Israel, France and Canada. The almost deserted *mellah* was soon taken over by Muslims arriving from the countryside. Rabat's twin town, Salé, also lost its Jewish population, around 6,000 in total. In 2007, only 120 Jews remained, mostly of an advanced age. Rabbi Raphael Encaoua, one of Morocco's most venerated Jewish *tzadiks*, is buried in the Salé cemetery.

In October 2007, a retired former accountant, who moved to Rabat from Casablanca, was asked why he had made the decision to stay on in Morocco and not leave like so many others of his Jewish brethren. He responded by saying he did not see the need; he held a good job with a pension. His wife was in a similar position with employment in the Post Office. Both had no problems with the Muslim community.

Asked what caused the majority of the Jewish community to emigrate, he replied "fear", and he said that most people sympathized with the Zionist goal of migrating to Israel. In response to other questions he said that his mother and grandmother, both from Fes, spoke only Arabic. Women never attended *Talmud Torah* (Jewish school), so consequently did not learn Hebrew. The traditional role for most women was to remain at home and take care of the children. The men of the poorer classes worked as porters in the *souks* and did the sort of jobs done by poor Arabs today: peddlers, shoe repairers and laborers in factories. The exodus from the *mellah* began in 1962, slowly at first, however, by 1967, most of the residents were gone.

The *Mellah*. Located within the walls of the Medina, the *mellah* was once home to a 16,000-strong Jewish community. Compared to most *mellahs* around the country, Rabat's *mellah* is relatively new. In 1808 Sultan Moulay Sliman (Alaouite dynasty) had it moved to its present position, and Jews were encouraged to move there from the previous location in the area of *Rue des Consuls*. Some Jewish families residing in grand villas converted to Islam, rather than moving to the new location and losing their homes and businesses.

Rabbi Shalom Izouwi Synagogue. Although no longer functioning, it has the interior fittings and furniture still in place. The 1960s Beth El Synagogue, with an empty Talmud Torah school attached, is outside the walls in the *Ville Nouvelle*. Friends socialize at the one and only Jewish club.

Cemeteries. There are two Jewish cemeteries. The old one is in the *Ville Nouvelle*. When it became full, a new one was created outside the city limits. The cemetery in Salé is the final resting place of Rabbi Raphael Encaoua, an important local *tzadik* with an annual pilgrimage.

Mausoleum of Mohammed V. Every Moroccan Jew regards the late King Mohammed V as a *tzadik* because of the way he protected them from deportation and the discriminatory laws passed by the Nazi controlled, French Vichy government in 1941. A visit to the Mausoleum of Mohammed V is valued as a pilgrimage. His two sons, the late King Hassan II, father of the present king, Mohammed VI, and the other, Prince Moulay Abdallah, lay at rest close by him. Every year, a delegation of Jewish elders places a wreath at the foot of Mohammed V's tomb to commemorate his life.

108

Strategically placed on a hillside that looks across the River Bou Regreg to the sister town of Salé, the mausoleum was commissioned by the late King Hassan II. The interior decoration, embracing the more striking aspects of Andalusian-Moorish architecture, took almost ten years to complete. The eyes are dazzled by the whole expanse of the carved mahogany ceiling covered in gold leaf.

Visitors from all religions, who are suitably dressed, can enter and view the tombs from an upper gallery.

Jewish Cemetery in Essaouira
Photo by Yehuda and Nurit Patt

Koutoubia Mosque
Marrakech
Photo by Ron Hart

11

South Atlantic Coast

Casablanca
Azemmour
El Jadida
Safi
Essaouira (Mogador)

The region between Casablanca and Essaouira was familiar to the Phoenicians, Portuguese and French, who were responsible for giving birth to the coastal ports spread out along this stretch of the Atlantic Coast. Much of the credit for the region's past economic success has to go to the Jewish communities that maintained a continuous presence in trading from these ports for almost 2,000 years. The Portuguese endowed the region with the impressive historic fortress towns still dominating parts of the coastline today. The French, on the other hand, brought contemporary development, building road and rail infrastructure, new towns, and more efficient ports.

A leisurely drive down the coast takes in miles of deserted golden beaches and passes through sparsely populated agricultural landscapes, where farmers work the land. The region between Safi and Essaouira is populated by indigenous Berbers. Apart from Casablanca, the urban centers with a large concentration of people rely on such industries as fishing, agriculture and tourism for their survival.

Casablanca

The exact origins of the small town of Anfa, now a pleasant suburb of the metropolis of Casablanca, remain a bit of a mystery. However, some records mention Jewish traders arriving with the Phoenicians and setting up trading-posts and settlements along the Atlantic coast as early as the eleventh century B.C.E. The Carthaginians came along in the sixth century B.C.E. and drove out the Phoenicians from Anfa and other coastal settlements.

When the Arabs and Islam came to Morocco during the sixth and seventh century C.E., Anfa was part of the Berber kingdom called *Berghouata*. In the eleventh century, the Almoravid dynasty, a Berber tribe from the Sahara, made several attempts to conquer Berghouata, but its inhabitants stubbornly refused to accept Islam. The annihilation of the *Berghouata* kingdom finally came in the twelfth century at the hands of the Almohads, a conservative Berber tribe from deep within the High Atlas Mountains. Their leader was the first Almohad sultan, Abdel al-Moumen.

In 1188, Yacoub el-Mansour, another Almohad sultan relocated several Arabs to the town and the surrounding region, with the aim of exerting stricter control. The port of Anfa then became a hub for the exportation of wheat and barley grown on the vast plains to the south in the regions of Settat, Berrchid and Ben Hmid.

The Almohads, who had no tolerance for Jews, adopted a policy of forced conversions and massacres, causing terror in the Jewish community, resulting in many fleeing to Christian Spain and to the mountains of Morocco's interior. Others who remained did convert, but some are reported to have practiced Judaism in secret.

In the thirteenth century, the Merenid dynasty overthrew the Almohads, and they recognized the importance of the Jewish role in the economy and treated them well. During the first quarter of the fifteenth century, the Merenids began to lose control of Morocco, and the Jews feared the loss of their protected status.

Sensing the fragility of the sultanate, the local Arabs around Anfa rose up in rebellion and won control of the town, eventually, creating a small republic. The Arabs then banded together with pirates and began commercial activities with Britain, Spain and Portugal. Some time later, the pirates of Anfa and the sultan of Morocco colluded with Britain to attack Portuguese merchant shipping on the high seas.

In 1468, the Portuguese, unable to tolerate the continued attacks on their ships, sent 10,000 armed men and a fleet of fifty ships to break the power of the pirates. Anfa was reduced to rubble. The small Jewish community was badly affected, and most moved on to other towns to re-build their disrupted lives. The pirates, undaunted by the Portuguese attacks, continued their harassment of the trade routes almost unhindered for nearly half a century. In 1515, the Portuguese returned and destroyed the town for the second time.

113

During the following years, Lisbon was expanding its empire and returned yet again in 1575. This time intending to stay, the Portuguese set about reconstructing the town and surrounded it with a thick defensive wall. They named the town *Casa Branca* after a white house that identified the area.

Constant attacks by local tribes, in due course, made Portuguese occupation costly and untenable. The final deciding factor was the massive earthquake of 1755 that wiped out Lisbon and caused considerable damage to Casa Branca. It left the Portuguese little choice but to abandon the outpost.

The Moroccan sultan, Mohammed Ben Abdallah, eventually managed to bring some semblance of life back to the town in the latter years of the eighteenth century. The sultan brought in Berbers from the Souss region and tribesmen from around Meknes to re-populate the town. He also arabized the name Casa Branca to *Dar el Beida* (The Spanish later changed it to Casablanca). The Jewish community managed to recover, but Casablanca's port was almost ignored for several years in favor of the port of Rabat, due to a dispute between a later sultan, Moulay Sliman, and local politicians.

The 1830s brought an upswing in Casablanca's fortunes. European economies were at an all-time-high, and the increase in demand for cereals such as wheat and barley and raw materials for the textile trade drove Europeans to import from outside their borders. Since Morocco was located close to Europe and had a milder climate, it developed an export trade with the thriving European cities. The port of Casablanca was back in vogue, drawing scores of Jewish traders and intermediaries from other coastal towns such as Tetouan, Rabat and Essaouira.

Britain was the first to think of opening a consulate in Casablanca, which it did in 1857, then followed by Spain in 1861, and France in 1865. By the 1870s, several European companies had opened agencies in Casablanca, and the town's economy continued to grow. The general population, too, had increased and stood around 20,000, of which 6,000 were Jews. The *Alliance Israélite Universelle* took responsibility for the education of Jewish children by opening two schools in 1897.

Anger and resentment about the Europeans' ignorance and lack of sensibility toward Moroccan and Islamic life reached a crisis point and, in July 1907, Moroccan rioters revolted, killing a team of European workmen transporting rocks from a quarry to a new harbour complex. The *mellah* was overrun with looters and Jewish businesses ransacked. Many people were killed in the town, including a number of Jews. The disturbances included the abduction of over two hundred women and children, both foreigners and Jews. The employees within the French consulate were also threatened by an angry mob.

The French, seeing this as an opportunity to advance their colonial aspirations, acted swiftly and sent a ship and several hundred troops to deal with the unrest. The locals put up a fight to keep control; however, the French won the day and initiated their plans for complete colonization, which they succeeded in doing in 1912 by declaring Morocco a French Protectorate.

The arrival of the French brought new influences in both the Jewish and Muslim communities. A European Jew living in Casablanca at the time expressed his opposition to the practice of child marriages between girls as young as eight years old and teenage boys, which were common in both the Jewish and Muslim communities. The *Alliance Israélite Universelle* was equally disturbed and went to great lengths to put an end to the practice; letters were written to the heads of rabbinical courts and other Jewish institutions in the major towns and cities, pleading for official condemnation.

Although a 2004 law establishes the minimum age for marriage at eighteen years old for men and women, exemptions can be granted by a court of law. Annually, thousands of fourteen and fifteen year old girls, primarily among Muslims, are still given permission to marry.

By 1912, Casablanca was considered the industrial and economic capital of Morocco, and it was a magnet for Jewish migration from the countryside and small towns in times of famine and drought, epidemics and other problems. The new migrants, who had no means of supporting themselves, lived in cramped conditions and abject poverty within the *mellah* of the Old Medina. The wealthy members of Jewish community established societies to care for the needy. The JDC (American Jewish Joint Distribution Committee) was also on hand to distribute food rations, medicine and clothing.

When the French created the New Medina, or New Town (in effect the city of Casablanca) with an infrastructure that included AIU schools, Jewish parents clamoured to have their children enrolled; the language of commerce and administration was French.

Moreover as the economy improved, more and more Jews opened businesses or took up employment in the new town. However, under the French Protectorate, most Jews were banned from setting up home there. The situation changed after Morocco gained independence; with the assurances announced by Mohammed V, the Jews of Casablanca began to build homes outside the old medina in the areas of their own choosing.

With the expense of World War II and the withdrawal of troops to defend the motherland, together with the problems associated with the war against nationalists in Algeria, the French found it more and more difficult to sustain a presence in Morocco.

The Moroccan political landscape was changing, and there were calls for independence from nationalist groups. The French had already sent the sultan, Mohammed V, and his family, into exile abroad, which caused the Moroccans to seek revenge by killing unprotected Europeans all over the country. The Americans and the British, strong allies of the Moroccan king, put pressure on France to relinquish the territory. Subsequently, Mohammed V was permitted to return in 1953 and, in 1956, Morocco gained independence.

116

Between the years 1948 and 1968, tens of thousands of Moroccan Jews came to Casablanca, with the intention of starting a new life or awaiting emigration. At its peak, in 1948-1949, Casablanca's Jewish community was estimated to be almost 80,000. That figure dropped dramatically to 60,000 in 1964, and further still to 37,000 in 1967, the majority leaving for Israel. The following year, the number stood at 17,000 out of a total of 22,000 around the country.

Neve Shalom Synagogue
Casablanca
Photo by Ron Hart

Today, the city has approximately 4,000 Jews, and there are no Jews living in the Old Medina. One of Casablanca's suburbs,

Derb Sultan, has a street called Derb L'Yehoud (Street of the Jews). The area has always been a hive of commercial activity. Although Jews owned and ran business in this part of the city, they did not actually reside there.

Casablanca is, today, a city of some 4 million people, many originally from rural regions. A rapid increase in construction over the last seventy years has turned what began as a small coastal town into a bustling and thriving city. A good number of Jewish businesses have benefited from this economic growth.

The city has a much heralded international financial district with its own Stock Exchange, set up by a Moroccan Jewish ex-banker, with years of experience working at France's PARIBAS. It also has several industrial zones, serving the national and international demand for Moroccan produced goods. The port is one of the largest and busiest on the African continent.

Casablanca has thirty-seven synagogues, twenty of which have daily minyans. The largest and the most beautiful is the Beth El (previously named The Temple), built by Algerian Jews who came (1920s). With a capacity for 300 worshipers, it is easy to make room for Jewish tourists and visitors who are welcome to attend the services. It was inaugurated in 1949 and renovated in 1995 and is a beautiful example of a modern Sephardic synagogue.

For the *Shabbat* meal, it is very likely that the visitor will receive an invitation to a private Jewish home where they are sure to experience the renowned Moroccan hospitality and taste real Moroccan cuisine. At other times, an invitation to dine at one of the Jewish community's private clubs is also a possibility.

A Jewish cemetery was created in the southeastern suburb of Ben M'sick in 1956, behind the French-created Christian cemetery. It is the final resting place of Rabbi Eliahou; one of Morocco's most famous and influential Jewish leaders. The rabbi was highly respected by the then king, Mohammed V. On the day of his funeral the king paid the rabbi the greatest honor by walking with the funeral cortège.

The story goes that before his death Rabbi Eliahou predicted he would be buried three times. The first burial was carried out on a site in Casablanca's city center, close to where the Hyatt Hotel stands today. Some time later, the remains of the body had to be moved again, this time to the cemetery in the old *mellah*. On the third occasion, due to no real guarantees of security for the rabbi's shrine and the fact that the rabbi had been declared a *tzadik*, drawing hundreds of pilgrims, his remains were moved to the cemetery at Ben M'sick.

On an organized guided tour you can ask to be taken to the Jewish club, which was repaired and renovated after being damaged by suicide bombers in 2003. The king, Mohammed VI, came in person to inspect the damage and apologize to the Jewish community.

The Environs of Casablanca

Azemmour

Seventy-five kilometers south of Casablanca along a modern toll road toward El Jadida is the Portuguese fortress town of Azemmour, constructed in the fifteenth and sixteenth centuries. The Phoenicians are said to have had a small settlement here at the mouth of the River Oum ou Rbia. Working with Jewish traders, they established links with other trading ports along this particular part of the Atlantic coastline. Not much else is known about the town's history before the Arab occupation of Morocco. Around 1377, Abd er-Rahman, the Merinid sultan, ruling from Marrakech, lost possession of the town to a dynastic rival, Abou el-Abbas, who governed in Fes.

The Portuguese took an interest in the town in 1468 and, with the signing of a treaty with the sultan of the day, began the construction of a fortified trading-post and manned it with a small garrison. Trade consisted of horses, wool products and corn from the nearby Doukkala region and areas further up the Oum ou Rbia valley. Jewish translators and intermediaries played an important role in making sure the passage of goods ran smoothly.

Tensions escalated in 1511, when the Portuguese were informed that their presence was no longer accepted. Unwilling to leave, Lisbon sent an army of 15,000 men and artillery to occupy the town. Some years later, in 1541, incapable of maintaining the occupation due to constant attacks and sieges by the armies of the Moroccan sultan, the Portuguese abandoned the town. At the beginning of the nineteenth century, the town was already in decline, with the Jewish community almost destitute. Salvation, however, came when, in 1821, the sultan, Moulay Abdel er-Rahman, invited Jews to return to a rebuilt El Jadida.

The old town or medina looks picturesque and is located at the mouth of the River Oum-er-Rbia. A walk around the whitewashed narrow lanes and along the river walkway is worth making the trip. The *mellah* was located at the north end of the medina, within the ochre-coloured section of wall, fronting the river. Entrance is through the gate known as *Bab del Mellah* (Gate of the Mellah).

The shrine of Rabbi Abraham Moul Niss (Carrier of Miracles) receives many visitors during the annual pilgrimage in May. However, visits are not restricted to this time. The story goes that he arrived from Israel (date unknown) to collect money. During his stay he ran into conflict, and he feared for his life. He hid in a deep alcove set in the town wall and remained there for the rest of his days. The Jewish community built a sanctuary for his tomb sometime after his death, which is in the old *mellah* close to the river.

El Jadida

Once a thriving commercial port, El Jadida is a short distance down the coast from Casablanca. The town is thought to be on the site of an ancient Phoenician trading post named *Rusibis*, where the Phoenicians worked closely with Jewish traders.

Later, Jewish merchants and intermediaries were present when the Portuguese built a small fort in 1502, known to the locals as *El*

Brija el-Jadida, or the shortened version, *El Jadida*. The Portuguese spent the next several years constructing a well-fortified town with a harbor, and gave it the name, Mazagan, which became the primary Portuguese trading-post in their chain of settlements up and down the Atlantic coastline. The Portuguese also took control of the nearby region of the Doukkala and cultivated vineyards and wheat crops for export to Portugal.

In 1562, the Saadian sultan, Moulay Abdallah, failed in an attempt to dislodge the Portuguese from this heavily defended garrison. When Spain controlled Portugal from 1580 to 1640, it controlled El Jadida before handing it back to Portugal, when the latter won its independence.

Around 1769, the fortress town was taken by Mohammed ben Abdallah, the Alaouite sultan, and the Portuguese were compelled to abandon the town and make an inglorious retreat back to Lisbon. To prevent the Alaouites from using the fortifications, they blew up most of the fort, leaving few spoils for the Moroccan victors.

In 1815 Sultan Moulay Abd er-Rahman started reconstruction, and later encouraged Arabs from the local region of Doukkala and Jews from nearby Azemmour to move to El Jadida, the new name he gave to the town.

In 1821 Jews moved into a corner of the town next to the sea. The entrance to the *mellah* was on the right of the Porte de la Mer at the end of the main street, just before the ramp leading up to the bastions facing the sea. Several Jews ran the *souk*, which used to be in the open space at the foot of the same ramp.

Up on the bastions is an old abandoned courthouse with a prison in its basement. The Jewish Star of David and the Muslim Crescent are still visible on the exterior wall. Both emblems were often used together as a sign of Moroccan ecumenism, indicating the strong union between the Islamic and Jewish religions.

The Jewish cemetery can also be seen from this vantage point, outside the fortress walls. The cemetery contains around 500 graves. Some tombstones mark the final resting place of former translators and other foreign consul employees, lending credence to the important role played by the Jewish community in Morocco's past trade with Europe and other parts of the world.

Despite the rebuilding, the port was little used until Portuguese traders arrived in the late 1800s with the permission of the Moroccan ruler. The town's fortunes started to pick up again with the large community of Jews working together with the Portuguese. By all accounts, mutual respect and religious tolerance helped form good relations and close friendships between the Jews and Muslims of the town.

During the years of the French Protectorate, the town reverted to its old name of Mazagan, and the subsequent expansion of a new town outside the medina included the building of several villas and a few hotels, a theatre and a central market. Most Jews left the old medina and moved into an area of the new town, living door to door with the general Muslim population. The synagogue they frequented was close to the central market, but it was closed toward the end of the 1960s. The wealthier Jews lived in the section of the new town to the south of the old medina, just beyond the landscaped gardens. They had their own synagogue, *Sha'ar Yamin*, which still exists, but has been closed for years.

Under the French, the development of the ports at Casablanca and Safi saw a decline in usage of El Jadida for shipping merchandise. Nevertheless, the town survived as a major player in the fishing industry. Shortly after Moroccan independence in 1956, the name El Jadida was restored once again.

At one time, the Jewish population was close to 5,000, with incomers from Safi and Essaouira. Many worked in trades associated with the local fishing industry. Although the bulk of El Jadida's Jews left for Israel during the 1960s, some businessmen and traders stayed on, not wishing to give up their lucrative businesses, particularly those involved in the business of grains and cereals. In 2008, two surviving Jewish residents, both elderly women, were all that remained of the former Jewish community. The town is without a working synagogue.

South of Casablanca (Atlantic Coast)

Safi

Historical evidence places the port of Safi as being used by the Phoenicians and later by the Romans and the Vandals. It handled cargo arriving from the Moroccan interior, much of which started its journey in sub-Saharan Africa. The same evidence mentions Jewish traders playing a major role in transporting precious metals from one trading-post to the next along the ancient Anti-Atlas caravan routes to its destination at the port of Safi on the Atlantic coast.

During the twelfth century, The Almohad dynasty built a fortified settlement close to the port, naming it *Asfi* (Esfi), as it is called today by all Moroccans. The town became a focal point for religious fanatics, whose intolerant practices caused many Jews to flee from forced conversions and persecution.

The Portuguese arrived at the beginning of the fifteenth century and immediately began building the Ksar-al-Bhur (Fortress on the Sea). The fortress was built to guard against attack by the Moroccan sultans from the landward side and safeguard the port. Confident of the respect the Portuguese had for the Jews, a new generation of Jewish traders returned to the town. The Jewish traders assisted the Portuguese in purchasing Moroccan goods from as far away as Marrakech, later to be exchanged for slaves and gold on the West African coast in countries such as Guinea. Less than two-score years later, the Portuguese abandoned the area, having lost Agadir, further south, to the Moroccan sultan, Mohammed ech-Sheikh, of the Saadian dynasty.

Good fortune came to Safi during the sixteenth century when there was a massive increase in the use of the port due to the interests of European traders. France had its principal Moroccan consulate in the town and various friendship treaties were signed. The port of Safi was considered the most important in Morocco. Some Jews held influential positions in the town, and they prospered. In the eighteenth century, Sultan Moulay ben Abdallah, an Alaouite, concentrated on developing the port of Essaouira, which left Safi in decline and almost forgotten.

Safi, or *Asfi*, made another come back during the twentieth century when a huge financial investment in infrastructure was made to support the growing sardine trade. Jewish fish merchants worked along the coast on the southside of town, and this part of the coastline is still known as *Jorf el Yehoudi* today. The 1970s Safi said farewell to the majority of its Jewish citizens when they migrated to Israel in unprecedented numbers, leaving only a handful of Jewish business people. More recently, the town was chosen as the site for a massive processing plant for one of Morocco's main exports, phosphate.

In 2007 there were only sixteen Jews remaining, all elderly, but still running their own businesses as grain merchants and dealers in the wholesale distribution of sardines. Local Muslims, Arabs mainly from the surrounding countryside, have replaced the Jews in the town's Jewish quarter (There was never an enclosed *mellah* in Safi).

The town is without a synagogue and a rabbi. Nonetheless, the small Jewish community receives a temporary boost when hundreds of Jewish pilgrims from around the world arrive each July. They come to visit the shrine of the Jewish *tzadik* and doctor, Rabbi Brahim Ben Zimirou, who came from Spain in the sixteenth century. His seven sons (Ouled Zimirou) are buried at his side in a separate complex from the Jewish cemetery. When alive, the sons won much fame and fortune as fortune-tellers. The Jewish cemetery in Safi overlooks the Atlantic Ocean, and is of a grand scale with hundreds of graves, which confirms the large size of the town's former Jewish community.

Essaouira (Mogador)

Essaouira is a picturesque town. Many Jews still fondly call it by its old name, Mogador. The old, walled town sits close to the beach with the waves of the Atlantic Ocean breaking nearby. Like most port towns along Morocco's Atlantic coast, Essaouira, has along history connected with international trade. Pieces of excavated pottery place the Phoenicians as having a small trading-post on the immediate off-shore islands, and Jewish traders are known to have been present as far back as the sixth century B.C.E. The Carthaginians were drawn to the area and built a settlement here, where they remained for decades.

124

In the first century B.C.E., King Juba II of Mauritania, which included the entire Maghreb, set up a factory for the production of purple dye on the largest island. The islands then became known as the Purple Islands. The Romans bought up huge quantities of the purple dye extracted from the abundant supply of a species of mollusc gathered from the seabed close to the shore. The purple dye was used exclusively for the robes worn by Roman aristocrats and nobles. The practice of mollusc gathering still continues today, during the months of July and August, along certain stretches of the Atlantic coastline.

There seems to be some uncertainty about the original name of the small settlement, which grew up on the shore opposite the islands. The Berber name *Amogdoul* is mentioned by some ancient historians and geographers. They claim it existed as a port of call or anchorage in the eleventh century and again in the fourteenth century.

The Portuguese, at the beginning of the fifteenth century, took control of the area, built a trading-post and garrison town within a fortress-like structure and named it Mogador. Jews played a large role in making the town successful. Under the Portuguese, some Jews rose to positions of influence, taking care of the affairs of the town. In the sixteenth century, the Saadian sultan, Moulay Abd el-Malek, fought for and won control of the town, sending the defeated Portuguese back to their homeland.

In 1760, Sultan Moulay Mohammed ben Abdallah, an Alaouite, came to power, and his reign brought a period of stability in which the Jews of Essauoira made political and economical progress. Moulay Mohammed was the person responsible for most of the town's architecture and grid layout as seen today. In the latter part of the eighteenth century, he instructed a captured

French architect, Théodore Cornut, to create a town based along the lines of European cities at that time. This was an example of the Alaouites' historical support of modernization. On completion of the construction, the sultan was so impressed that he named the town Essauoira, derived from the Arabic word for picture, *teswira*.

In a move to attract European business, Sultan Moulay Mohammed declared the importation of goods free from customs duties. His plans and efforts drew hundreds of foreign merchants to come and live in the town and many countries set up consular offices with Jews as their representatives. To protect their investment, the foreign governments issued their Jewish consuls with documents, which took them out of the sphere and influence of Morocco's central power. Essauoira has an old Christian cemetery where foreign residents are buried.

The town's prosperity was even more enhanced by the influx of a large number of Jews from around Morocco, especially from Agadir, which had lost its previous dominance and importance to the new town. Many Jews made their living as wholesalers of sardines and anchovies. Essauoira, formally Mogador, was now considered one of the principal ports dealing with Europe. In 1867, the *Alliance Israélite Universelle* opened more than one school in the town to accommodate the large number of Jewish children.

When the French moved in under the Protectorate, the town's name reverted to Mogador and the bulk of trade moved to the new port in Casablanca and other more efficient ports such as Tangier. From the 1920s to the 1960s was a dismal period for the people of Essaouira; due to the changes made by the French, unemployment was rampant. The younger generation of Jews, dissatisfied and frustrated, drifted away to the larger towns, Marrakech, Agadir, and Casablanca. By the end of the 1960s, most of the remaining Jews had left the *mellah* to join relatives in Israel.

In recent years Essaouira has undergone major renovation since a group of former residents, most of them Jewish, formed an association to bring life back to the town. Their efforts have been rewarded. The fishing and resort town today attracts thousands of visitors and tourists, in particular Jewish tourists who come to learn about its rich Jewish heritage. As a gesture of confidence, dozens of foreign Jewish businessmen have invested in the town's appeal by buying up property.

As part of its program of promotion, the town also holds a well-attended annual music festival, normally toward the end of June. International musicians are invited to perform in front of thousands, by no means all Moroccan. So many people come that finding accommodations during the festival is difficult.

The Mellah. Parts of the Mellah received restoration work; especially the former home of one of Morocco's better known Jewish *tzadiks*, Rabbi Haim Pinto. The house was built in 1860, with a synagogue incorporated on the upper floor. It is open to Jewish visitors, and the guardian and holder of the keys is a young local Muslim.

Jewish Stars of David have survived over the doorways of some dwellings, an indication of the religious identity of former occupants and proof of the acceptance of the Jewish community in Essaouira. The Jewish inhabitants of Essaouira were, at one time, 40 percent of the town's population. Chronic overcrowding resulted in the town elders having to add two more separate Jewish quarters, making Essaouira the only town in Morocco with three *mellahs*.

The Jewish Cemeteries. A short walk outside one of the town's historic gateways, and you come upon two Jewish cemeteries. The oldest, dating from 1776, houses the shrine of Rabbi Haim Pinto, an extremely popular Moroccan Jewish *tzadik*. He is usually referred to as Rabbi Haim Pinto Ha-Gadol (the Elder) to avoid confusion with his grandson of the same name, also a *tzadik*, but buried in the old Jewish cemetery in Casablanca. It is not unusual to see up to ten coach loads of international Jewish pilgrims arriving during the days in September set aside to commemorate his memory; upwards of 6,000 pilgrims visited in 2007. Former Jewish residents of the town speak of the terminally ill and dying staying close to the Rabbi's shrine until the last hours, before passing away. Countless pilgrims shed tears over the tomb, which is within a sanctuary dominating the cemetery.

The other cemetery, very close by, was created out of necessity as an overspill. The custom, set under *Megorashim* rules, was to bury the dead with their heads pointing toward the cemetery gate and the gravestones of females were engraved with a hair design or human form. The plain gravestones mark the resting place of a male. Both cemeteries are well maintained and open to Jewish visitors on request.

The Medina. Many of the financially successful Jews who held positions of influence had their homes outside the *mellah*, where they even built their own private synagogues. Commemorative plaques mark out the buildings, which were synagogues previously, and one or two are on hold for future possible restoration. One of the town's large monumental gateways still bears Jewish insignias.

Patio of House. Fes. Photo by Gloria Abella Ballen

12
Fes and Environs

Meknes
Fes
Sefrou

❀ Fes is a region of surprisingly natural beauty: rolling hills, abundant rivers, cedar-covered slopes and lush green pastures. In this ideal setting the first of Morocco's royal dynasties, the Idrissids, chose to build their capital, Fes, in the year, 808 C.E. Jews had already settled in the region, as archaeological evidence found at the Roman ruins of Volubilis, north of Meknes, has testified. Thousands more arrived over the centuries from other North African countries and the Iberian Peninsula, escaping from anti-Semitic persecution. Many chose to start a new life in Fes, while others settled in the surrounding towns such as Sefrou and Meknes. Their intellect, as well as their skills in commerce, handicrafts and agriculture, played a vital role in the region's economic success. Today, the entire region depends on agriculture, in particular the cultivation of olives, pears and grapes.

Meknes

The Berber tribe, the Meknassa, built a settlement here in the tenth century C.E. and named it Meknassa ez-Zitun (Meknes of the Olives), close to the Oued Boufkrane (River Boufkrane). Abd el-Moumin, of the Almohad dynasty, occupied the town around 1146, and many Jews fled, due to harsh treatment and pressure to convert.

When Almohad rule finally ended in the thirteenth century, the Merinids took control of the town, and the Jews returned in large numbers. The following period was one of prosperity and building projects, such as great mosques and *madrasas*. The town grew rich from the sale of agricultural produce: olives and olive oil, grapes, wheat and citrus fruit, and Jewish merchants had an important role in this development.

In the fifteenth century, the town went through a period of instability as a result of family squabbles between various factions in the Merinid families, as princes fought among themselves over claims and counter-claims for the throne.

Stability, however, returned with the Saadians (sixteenth century), who granted several privileges to Jewish merchants in the country. In 1672, with the financial assistance from the Jews of Meknes, the second Alaouite ruler, Moulay Ismail (1672–1727), came to power and soon after made Meknes his capital and, therefore, an imperial city. Moulay Ismail was *khalifa* (deputy) of Meknes when he heard of the death of his predecessor, Moulay er-Rachid, who passed away while on a visit to Marrakech. He moved quickly to consolidate his power.

The main factor in Ismail's choice of Meknes was attributable to its central position from where he could control the lands between Fes and Marrakech, the *Bled el-Makhzen*, formally the only part of Morocco under any real control of the sultans. The *Bled el-Siba,* the rest of the country remained, more or less, off-limits or uncontrollable for many Moroccan rulers until its pacification under the French Protectorate during the 1930s.

Important individuals in the Jewish community made Moulay Ismail's proclamation and transition to the throne faster and easier than it would have been. In appreciation of their actions he rewarded a favored circle of Jews, and some were appointed to high office within the royal palace. Others worked in the diplomatic field and were entrusted with the signing of foreign treaties. Historical records demonstrate that the Jews close to the sultan exerted their power of persuasion over him, which assisted in protecting the country's Jews.

Although the tax burden on the Jews was unreasonably high, Ismail did give them protection. He also allocated the Jewish community a strip of land to build a *mellah*, which was close to the sultan's storehouse for salt. The storehouse was later enclosed within the *mellah,* with only a small group of trusted Jewish businessmen authorized to manage it. Despite Moulay Ismail's reputation as a cruel and sadistic ruler, the Jewish community was treated well.

Under Ismail, Meknes took on a new form with a series of massive building projects. Some of the finer decorated pillars, he brought from older buildings in Marrakech and Volubilis.

Extravagance, excess and self-indulgence characterized his reign, and moderation was not a value for him. Twenty-five kilometers of defensive walls surround the town, and he constructed magnificent ornamental gateways and stables for well over 12,000 horses, a huge complex of palaces to house his harems and hundreds of offspring. He had thousands of slaves and is reported to have made a sport of decapitating them, especially African and European slaves. He imposed high taxation rates to pay for the building projects and his military campaigns.

When Moulay Ismail died in 1727, his son, Moulay Abdallah, made a conscious effort to carry on the construction of Meknes, which was then followed up by his grandson, Moulay ben Abdallah. Jews did well under Moulay ben Abdallah, who also granted favors and allowed certain Jews to climb to positions of influence and political responsibility.

However, Abdallah's preferential treatment of the Jews caused resentment among the larger Muslim community, who following the sultan's death took revenge by attacking and looting the *mellah*. Instability caused the decline of Meknes, and the capital was moved to Fes.

Two explanations are put forward for today's extensive damage to the former grand palace complexes built by Moulay Ismail. One says the complex was a victim of a massive earthquake, which spread devastation as far away as Europe in 1755. Another explanation claims that successive sultans allowed the deterioration of the site through a lack of interest and the high cost of maintenance. It is also most likely to have been cannibalized for building materials by local people over the years.

Moulay al-Yazid (1790-92), the successor to Moulay ben Abdallah, was revengeful and made no effort to conceal his hatred for Jews after he was refused a loan while the heir to the throne. Rounding up his father's Jewish courtiers, he then had them hung by their feet outside the gates of Meknes, where they stayed until death brought them relief after days of suffering.

Robert Kerr, a Christian missionary, visited Meknes toward the end of the nineteenth century. What he discovered left him profoundly shocked; the population, he estimated to be between 40,000 and 50,000, of which 5,000 to 6,000 were Jews. The *mellah* was the filthiest he had come across during his tour of the country, and Jews did not share the same freedoms found in Fes or the major coastal towns. One example was that the Jews were forced to remove their footwear whenever they passed through the Muslim quarter, especially in the vicinity of sacred places such as mosques.

Long before the period of the French Protectorate, Jews were granted authorization to build a new *mellah* (adjacent to the old *mellah*), and the majority later abandoned the old *mellah*, leaving the Muslims to move into the abandoned quarter. Several synagogues and community associations were established. Jews worked as silversmiths, tailors and grain sellers, citrus and olive dealers, and in occupations connected to the wool trade. Meknes is renowned for its good quality wines and excellent olives. It is thought that it was Jews who spread the cultivation of grapevines and olive trees around Morocco, even before the Romans arrived.

For a time after the signing of the Treaty of Fes in 1912, Jewish merchants in Meknes prospered supplying the French military garrisons around the town until they were eventually replaced by French colonial suppliers. The French used Jews as intermediaries and interpreters between themselves and the greater Muslim population, and even went a step further by promoting Jews to the rank of military officers, which caused divisions between Muslims and Jews.

In 1937, unable to tolerate the negative effects of French policies, Muslim rioters stormed the *mellah*, raided Jewish commercial premises and left buildings completely destroyed. The French turned a blind eye.

Two years later, in 1939, riots were sparked off by a dispute between youths over a Jew who had converted to Islam, culminating in an attack on the unwalled new *mellah*. The total number of casualties included three dead Jews. On this occasion the French authorities again did nothing.

After the establishment of the state of Israel in 1948, tensions related to the Arab-Israeli War caused some Jews to emigrate to Israel. However, the bulk of Meknesi Jews left in the mid-sixties. Today, the Jewish community numbers around 180, including a few young children. Supplies of kosher food have to be transported from Rabat. The Meknes *mellah* is the only one in the whole of Morocco with streets named after rabbis and, in years gone by, the town was known as Little Jerusalem.

What to Visit in Meknes

Barroukh Toledano Synagogue. Constructed in the nineteenth century by the Toledano family, Sephardim who originally came from Toledo in Spain, the Barroukh Toledano synagogue is situated in the new *mellah*. Restoration was carried out (2005-2006) by the Foundation for the History and Culture of Moroccan Jews (based at the Jewish Museum, Casablanca) and also by the local Jewish community.

Beth El Synagogue. The only synagogue in use today, the Beth El synagogue, dates from the 1930s and is located in the new *mellah*.

Aim-Habbonim School. The education of children was seen as paramount for most Jewish parents. For decades the majority of the Jewish children of Meknes received their education in the Aim-Habbonim School, which is no longer in use. The building, now eerily silent, has stood for over 250 years and also included a synagogue.

Jewish Cemeteries. Many cemeteries can give a clear indication of how long a town or its population has been in existence. The site of the old Meknes Jewish Cemetery has been dated to be around 600 years old and is the only one in Morocco where the tombs of important rabbis were placed into the walls. Three of the better known tzadiks are: Haim Messas, David Boussidan and Raphael Berdugo. The newer of the two cemeteries is located in the modern part of town.

134

Entrance to Tomb of Moulay Ismail, Meknes
Photo by Ron Hart

Fes: The First Imperial City

The most ancient of the imperial cities, Fes was founded by Idriss II around 789 C.E., having been drawn to the area by the abundance of fresh water and the green and fertile location. Some evidence suggests that a tribe of Berber Jews had once settled on the site. The original population of Fes was predominantly Berber, but in the early 800s there were major immigrations of Arabs and Jews into the city.

Realizing the importance of Jews to the realm's economy and as a source to his own wealth, Idriss II encouraged Jews to come and live in his new city. Around 8,000 families, many of them Jews, fleeing from the tyrannical King el-Hakim, the Muslim ruler in Cordoba, Spain, settled on the eastside of the river (Oued Fes) in 817 and 818. Thus creating Quartier Adouat el-Andalus (in Fes el-Bali), as it is known today. So many Jews lived in Fes that it became known as the City of Jews.

In 824 the Muslim population received a boost when Arabs from Kairouan in Tunisia settled on the west bank of the river, called Quartier Kairaouine today. Both Muslim and Jews held to their own customs, and the Jews were permitted to retain their structures of legal and religious institutions. Although the Almoravid dynasty (eleventh century) later chose Marrakech as their capital, Fes held its own and continued to grow and prosper.

This historic city became the spiritual center and the focal point for religious and academic studies for both Muslims and Jews, with a large concentration of synagogues, mosques, *madrasas* (Koranic schools) and universities. Jews were renowned for their exceptional skills in the making of gold thread, lace, embroidery and tailoring, all in great demand by the high society in Fes. They were also responsible for creating the Moroccan *djallaba* for both men and women and the *caftan* worn on special occasions by women, both Jewish and Muslim.

The Jews of Fes were the victims of occasional attacks over the centuries and many of the families in the old city (Fes el-Bali) were Jews who converted to Islam but kept their original Jewish names.

One street in the city also retains its original name; Derb L-Yehoud (Street of the Jews).

During the years of Almohad rule (twelfth century), Marrakech and Rabat were the two towns that received most of this dynasty's attention. Ongoing commercial relations with Muslim Spain maintained Fes as an important part of the country's economy during this period. The Almohads controlled both Morocco and Muslim Spain, where they embarked on a campaign of the spiritual renovation of Islam. That in turn resulted in persecutions and forced conversions of Jews. Thousands of Jews fled Morocco while many Spanish Jews were fleeing from Muslim Spain and becoming part of the Jewish community in Fes, which suffered less persecution.

The family of Moses Maimonides (1135–1204) followed this route in escaping persecution in Spain, and he lived in Fes as a young man from 1159 to 1165. Under pressure from the Almohad rulers to convert to Islam, he escaped to Egypt, subsequently becoming the physician to the Egyptian Sultan. The building where he is purported to have lived still stands in Fes today. Maimonides became one of the most important Jewish scholars of all time, and his *Mishneh Torah* is still required study in many Jewish schools. As a scientist and religious scholar, he is one of the first to explore the complicated relationship between science and faith, and his *Guide for the Perplexed* continues to be the classic work on that subject. He is also respected in the Arab world and is considered to be an Arab scholar. Much of his writing was in Arabic.

In the latter part of the thirteenth century, the Merenids overthrew the Almohads and made their capital in Fes. They organized the construction of the religious *madrasas* and much of Fes el-Jdid (New Fes). The original, older part of the town became Fes el-Bali (Old Fes). In the proceeding years, the Jews were given preferential treatment and special concessions. The Merenids were aware of the Jews' skills in running the economy and their importance in dealing with foreign trade, as a result of their international contacts. Seething resentment of the Jews' privileged position later came to a head in 1276, when Muslim rioters took to the streets of Fes attacking the Jewish population.

By 1438 the Merenids were losing control and attacks on Jews and their property became more frequent. The Jewish community in Fes el-Bali was moved to a former military garrison next to the royal palace in Fes el-J. Later, it became a salt market. Through time, the area became known as the *mellah*. The Fondouq el-Yehoud (Fondouq of the Jews, Inn of the Jews) in the former Jewish quarter of Fes el-Bali is a present reminder of this stage in the imperial city's history.

In 1492 Andalucia came under the control of Catholic Spain, and King Ferdinand and Queen Isabella issued their "Edict of Expulsion," giving an ultimatum to all Jews and Muslims to convert to Catholicism or leave their realms. There were more than 165,000 Jews of Spanish origin at the time.

Fes was chosen as a destination by a large number of Jews fleeing Spain, who later became known as Sephardim (Hebrew for Spanish) or *Megorashim* (the banished) by the already established Jews, *Toshavim*. For various reasons already explained (see under The Sephardim) the two communities led almost separate lives for four centuries.

Fes fell into the hands of the Saadians in 1554. The Saadian dynasty originated from the southern end of the Draa valley and had long since made Marrakech their capital. The ruling sultan appointed a close family member (usually a brother) to govern Fes on his behalf. Despite this arrangement, Saadian control in the city was frequently challenged by family disputes and attempts to gain control by local Berber tribes. It was only later during the reign of the Saadian, Moulay Ahmed el-Mansour (1578-1603) that order and stability in the city were restored.

Further political turmoil returned to the city following the death of Moulay Ahmed el-Mansour, when three of his sons quarrelled over the right to succession. At one point, the country had two sultans; Moulay Zidan ruled from Fes, while Moulay ech-Sheikh el-Mamoun ruled from Marrakech. The people of Fes had to chose which one to support.

Eventually, the Saadian sultans began to lose power and attempts to undermine their authority intensified. As a result, the Jews were given the monopoly on several commodities as a way to increase taxes in order to defend against the military challenges to their rule.

In 1640, the Saadian sultan, Mohammed ech-Sheikh el-Mamoun, lost control of Fes to Berber *marabouts* (a religious brotherhood). Under the *marabouts*, Fes went into serious decline, forcing the inhabitants to give their backing to the Alaouite charif, Moulay Mohammed to seize the city. The *marabouts* later managed to regain control and held the city until the appearance of another Alaouite, Moulay er-Rachid, the first of the Alaouite dynasty, who took power in 1660.

Without the financial assistance of a circle of Jewish merchants from Taza, northeast of Fes, it might not have happened at all. Moulay er-Rachid had already taken control of Taza, and had bigger ambitions to rule the whole of Morocco. Lacking the necessary funds to present a challenge to the throne, he was given financial backing by Jewish merchants, and secretly entered the *mellah* of Fes. Accommodations were supplied by one of Fes' prominent Jews.

Following his successful accession to the throne, Moulay er-Rachid looked favorably on the Jews, and many prospered under his reign. A similar strategy of help and financial support was adopted to bring his successor, Moulay Ismail, to power. On that occasion, it was with the Jews of Meknes, where Moulay Ismail decided to have his capital.

The closing years of the eighteenth century started well for the Jewish community in Fes. Sultan Moulay Mohammed ben Abdallah (Alaouite dynasty) brought prestige back to Fes by making it his capital. From here, he worked closely with the

Jews and even appointed a few to serve in his government. After the death of Mohammed ben Abdallah, his son Moylay el-Yazid used his power as the new sultan to persecute the Jews.

Under the Alaouite kings, the Jews were permitted to rebuild their communities and businesses but still within the confines of the *mellahs*. Life for the Jews of Fes returned to some semblance of normality, and a few prospered. By the middle of the nineteenth century, the European powers, Britain, France, Spain and Germany began to show an in earnest interest in adding Morocco to their colonies. After a period of threats of war, squabbling and, finally, negotiations, parts of Morocco were divided between France and Spain.

In 1912 the French moved the center of their administration to the coastal town of Rabat; away from the troubles and stresses with having to deal with tribal rebellion and other insecurities, much to the disapproval of the Fassi (Fessi) royal hangers-on and political elite. The French colonists later added a new sector to Fes by constructing the *Ville Nouvelle*, with wide avenues and landscaped gardens.

Emigration to Israel began in Fes, first as a trickle, in the 1950s, progressing to a flood as the decade ended. Remnants of the middle-class Jews who had stayed because of business commitments choose, in the 1960's, to go to Canada and France rather than face the problems Israel was experiencing with its Arab neighbors.

What to see in Fes

Slat Sadoune, circa 1920s, is one of the synagogues still in use. The other, Beth El, is located under the Jewish community center, Maimonide, where visitors to Fes will be warmly received. The center includes a kosher restaurant.

Mellah. Fes' fifteenth century *mellah* is crowded into the southern corner of Fes el-Jdid, fairly close to the Royal Palace. History reminds us of the time (fifteenth century) when it was necessary to vacate the original *mellah* in Fes el-Bali (Old Town) due to constant attacks by disgruntled Muslims. The hope was the Jews would be better protected by living on the doorstep of the sultan; however, later historical events proved otherwise.

It was the local population that subsequently gave the area the name, *mellah,* derived from the Arabic word *mleh*, meaning salt. Whenever they had the need to buy salt, they would say, for example, "We need to go to the *mellah* to buy salt." The name *mellah* then came into common use to describe a Jewish quarter, whether it was enclosed or open.[2]

The *mellahs*, the name given to Jewish quarters in Morocco, were usually constructed near to the royal palaces or the *kasbahs* of the local *caids*, making protection of the Jews a much easier task. Some were enclosed behind protective walls with gates that were locked on *Shabbat*, so no business could be conducted, and also at night to keep harm on the outside.

Mellah as an expression was not in common use in the Spanish controlled north of the country. Instead, the Jewish quarter was called *La Calle de Judío.* The houses standing today in the *mellah* are mostly from the eighteenth and nineteenth centuries and easily identifiable by their small windows and ornate iron grills. The *Rue des Mérinides* provides the best examples. The narrow lanes were once cramped with Jewish shops and their customers, with a most welcome respite each *Shabbat* when the whole of the *mellah* closed down. The *mellah* once held around 30,000 Jews, and the vast majority lived in substandard housing and poverty. By 1947, the estimated count was 23,000. Today, the Jewish community in Fes has approximately 100 people, and all are residents of the French built *Ville Nouvelle.* Muslims now occupy the *mellah.*

---

2   A myth developed that in accepting the monopoly for selling salt, Jews were expected to salt (and hence preserve) the decapitated heads of those executed by the ruler. There is no evidence that Jews were involved in any such acts.

Ibn Danan Synagogue. In all, there were twenty-eight synagogues in Fes, mostly closed now. The most famous and most visited is the restored seventeenth century, Rabbi Ibn Danan Synagogue. A plaque above the entrance informs of the name of the synagogue in Arabic, Hebrew and Roman lettering. It also indicates the seventeenth century as the date of construction and 141 1998-1999 as the period when the last restoration was done. The interior walls are covered in tiling. The Ark is of elaborately carved dark-wood. A visit to this unique synagogue is a must. It is now a UNESCO World Heritage site.

Rabbi Ibn Danan Synagogue, Fes
Photo by Gloria Abella Ballen

Jewish Cemetery. It is located immediately behind the south wall of the *mellah*, and it is one of the best-maintained Jewish cemeteries in Morocco. There were originally two entrances in use: one directly from the *mellah* and the other through the main entrance or gate. Burial society members have ensured the whitewashed tombs were set in neat rows. The most venerated *tzadiks* are marked out by their separate shrines. One section comprises of the unmarked graves of the victims of a plague. Another section was set aside for the *Cohanim*, or priests.

The grave of Abraham Ibn Attar, the writer of *Gour Ayer* (The Book of Jewish Law), who died in 1665, is to be found there among many other Jewish notables and scholars. The two most visited *tzadiks* are Rabbi Avner Ha Zarfati and Lalla Solica, considered as a martyr to her faith. The original mourner's bench is still in place, as is a fountain used for ablutions. A charity box is conveniently located close to the main gate. Like the Ibn Danan synagogue, the Jewish cemetery is now an UNESCO World Heritage site.

The Story of
Lalla Solica Hachwelle

Countless numbers of Jews come to pray at the graveside of the martyr, Lalla Solica Hachwelle. There are numerous stories about her heroic deed when she was put under great pressure to renounce her Jewish religion and convert to Islam. The following is perhaps the most common version.

Lalla Solica was born in Tangier in 1817. The family later moved to Fes. Once while walking near her parents' home, she was seen by one of the sons of the then Sultan, who immediately fell in love with her. As was the custom and in many cases still is, the son asked her parents for her hand in marriage. and they gave their consent. She refused because it would meant that she would have to convert to Islam.

To force her hand, the Sultan's son went to the office of the *caid*, a local government administrator and denounced her. He claimed that Solica could not turn down his proposal of marriage as she was no longer Jewish, having previously converted to Islam of her own accord. During a meeting with the *Caid*, Solica protested that she had not converted. When called before the Sultan, she categorically stated she had never gone through conversion. Eventually, she was accused of being an apostate and condemned to death in the year 1834.

Habanim Synagogue. Located within the Jewish cemetery, the Habanim Synagogue is now home to a museum with a collection of various artifacts donated by or left behind by previous occupants of the *mellah*: photo albums, books and personal items such as clothing. The Jews of Fes kept scrupulous records of births, marriages and deaths etc. The museum has records going back many generations.

143

Jewish Cemetery Fes
Tomb of Lalla Solica on right blackened from the smoke of memorial candles
Photo by Gloria Abella Ballen

Three in One

Today, Fes is comprised of three distinct parts: Fes el-Bali (the Old Town), Fes el-Jdid (the New Town) and the *Ville Nouvelle*, constructed by the French.

Fes el-Bali (Old Fes). The Jews expelled from Spain in the fifteenth and sixtieth centuries, brought skills and knowledge in the dying of wool and animal hides. Mindful of any competition, they formed tanners and dyers guilds. Morocco leather, as it was known, could fetch a substantial price on the international market, in particular, the fine soft leather made from the skin of a goat, used in bookbinding and much admired by ardent book collectors.

Very little has changed in the tanning process that has survived for centuries, which gives the site of the tanneries a particular medieval appearance. Men stand knee-deep in large vats filled with a concoction of cow urine, pigeon droppings and ash. Their job is to tread on the hides, keeping them submerged. Commercial dyes were added later; mostly chemical dyes, unlike the natural vegetable dyes used in earlier days. At the end of this process, the treated skins are laid out on the rooftops to dry in the sun.

Dye Vats for Leather, Fes
Photo by Gloria Abella Ballen

Fes el-Jdid (New Fes). The Merenids took great care when plans were drawn up for their new city. The intention was to build a city that could be easily defended from the occasional unrest caused by the rebellious Berber tribes living in the not too distant mountains. Construction got underway in about 1273, on the orders of the second sultan, Youssef Yacoub, and was ready for occupation within three years, with the inclusion of the *Dar el-Makhzen,* and the royal palace and a network of military garrisons.

Ville Nouvelle. There is no mistaking that the *Ville Nouvelle* was built by the French. In contrast to the older Fes el-Bali and Fes el-Jdid with their narrow lanes, there are wide tree-lined boulevards, beautifully landscaped gardens and many of the original French constructed buildings that still remain intact. The life-style of its inhabitants bears traces of the former colonists: outdoor cafes every few meters, small boutiques with French names, and elegant Fassi women sporting the latest fashion trends, speaking only French. Fes' small Jewish community is located in this section of the city. Many of the residents are in their older years, but there are a few young children. Jews are mostly self-employed as business people. Most of the kosher food is delivered from Rabat.

Although decidedly hot and humid, the streets are full of activity in summer evenings, as people emerge from their homes to stroll along boulevards lit by a spectacular display of lights. Many people sit at tables outside the many cafes, surrounded by family and friends, just like the French used to do.

Sefrou

Some thirty kilometers to the south of Fes is the ancient and walled town of Sefrou. The association between the town and the Jews has a long history going back to pre-Islamic times. It was formally the home territory of the Ahel Sefrou, a Berber tribe living on the lower slopes of the Middle Atlas Mountains. Around the time when Islam was making inroads into Morocco, the tribe converted to Judaism. They also built a settlement on the banks of the Oued el-Yhudi (River of the Jews), as it became known.

In the ninth century, during the construction of Fes, Sultan Moulay Idriss II was a frequent visitor. He seems to have spent a good part of his time in the area carrying out his personal crusade of forced conversions, and from all accounts he succeeded.

Sefrou was an important commercial center on the caravan routes that ran between Fes, in the north, and the region of Tafilalt, on the edge of the desert to the southeast. By the twelfth century, the town had grown to a considerable size, and under the Merinids in the thirteenth century, it expanded even further when hundreds of Jews arrived from the area of Tafilalt and the southern reaches of neighboring Algeria.

The Medina, the original old town, is separated from the rest of the town by the Oued Aggai (also known as Oued el-Yhudi). The area of the *mellah*, situated on the south bank, took up almost half of the town, and at one time the Jews made up nearly half the population (4,000 Jews of 10,000 population), prompting the town of Sefrou to be known as Little Jerusalem. Most of the buildings are from the nineteenth century, as are the ramparts that enclose the old town.

The Jews were restricted to the area of the *mellah*, which over time created serious problems of overcrowding and a shortage of suitable housing. Jewish landlords or owners of property took advantage of the huge demand for accommodation by building houses three stories high. In many instances, a whole family occupied a single room. Life for most in the dank, dark and gloomy narrow streets was miserable and harsh.

From around 1912 onwards, the younger members of the Jewish community began to move to the larger urban centers, especially Casablanca, in search of gainful employment.

During the early years of French Protectorate, the local Jewish landowners prospered. However, the good-life came to an end in 1941, when the, Nazi controlled, French Vichy Government passed laws discriminating against Morocco's Jewish population; credit facilities to Jews were curtailed and times became difficult for fruit growers and others involved in agriculture.

In 1950, disaster struck when the nearby river broke its banks and flooded part of the *mellah*, resulting in the loss of twenty-one lives. Over the years, the nearby *Kef el-Yhudi*, also known as *Kef el-Moumin*, a cave of pilgrimage for both Jews and Muslims, received many pilgrims who prayed for a better life. Prayers were eventually answered when most of the Jewish community abandoned their homes and departed for Israel in the 1950s.

One of the town's remaining Jewish structures is the now vacant orphanage and school, Aim-Habbonim, which includes an unused synagogue. It is also possible to see what was once the *mellah*. The houses here, now inhabited by Berbers, were abandoned by the Jews in the 1950s. Look closely at the door posts, and it is possible to make out the marks left by the *mezuzah*.

Sefrou's Jewish cemetery is located on the main road, at the entrance to the more modern area of the town, coming in from the direction of Fes. The cemetery gates are easily identifiable from the large Hebrew inscriptions. Funding for the restoration and maintenance of the Jewish cemetery is in the hands of former Jewish residents now residing overseas. The cemetery contains monuments that commemorate the merchants who met their deaths in a fatal truck accident while travelling to the region of Tafilalt and the victims of the flood of 1950.

Many former residents and their descendants return for the annual pilgrimages honoring Sefrou's *tzadiks*: Eliahou Harraoch, David Arazil, Moshe Elbaz and the Masters of the Cave.

Sefrou today is predominately inhabited by Berbers, a fact that can be substantiated by its calmness and the lack of loud music, as opposed to Arab dominated towns, which are normally noisy with music blaring out of cafes and shops.

The region of Sefrou is famous for the cultivation of cherries. Each year, in June, the town holds a very popular Cherry Festival, when a Cherry Queen is chosen. Celebrations last three days and include dancing, street processions and folk music.

13
Northeast

Taza
Oujda
Debdou
Figuig

The Northeast Passage, as it is sometimes called, runs from Fes to the town of Oujda on Morocco's north-eastern frontier with Algeria. It is the historical route taken by the Romans, the Jews, the Arabs and, lately, the French as the landward entrance to the interior of Morocco.

149

It was also a much used section of the ancient caravan routes that wound their way up from the desert ports in the far south of the country, a fact that allowed several Jewish communities to settle in this region; the small towns of Guercif and Taourirt are just two examples. The two principle towns are Taza and Oujda, with the latter at the end of the route and close to the Morocco-Algeria frontier.

Taza

The town of Taza is at a distance of approximately 116 kilometers northeast from Fes. The nearby Taza Gap, a long natural corridor or wide pass running between the Rif Mountains and the Middle Atlas, is the only feasible or practicable route connecting Eastern Morocco to the interior and the west of the country.

The Romans, the Arabs and the French are known to have invaded Morocco via the pass from Algeria. A large number of Jews would have come through the pass in the sixth century C.E., fleeing in advance of the Arab armies marching in a westerly direction through the countries of North Africa. As the Arab invaders progressed, they caused panic among Jewish inhabitants who refused to embrace Islam.

Before the Arab invasion the region was inhabited by a Berber tribe, the Meknassa, who split away from the larger tribe by the same name. In the latter part of the seventh century, they built a small *ksar* (fortified settlement) and gave it the name *Meknassa Taza*. The Meknassa tribe are said to have accepted the authority of Idriss I and his son, Idriss II.

In 1074, the Almoravids took control of the town and surrounded it with a defensive wall and built a mosque. The succeeding dynasties, the Almohads and Merenids, also added mosques and *madrasas*. The Saadians (fourteenth and fifteenth centuries) are credited with making Taza the best fortified town in the eastern region of Morocco.

The Jews of Taza were instrumental in assisting Alaouite rulers to come to power in the seventeenth century. They helped the founder of the Alaouite Dynasty, Moulay er-Rachid and later Moulay Ismail (1672-1727) with the funds needed to launch their bids for the throne. Toward the end of the seventeenth century and the earlier part of the eighteenth century, Moulay Ismail built *madrasas* and a few other buildings in the town. Although Taza had lost some of its importance commercially, it played a vital role in controlling the eastern flank of the country and preventing attacks by enemy forces from Algeria.

The rebellious local tribes of the Taza region had been a thorn in the side of most sultans. Under Moulay Abd el-Aziz (1894–1907), Morocco's economy was in dire straits and the sultan's influence had grown pitifully weak, making the situation ripe for rebellion.

Taza was overrun by the local tribes led by a upstart named, Moulay Mohammed. However, history has registered him as Bou Hamara, translated as "The father of the female donkey." "El Rogui" (The Pretender) was added to his name, after he had himself proclaimed sultan in Taza.

A disastrous attempt was made in 1903 by Abd el-Aziz' troops to dislodge Bou Hamara from inside the town. Although the troops were able to enter by blasting the gates with cannon fire, once inside, they found the going tough, with the intense fighting lasting two days. Local tribes arrived in support of Bou Hamara and trapped the sultan's troops within the walls, resulting in a massacre.

Jews managed to escape the turmoil and re-settled in the northern town of Debdou and the Spanish town of Melilla.

Later, the sultan sent new troops, and they captured the rebels and sold them in the souk.

Following some political skulduggery involving a member of the Glaoui family, Moulay Hafid replaced his brother, Moulay Abd el-Aziz, as sultan in Fes. El Rogui was eventually captured in 1909 by Hafid's troops and taken to Fes, where he was paraded through the streets in a cage prior to his subsequent execution.

151

In 1914, French troops occupied Taza and made it into a garrison town, from which operations were carried out to subdue the rebellious tribes in the neighboring Rif Mountains. Under the French, Taza was one of the few towns in the country without a *mellah* or Jewish quarter. The Jews and Muslims lived together in a mixed community, but the Jews had majority control of the local souk. After Moroccan independence in 1956, Taza continued as a garrison town, protecting and controlling the Taza Gap from any insurgency from Morocco's neighbor, Algeria.

In 2008, only one elderly Jewish woman remained, who had an "adopted" Muslim woman of about twenty years of age living with her. It's quite possible the young woman was taken on as a domestic when she was young and remained mainly in that capacity. Several Muslims visit the elderly woman in order to receive her special blessing (*baraka*) as a female descendant of the Cohanim.

Taza's souks were the domain of Jewish merchants and stallholders for several centuries. The original old Jewish quarter once stood below the plateau of the medina, next to the road that descends down the east side to Avenue Moulay Youssef. It was abandoned at the beginning of the twentieth century, after it was severely damaged during the tribal skirmishes to take control of the town.

Oujda

Located on Morocco's northeastern extremity, Oujda has always played an important role in the history of the country, both from a political and commercial point of view; the town is the principal gateway connecting Morocco with Algeria and the other countries of North Africa.

According to historians, there was a Berber settlement on the Oujda plain long before the arrival of the Romans or the Muslims. It is also understood to have been one of the main entry points for the thousands of Jews who migrated from further along the North African coast throughout the centuries.

The town was founded in the tenth century by the Magrawa, a nomadic tribe who wandered the land as far south as Tafilalt. It remained independent until the Almoravids took it by force in the eleventh century. The Almohads laid claim to the town in the early part of the thirteenth century and turned it into a fortress town. The Merinids lost control in 1271 to the Ziyayans from Tlemcen, in Algeria, but were able to win it back in 1296. The town walls were later strengthened and construction was carried out on a *kasbah*, a palace complex and a mosque, which included a *hammam*.

In 1352, the Merinids foiled another attempt by the Algerian Arabs to conquer Oujda in a fierce battle that took place on the Oujda plain. Also, under the Merinids, the small Jewish community of Oujda were given control of all cross-border trading in order to collect more taxes to fund the huge building projects the dynasty was commissioning in the central part of the country.

The strength of the Saadians was put to the test on several occasions by the Ottoman Turks, who had occupied Algeria. In a desperate effort to gain more revenue to pay for their military campaigns, the Saadians granted even more trading concessions to the Jewish merchants. Despite the Saadian attempts to hold on to the town, the persistent Turks took Oujda in the sixteenth century and from that base eventually took Fes in 1579.

The Alaouite sultan, Moulay Ismail, brought Oujda back under Moroccan control in 1690, but some time later, the Turks seized it yet again. In the early years of the nineteenth century another Alaouite, Moulay Sliman, routed the Turks for the final time, and Oujda has been part of Morocco since then.

In 1844 and again in 1857, the French, who had already colonized neighboring Algeria, occupied the town. Then in 1907, French troops, taking advantage of the weakness of the young Moroccan sultan, Abd el-Aziz, marched into Oujda, before going onto Fes, to begin almost fifty years of occupation on Moroccan soil.

153

During the years of the French Protectorate, the French enlarged the town by constructing the *Ville Nouvelle* (New Town), which accounts for the town's more modern appearance today. With the assistance of Israeli and foreign Jewish agencies, many of the poor among Oujda's Jewish community began to emigrate to Israel after 1948. The French responded by placing a total ban on emigration to Israel. In an effort to overcome the restrictions, the Israeli secret service set up a clandestine emigration network through neighboring Algeria, and Marseilles, France.

Tensions among the Muslim population reached their peak when it became evident that Israel was gaining the upper hand in the first Arab-Israeli War (1948). Out of revenge, the Muslims attacked the Jewish quarter, causing several fatalities and injuries that included young children. The attacks on the Jews lasted three days and damage to Jewish businesses and housing was extensive. The Pasha of Oujda visited the families of the victims to express his sadness regarding the unprovoked attacks and was later jostled by an angry crowd at the Grand Mosque.

Some think the violent unrest was fermented by the French. Whatever the origin, it strengthened the Zionist movement because it led Jews to fear what might happen to them after Moroccan independence. Between 1948 and 1956, the year of independence, more than 90,000 Jews emigrated to Israel at a rate of approximately 1000 people per month.

The author, Raphael, interviewed an elderly Jewish woman in her home in Oujda in1995 as a representative of the Casablanca based Foundation for the History and Culture of Moroccan Jews. During the course of the interview, she divulged that she had been a witness to the 1948 attacks and was certain the main body of assailants were Algerian Muslims from across the border. She also stated that realizing the Moroccan government was incapable of protecting the local Jewish community, Oujda's Jews were left with no other choice but to leave as soon as it was physically possible.

Oujda's close proximity to the Algerian border has given the town a reputation of being a smugglers' paradise; contraband goods have been crossing the frontier for centuries, though at a substantially reduced level since 1994, when Algeria closed it down due to political conflicts with Morocco. The closure has unfortunately affected the local economy to the point that companies and hotels that relied on the cross-border traffic, are struggling to survive.

Six kilometers to the southeast of Oujda is an oasis with the *marabout* or shrine of Sidi Yahia, who is venerated as a *tzadik* by Jews, Muslims and Christians alike. According to local folklore, he is the St. John of the Bible. In the past, Jewish pilgrims made animal sacrifices and later shared the meat with the poor and sick, who often spent several days at the site praying for an improvement in their circumstances. In 2008, there were only seven Jews living in Oujda.

The small Beth El synagogue, situated under the CTM bus station, is closed for services, but the interior installations are still in place. The large cemetery consists of a memorial to the adult victims of the pogrom of 1948 and another one dedicated to the children massacred during the same disturbances. As is common across Morocco, a local Muslim man is in charge of the security of the cemetery.

Debdou

The small town of Debdou, southwest of Oujda, was once the capital of an independent state governed by a Berber tribe. In the thirteenth century, it consisted of little more than a fortress on a pastoral plain. Debdou was also located on the important caravan routes that came up from Tafilalt in the south and continued into Northern Algeria. The year 1391 saw the arrival of two groups of Jews from Spain; one from the large Cohen-Scali family from Seville and the other from the Murciano family of Murcia. Their rivalry divided the Jewish community into different synagogues.

155

By the beginning of the fifteenth century, Debdou was under the rule of the Merinid princes, who had the task of defending the by now much larger town against cross-border attacks from the Arabs in Algeria. A European witness reported seeing a thriving Jewish community in 1596. The town had the distinction of being an important center for North African Judaism, and its scribes produced Scrolls of the Law for many of the communities of Morocco and its neighbor, Algeria.

The Jews worked as merchants, tailors, jewelers, weavers of cotton thread and wool. Several were employed in the local orchards, which produced olives, grapes, pomegranates and peaches. The cultivation of figs and their by-product, the distilling of *mahiya*, were also very popular. The women were renowned for their fine embroidery work.

In 1745, a cholera epidemic ravished the Jewish community. As a consequence, 300 families moved away, leaving a total of 160 Cohen-Scali families (*Megorashim*), 110 Murciano families (*Megorashim*) and 60 indigenous (*Toshavim*). Nevertheless, the remaining Jews still made up two-thirds of the town's total population. Debdou is said to have had seventeen synagogues, which mostly followed the rituals and customs brought over from Spain by the *Megorashim*. Today, only three unused synagogues remain. At the turn of the twentieth century, the region of Debdou had a Jew, David Cohen-Scali, as its governor.

Rapid emigration to Israel began shortly after 1948. The first groups of emigrants left through the clandestine network taking them through Algeria and Marseilles. The town also suffered during a spate of attacks on the Jewish community, as happened in other northeastern towns. Figures for 1950 put Debdou's Jewish community at around 1,000 people. By the middle of the 1950s, the large *mellah* was completely empty of Jews, the majority settling in *moshavim* cooperative settlements in Israel.

As evidence of how large the former Jewish community really was, Debdou has two cemeteries, the oldest said to date back 900 years. The other cemetery consists of graves dating from the early years of the twentieth century to the 1950s, and a good number have Spanish inscriptions. It also has a sizeable list of revered Jewish tzadiks: Mardoche Ben Moche Cohen, Jacob Cohen, Ishak Ben Moche Cohen and Moche Ben Sultan. Their graves are easily identified by the nooks used to burn candles. Several of the former Jewish community come from around the world to attend the annual pilgrimages.

Figuig

Out on its own to the southeast and literally on the border with Algeria, Figuig consists, essentially, of a huge *palmeraie*, a palm tree grove, with around 200,000 trees, and seven *ksour* (fortified settlements). Given its position, it is not hard to imagine its strategic and, at one time, commercial importance. For centuries, it was a busy trading-post and way station for both goods and travellers between Morocco and Algeria; for instance, from the fourteenth to the early nineteenth century, Jewish traders transported goods from as far as Tafilalt in the south of Morocco to the port of Oran in Northern Algeria.

With the advent of modern forms of transportation, first, shipping and then airlines, the town quickly became an isolated outpost.

Figuig has been the object of cross-border skirmishes throughout its long existence. The Saadian sultans lost control of Figuig to Arabs from Algeria in the early part of the seventeenth century and again in the first quarter of the eighteenth century.

In 1963, Moroccan and Algerian soldiers fought a battle in the town, which eventually ended with a ceasefire agreement. The seven *ksour* or small settlements, in the past, housed distinctly separate communities, each looking after their own particular section of the *palmeraie*. Evidently, there were often disputes between the communities over water rights, and the defenses of the *ksour* were continually re-enforced and altered.

Recent research has brought to light that a Jewish community once inhabited one of the *ksours,* fortified settlements. Figuig was also the site of a center that trained young men who later joined Jewish communities around Morocco and Algeria as teachers and aids in the synagogues. It is difficult to determine how many Jews actually lived in the *mellah* of Figuig; one estimate puts the number at one hundred; because cross-border controls were often lax, numbers within the Jewish community fluctuated as families came and went, depending on where they could find the best opportunity to make a living, whether in Morocco or across the frontier in Algeria. There are two Jewish cemeteries, and one tombstone inscribed with Hebrew lettering is dated 1923.

The inhabitants today are Berber Muslims and many work far from home in other parts of the country or in Europe. Typical of many Moroccans, they return from time to time and build new houses, looking forward to their retirement years to be spent with their families in their own *bled*.

14

Central Region

Marrakech
Ouirika Valley
Aghmat
Amizmiz
Tiz N'Test
Ait Ourir
Sidi Rahal
Tazerte
Demnate

❀Marrakech

Moroccan Jewish history tells us that this imperial city started out as a small oasis settlement along the caravan routes that came up from sub-Saharan Africa and ran along the full stretch of North Africa. Berber Jews, who were already settled there, did most of the trading. The credit for the foundation of Marrakech as a city goes to the Almoravids, a nomadic Berber tribe from the Atlantic region of the Sahara. One of their leaders, Bou Bekr, is said to have established an important trading-post or market around 1070 C.E., including a *kasbah* on the site of an already existing settlement, thought to go under the name Martok.

The city came into prominence later in the eleventh century when it was chosen by Youssef bin Tachfine, the first of the Almoravid dynasty, as his capital. After conquering northern Morocco and going on to defeat the Christian rulers of Andalusia in Southern Spain, Marrakech subsequently became the capital of the Moorish empire, also incorporating a large region of North Africa.

Under Ali ben Youssef, successor to bin Tachfine, Marrakech and the Jewish traders benefited immensely from the trading of goods and services between Morocco and the Moors in Andalusia. The huge financial gains allowed for the construction of a new and larger city. Besides the grand palaces and mosques, an underground system of channels and conduits was successfully installed to counter the shortage in the much needed supply of water.

Jewish and Muslim scholars and craftsmen arrived from Andalusia and introduced their Andalusian culture to the city's elite. The period became to be known as The Golden Age. Jews were prohibited from living within the city walls. Their movement was restricted, and it was forbidden for any Jew to enter through the gates of Marrakech at night.

Around 1145, the Almohads, a Berber tribe from deep within the High Atlas Mountains, took control of Morocco and Muslim Spain. The Almohads were Islamic fundamentalists, bent on a purely Islamic state, and they expelled Jews from Marrakech. Some Jews escaped to the mountainous regions, staying just out of reach of the Islamists, while others left Morocco altogether.

The Almohads also destroyed much of the city built by the previous Almoravid dynasty, said to have been an act of religious purification. The first Almohad sovereign, Abd el-Moumin, decided Marrakech should remain as the capital of the Moorish empire. He immediately set about the reconstruction of a much grander city. The city's most famous landmark today, the *Koutoubia* mosque, was built during his reign. The city expanded way beyond its former boundaries with the accession of the third sultan, Yacoub el-Mansour (1184-1199), an unrelenting and indefatigable builder of several palaces, ornamental lakes and gardens and, even, a hospital.

After the downfall of the Almohads (thirteenth century), mainly due to internal family squabbles for the right to rule, which led to brother killing brother, the Merenids came to power and moved the capital to Fes. As a direct result, Marrakech lost much of its importance and remained on the sidelines for most of the next century. However, many Jews, who had by now returned, stayed on. After all, the city was still of some great importance on the caravan routes bringing merchandise from as far away as Timbuktu.

Although Fes was their capital, Merenid sultans stayed for months at a time in Marrakech. As they were always accompanied by Jewish jewelry makers from Fes, who were *Megorashim*, with different customs and ways of worship from the local Marrakchi *Toshavim*, it was necessary to build a separate synagogue. It later became known as the Synagogue El Fassiyin. In addition, many privately owned synagogues were erected by individual Jewish families and eminent community leaders.

Family feuds were also partly to blame for the demise of the Merenid dynasty, which then lost out to the Saadians in 1521. The Saadians originated from the Draa valley. The Saadians continued with the construction of Marrakech, adding *madrasas* and palaces. They also took back partial control of the Atlantic coast from the Portuguese, who had colonized it during the earlier part of the century. Furthermore, the dynasty made great strides in developing the sugar cane plantations in the region of the Souss, bringing in huge profits from exportation to many countries around Europe.

The Saadian sultan, Moulay Abdallah el-Ghalib (1557–1574), moved the Jewish quarter from its original site (where the Great el-Mouassin Mosque stands today) much closer to the royal residences and had it enclosed within a protective wall. The move was most likely made because of attacks by local Muslims, or purely for the reason that the sultan was well aware the Jewish traders were the life blood of the town's economy.

The Jewish community was also granted a plot of land to create a cemetery. The whole complex was formerly separate from the rest of the city and was more or less self sufficient with its own *souks* and rabbinical courts *etc*. This is today's old *mellah*.

In 1591, the greatest and most heroic of the dynasty, Abou el-Abbas, hailed as *el-Mansour* (the Victorious), marched at the head of an army made up of black soldiers and Christian mercenaries and conquered Timbuktu along with the lucrative caravan trade routes. He returned with large shipments of gold, slaves and other items of great value, earning for himself the further epithet *ed-Dehbi*, the Golden One.

Some of the new wealth went into the construction of the *El Badi* palace, at the time, the finest and largest in the south of Morocco. However, military campaigns and constant attacks from family rivals bore heavily on the royal coffers. A decision was, therefore, made to give the Jewish merchants the monopoly on sugar imports and more control on trade routes to raise tax revenue.

In 1660, the first of the Alaouite dynasty, Moulay er-Rachid, claimed the Moroccan throne and took up residence in Fes. His successor, Moulay Ismail, who detested the people of Fes, moved the capital to Meknes, from where he made a devastating attack on Marrakech, destroying much of the Saadian-built properties, including the *El Badi* palace. However, in a shrewd move, he carted several pieces of the finest decorated masonry back to Meknes and incorporated them into the construction of his huge palace complex.

A black cloud descended on the city during the short reign of Moulay al-Yazid (1790-1792), who disliked Jews. The Muslim elite of Marrakech did their best in protecting the Jews by concealing them in their homes and farm properties.

The development of regular shipping lanes throughout the seventeenth to the nineteenth century from the West African coastal ports directly to Europe sounded the final death knell for the once successful overland caravan trading routes. As a result, Marrakech became a provincial backwater and was almost forgotten, but it was never ignored by the Alaouite dynasty. As a matter of fact, sultans frequently visited when restoration and further building work was being done.

Under Moulay el-Hassan (1873-1894), who was proclaimed sultan in Marrakech, before being given the approval by the *Oulema* in Fes, the old *mellah* was extended due to overcrowding. His son, Moulay Abd el-Aziz, who inherited the throne while still a child, lived in the city from 1895 to 1901. His Grand Vizier and protector, Bou Ahmed, built the massive *Bahia Palace*, made it his home, and ruled on behalf of the boy-king.

In 1912, under the French Protectorate, T'hami el-Glaoui, of Telouet fame, was declared Pasha of Marrakech, after giving his assistance in rescuing French hostages held in a suburb of the city. Glaoui took no time in making the city and the lands beyond the High Atlas Mountains his personal fiefdom, which he held onto until his death in 1956, coincidently, the year of Moroccan independence.

Following independence, Sultan Mohammed V decreed that the Jews were no longer under any obligation to live within the *mellahs* around the country. Evidence came to light in the late 1990s that el-Glaoui was an accomplice in the French government's plan to register all Moroccan Jews, along with their ownership of property in preparation for their expulsion to the Nazi camps in Eastern Europe.

When Marrakech's large Jewish community left for Israel and other lands during the 1960s, the city's economy floundered, causing mass unemployment among the Muslim inhabitants who took over the *mellahs*, old and new. From the 1960s to the early 1980s there was an influx of tourists to the city, mainly hippie types and backpackers on low budgets. The government, under King Hassan II, realized the potential in developing the city as an upscale tourist destination. Unlike the city's past history when monuments and grand palaces were the mode, it was decided to construct several grand hotels and improve the city's infrastructure.

In a few short years, Marrakech has been transformed into a city of which any country would be proud: foreign and national investment is pouring into the city in the way of major construction of new apartments, luxury villas and a new train station. Some of the investors are said to be international Jewish businesses.

The once littered streets are now cleaned on a daily basis, and landscape gardeners are in fashion. A coat of red ochre, or pinkish paint, the colours of the soil in the mountains looming high over the city, has been added to anything that does not move, giving the city a warm and welcoming glow. Some Moroccans have given it the name *L'Medina Hmera* (The Red City). Marrakech (Morocco City on some nineteenth century maps) is now the darling of international tourism and is poised to remain so for many years to come.

The Mellahs. The old *mellah* in the Old Medina of Marrakech was constructed in the sixteenth century, during the reign of the Saadian sultan, Moulay Abdallah el-Ghalib (1557–1574), who made the decision to move the Jewish quarter closer to the royal palace to give more protection to the Jews. Further extension took place in the reign of the Alaouite sultan, Moulay el-Hassan (1873-1894). Muslims took over the vacant residential and commercial properties in the old *mellah* when the Jewish community abandoned everything to begin a new life in Israel, France and Canada. However, with a little bit of imagination, it is possible to have some idea of how the former Jewish residents lived and worked.

Located on a narrow street that retains its original Jewish name, Rue Talmud Torah, the Slat Laazama (*Megorashim*) is the only synagogue in the Old Medina still open for religious services. The synagogue is in the interior of a walled complex, which, until the departure of the majority of local Jews to Israel, served as a Talmud Torah school. The school also received rabbis from the new state of Israel who attended training seminars. Their visits were considered necessary due to the hundreds of European rabbis who perished during the Holocaust, leaving a void in knowledge and the procedures of rabbinical duties.

Restoration of the building was carried out in 1956. Around the walls of the inner courtyard are several framed photographs depicting the tombs of Morocco's better known Jewish *tzadiks*. The upper floor of the riad-style complex has been put to good use: the former classrooms have been converted into an Old Age People's Home, with small apartments for elderly people with no regular income. It is supported by donations from the local Jewish community organization. In 2008, approximately six Jews were still living within the old *mellah*. There are no facilities for Shabbat within the Old Medina.

Nearby is the enclosed Jewish cemetery, the Beth Haàlmim. The original graves are now completely covered below ground level, with a second level or tier of tombs established on top, leaving only a small area for future internments. The whitewashed mausoleum of Marrakech's most venerated Jewish *tzadik*, Rabbi Hanania Cohen, is a prominent feature within the cemetery.

Maintenance and security of the cemetery is in the hands of a local Muslim family, paid by the Marrakech Jewish community.

Construction of the new *mellah*, a spill over from the old, began in the nineteenth century and quickly expanded to include a market run by the Jews. During the years under the French Protectorate, Jews were not allowed to live in the French or European quarter, which was the *Ville Nouvelle* and the trendy suburb of Guéliz. However, they were permitted to work there and later obtained authorization to build a few synagogues near their places of work. In the years following Morocco's independence, the Jews were free to live wherever they pleased.

Before the majority of Jews left for Israel or France during the 1960s, almost every street in the *mellahs* boasted a synagogue, mostly owned by private individuals or a family. Today very few are actually in use or even exist. With the right guide, it is possible to visit the closed Betioun Synagogue in the new *mellah*, recently restored and privately owned by the family of the same name.

The Beth El Synagogue, located in the modern suburb of Guéliz (Impasse du Moulin, opposite the American Language Center), is privately owned. Built in the 1960s by a member of the Kadoch family, it holds services for Shabbat and important feast days.

The new *mellah* once had everything to service the community, including a clinic and a home for the elderly. The jewelers' *souk* was once the exclusive domain of Jewish craftsmen, now run by Muslim artisans. Many of the designs mirror the skills and creativity of the former Jewish jewelers. However, there is a caution; local dealers will offer "genuine" antique Jewish jewelry or other "old" Jewish artifacts, such as plates and lamps with Hebrew writing, much of it misspelled.

Historically, local Jews, as well as Muslims, have been known for the practice of beliefs against the evil eye and other occult dangers. Local herbal remedies are also used for many ailments in addition to the use of western medicine. A European traveller to Marrakech in 1891 found the city infested with scorpions. Local Jews sought the services of a rabbi who visited their homes and drew a picture of a scorpion on a piece of paper, which was then stuck firmly to the doorpost. The paper included some Hebrew inscriptions, said to contain a magical spell. A Jew later swore he had been an eye witness to a large scorpion stopping, as if stupefied, while it was about to enter a house through the front door.

166   In the past, Jewish fortune-tellers, clairvoyants, palmists and herbal or traditional healers existed, and business was plentiful, especially with affairs of the heart, personal wealth and problems of a sexual nature. Clients included Jews and Muslims, even sultans, who sought their services, hoping to receive some good news about the future or maybe just some Jewish *Baraka,* good luck or a blessing.

In 2008, around 240 people made up Marrakech's Jewish community, the majority old and frail. The last circumcision was said to have been in 2001, and new births looked very doubtful. The one and only kosher restaurant in Marrakech, the Primavera Hotel-Restaurant, is situated within a hotel complex on the road to Casablanca, some distance from the city center, and it does include its own synagogue. Its speciality is Moroccan-style food with a seating capacity for 100 diners. Shabbat meals with a Jewish family can also be arranged.

Rabbinical Court in Marrakech, 1950s
Photo Courtesy of Mordekhai Perez and Isaac Ohayon

Environs of Marrakech (South)

Ouirika Valley
The long stretch of the Ouirika Valley, in the foothills of the High Atlas Mountains, and within easy reach of Marrakech (62 km), was home to several Jewish families before they departed for Israel (1950s and 1960s). There were eighteen Jewish quarters or settlements in total, spread up and down the valley. The valley's fertile soil together with the rivers and streams were ideal for the cultivation of fruits and nuts, apples and pears, hazelnuts, and the growing of *neanaa,* green mint used in the making of Moroccan mint tea, all which helped subsidize the seasonal incomes of the inhabitants. The Jews were also instrumental in the production of pottery and the making of beaded jewelry, still carried on by local Muslims today.

The indigenous inhabitants of the valley are Berbers, and the language spoken is Tachelhite, a dialect of Tamazight (pronounced Tamazirrt), the principal language of Morocco's Berbers. This language uses a clicking sound rather than the utterance of a word when answering yes to questions. In addition to Tachelhite, they speak Moroccan Arabic, both of which the Jews also spoke. The two communities lived a harmonious coexistence for hundreds of years because they had so much in common, including mutual respect.

Rabbi Salomon Bel-Hench (meaning Son of the Snake), who died more than 500 years ago, is buried in the valley at Aghbalou (Arrbalou). It is said he got the name, Son of a Snake, because a huge snake used to crawl in and out of his grave at certain times, which was taken as a sign he was showing himself to the pilgrims.

The cemetery with the rabbi's shrine is easy to find; it is on the left of the main road, just before Aghbalou, approximately 100 meters before the fork in the road which goes to Setti Fatma, in one direction, and the other, to the winter ski resort of Oukaimden. There is a large plaque bearing his name and also Hebrew inscriptions on the exterior of the walled cemetery.

The *tzadik's* shrine is looked after by Hanaya Alfassi, one of the last two surviving Jews in the valley. Hanaya's mother, who preceded him as the guardian of the *tzadik's* shrine, is also buried there. When interviewed, Hanaya, a fit 80-year-old male, had an interesting story to tell about why he stayed behind when the valley's other Jews left for Israel in the 1950s and 1960s.

As a much younger man he found difficulty in leaving the area where the local rabbi *tzadik* lay buried. After having discussed the problem with his wife, the couple decided to remain and look after the rabbi's shrine. Hanaya worked on maintaining the site for the few pilgrims that came by from time to time. Many years passed with the couple longing for the company of their former Jewish neighbors. Occasionally, they received messages from their family and friends urging them to join them in Israel.

During the 1970s Hanaya and his wife decided the time was right to leave the Ouirika valley and emigrate. Travel dates and arrangements were fixed by the representative of the Jewish community in Marrakech; the couple would fly to Israel via Marseilles, France. On the morning of their departure from the valley, Hanaya and his wife packed what they could physically carry and then made their way to Marrakech, where they would spend the night.

That very evening in Marrakech, Hanaya suffered some kind of seizure and went into a coma for three days. On gaining consciousness, he told his wife that the rabbi *tzadik* had appeared to him in a dream and asked him to return to the valley and remain there to look after his shrine. The couple eventually returned to Ouirika once Hanaya had made a full recovery. From that day on, Hanaya has rarely left the area of the rabbi's shrine, except for the odd trip to Marrakech to attend special feast day services at one of the synagogues and to visit the grave of his wife, who died in 1998 and lies buried in the Jewish cemetery.

A few years ago, the author, Rafael Elmaleh, lived in the valley for one month, having been sent by the Jewish Foundation in Casablanca to do research on the former Jewish population. Throughout his time in the valley, which coincided with the feast of Passover, he lodged with a Berber family. He made matzah (unleavened bread) intended for his Passover meal. On seeing the bread, the lady of the house became excited and explained how, as a young girl, she had been invited to share it with her Jewish friends. She then took a piece and placed it in a display cabinet, saying she hoped it would bring her Jewish *baraka*, good luck or a blessing.

The valley's peaceful ambience led a former Jewish resident to return from Israel and build a house with the intention of living there permanently. The local Berbers know him as a fortune-teller. Over a glass of Moroccan mint tea, he said he had only emigrated to Israel because everyone around him had decided to go. He went on to say that all the years spent in Israel were years of regret, and he had often dreamed of the opportunity to return to Morocco.

Years of instability caused by the Israeli-Palestine conflict convinced him life would be better returning to the place of his birth. He showed some impatience talking about the situation in Israel. He said that Jews and Muslims there did not know how to live alongside each other, in contrast to Morocco where Jews and Muslims have lived in close proximity for thousands of years. Then, looking up and down the valley, his demeanour turned to one of content as he said, "If I had my way, I'd change the name of the valley from Ouirika to Eureka." A great deal of pleasure can be derived from visiting some of the traditional-style Berber villages where the Berber Jews and the Berber Muslims in the not so distant past lived together in relative peace and harmony.

In the village of Tafza, thirty-seven kilometers from Marrakech, the family of Mohammed Iouizalne often receives tourists to share Moroccan mint tea on their terrace and gain some knowledge of local daily life. There is an old Jewish cemetery on the hill behind the village. Unfortunately, years of soil erosion and neglect have left no traces of the tombs. It is remembered locally as a sacred place, and it is the custom for single local women to carry buckets of water to the site to wash themselves, done as an act of ritual purification one week before getting married.

Aghmat

At the northern end of the Ouirika Valley lies the region known as the *Bled Aghmat*, where the ancient town of Aghmat is believed to have been in existence many years before Islam entered Morocco. The town was inhabited by a Berber tribe said to have converted to Judaism.

The first Arabs invaded the region in or around 705 C.E., and their leader, who became the first Arab *caid*, built a mosque in the town. In the beginning, several Berber tribes resisted the rule of Arab governors by joining forces with their Jewish neighbors in opposition. However, during the reign of Idriss II (791–828), the region of Aghmat was put under control from Fes and remained in the hands of the Idrissid dynasty after his death.

By the end of the tenth century, the town had gained some importance and was the capital of a small principality, stretching to the plains of Chaouia, south of Marrakech, and well into the High Atlas Mountains.

In 1058, the Almoravids brought the town back into the Moroccan kingdom around 1070 and encouraged Jews to move there to help in its development. Although the town later fell into economic decline, it remained an important center of learning for Jewish scholars. The Almoravids, after adding Seville and Cordoba to their empire, placed the local ruler in exile in Aghmat. After his death, his tomb became a place of pilgrimage for both Muslims and Jews. During the 1970s, a mausoleum was built over the tomb.

When the Almoravids lost the town to the Almohads in the middle of the twelfth century, the Jewish population fled to escape persecution and forced conversions. The town later experienced a period of calm under the Merinid dynasty, and many Jews felt confident enough to return. Written evidence from 1860 recorded a total population of 5,500 in the town, which included 1,000 Jews.

It should be said here that there were two places with the name Aghmat; Aghmat Ouirika was the main center of commerce. Aghmat Ilane, a short distance away, was probably considered a Muslim holy place, as it was prohibited for foreigners to reside there. These days, although Aghmat still exists, there are very few traces of its past importance.   171

Amizmiz

At a distance of fifty-seven kilometers south of Marrakech, lies Amizmiz. The small market and administrative town serves the district of the Oued N'fis valley. The layout of the town has an interesting concept; distinctly separate sectors or quarters separated by a rugged ravine, consisting of a *Kasbah*, once controlled by the Glaoui family. There is also a former Jewish quarter and a *zaouia,* the base of an Islamic religious fraternity, which usually included a *marabout*.

Amizmiz was for centuries on the main trading and transport route that cut directly across country between the region of the Oued N'fis and Essaouira port, which might explain the strategic positioning of the *kasbah*; the local *caid* or tribal chief charged taxes or duties on all goods passing through the territory under his jurisdiction.

The once common combination of *kasbah* and Jewish quarter comes into play here; the Jews were responsible for the collection of the revenues in return for the *caid's* protection and were, in addition, given certain trading privileges, particularly at the weekly local *souks*. Jews made up a fifth of the Amizmiz population around 1940, but left with the first wave of immigrants shortly after the formation of the state of Israel in 1948. Near Oued Amegdoul, the only indication of a former Jewish presence is the shrine of Rabbi Raphael Cohen, or Mul Amegdoul, as he is known to Muslims. The shrine was restored by the Ohayon family, which has roots in Amizmiz.

The highlight of the week is the large Tuesday market when Berbers from the tribal areas in the surrounding mountains come to town to trade. Merchants come from Marrakech to buy the inexpensive red clay pottery that is popular with Moroccan housewives for tajine dishes and storage pots.

Tiz N'Test

172

Not a town or village, Tiz N'Test is, in fact, the name of the incredible pass that cuts through the High Atlas Mountains. It links Marrakech to Taroudant, on the Souss Plain. With its dizzying twist and turns, medieval-style *kasbahs*, amazing views and picturesque, traditional Berber villages, the pass has some of the most spectacular scenery Morocco has to offer.

The credit for this skilful feat of engineering goes to the French, who built the road after they gained control of the High Atlas Mountains and the Souss Plain. They gained control with the assistance of T'hami el-Glaoui, the richest and most powerful man in the Morocco of his day. The original pass, a narrow and winding dirt track, was an important trade route, though, often mired with difficulties due to seasonal bad weather and danger of attack from roving tribes of Berbers, as many over-optimistic sultans discovered during their attempts to bring the local inhabitants under control.

No evidence of a former Jewish community along the extreme mountainous section of the route has come to light; the assumption being the lack of any real security in the past. However, there is some confirmation of former Jewish settlements at Tahanaout, Asni and Ouirgane (Wirgane), small market towns on the flatter Marrakech approaches to the Tiz N'Test Pass.

The road through the Tiz N'Test Pass becomes interesting shortly after passing through the town of Tahanaout. It starts to climb steeply through a stretch of red ochre-coloured foothills and continues along a high precipice cut through the Gorges of Moulay Brahim, and then flattening out just before arriving at the regional market town of Asni. The small town is practically deserted most days of the week, but on Saturday, market day, it is filled with hundreds of *djallaba*-clad Berbers from the surrounding mountain villages, many arriving, as they have for centuries, on the back of mules.

The *souk* used to be run by Berber Jews, travelling up from Tahanaout, further back on the road. The original market day was held on Thursdays, to comply with the rules of *Shabbat*. These days, the souk mostly offers everyday necessities; nevertheless, the whole scene brings to mind vivid images of a time long ago.

Further along the main Tiz N'Test road is Ouirgane (Wirgane), once a small, sleepy riverside village up until 2008. Now it sits on the eastern flank of what looks like a huge lake, but in actual fact, is the Ouirgane Barrage, built to store much needed water.

Very close to Ouirgane is the small village of Anrhaz, only a short distance from the confluence of the Oued N'fis and the Oued Ouirgane. It appears to have had, at one time, quite a substantial Jewish community. A whitewashed shrine complex is the final resting place of five rabbi *tzadiks* (*tzadikim*, holy men). And just outside the walls is what remains of an ancient Jewish cemetery.

The most important *tzadik* is Haim Ben Diwan, the son of Morocco's most venerated Jewish *tzadik*, Rabbi Amram Ben Diwan, buried near the northern town of Ouezzane. It is said Haim arrived in the area in the eighteenth century to collect donations for a *Yeshiva* (Rabbinic school) and spread Jewish awareness among the local Berber Jews. Several miracles have been attributed to him. One, which is often told, is that the earth opened up by itself at the time of his burial to receive his physical remains.

The local Muslims often visit his shrine to receive some Jewish *baraka*, or blessing, but being unaware of his real name, they call him Mul Anrhaz, after the village. Haim Ben Diwan's sanctuary, built by his descendants, includes the bodies of two others, claimed to be his disciples. In an adjacent room are the tombs of Rabbi Mordekhai Ben Hammou and Rabbi Abraham Ben Hammou, father and son respectively.

In 2008, the accommodations built within the complex for pilgrims looked neglected and uninhabitable. Private rooms, toilets and hammams were in a bad state of disrepair, leading to the conclusion that no one actually stays overnight anymore. Perhaps, some pilgrims lodge at the large villa a few meters away on the periphery of the complex. It is understood to be the property of a descendent of one of the rabbi *tzadiks*. Security of the complex is in the hands of a local Muslim, who is generally present in the daytime and will open the gate to visitors. The annual pilgrimage is held during *Lag Baomer* (May), and prayers are conducted at a small on-site synagogue. A cemented platform provides a place for the ritual slaughtering of animals.

174

Beyond Ouirgane, the road slices through the spectacular gorges of the Oued N'fis, then on to the Berber village of Ijoukak. Approximately six kilometers more, next to the river, is the old village and the ruins of the *kasbah* of Taalat N'Yacoub, former seat of the Goundafa tribal chief, by the name of Tayeb el-Goundafi.

The *kasbah* was constructed in the latter part of the nineteenth century by his father, a feudal lord, who initially refused to relinquish his independence to the central power of the sultan, Moulay el-Hassan. He did, however, later change his mind by sending his son, Tayeb, a childhood friend of the sultan, to make peace and express his acceptance of the sultan's authority. It has also been said that he presented one of his daughters in marriage to the sultan, as a gesture to cement good relations.

The nineteenth century Scottish traveller and writer, R. B. Cunninghame Graham, spent a few weeks as a virtual prisoner of Tayeb el-Goundafi at the *kasbah* but, fortunately, was able to keep a diary of daily events. He later published his experiences in a book *Mogreb-El-Acksa*. The book gives an amusing and very descriptive insight into the history of Morocco, and Moroccan life, within and around the confines of the *kasbah* during his short stay.

Tayeb's moneylender was a Jew who travelled around the south of the country, offering his services to the local tribal chiefs and governors. We also learn the *kasbah* was frequented by Jewish peddlers and traders.

Another European visitor, on this occasion an honored guest to the *kasbah*, later related a story, whether true or false, told to him by Tayeb el-Goundafi. One day Tayeb proudly displayed for his inspection a selection of beautifully made daggers and jewelry. Tayeb's father had asked a Jew from Amizmiz to make the fine items, which took two years to produce. After being paid the agreed price on delivery, the Jew went on his way. Immediately after, on the orders of the cunning employer, the Jew was murdered and robbed of his fee as he rode along the Nfis valley. Tayeb boasted that the collection had not cost his father a single cent.

The next point of interest along the route is the mosque in the village of Tin Mal, reached by an access road on the right. The founder of the Almohad dynasty, Abd el-Moumin, built the mosque in 1153-1154, with the intention of making it a mausoleum for the Almohad dynasty. He and two of his successors were buried there. It was from this site that Abd el-Moumin set out to take control of Morocco from the Almoravids, which he finally succeeded in doing in 1146. Not content with this major accomplishment, he went on to conquer the whole of the Maghreb (Algeria and Tunisia) and also Muslim Spain.

After the capture of Marrakech from the Almoravids, Abd el-Moumin made the red city the capital of the Almohad empire and Tin Mal became a place of pilgrimage, particularly for the High Atlas Berbers. In the thirteenth century, the Almohads lost out to the Merinids, and the remnants of the dynasty fled to make their final stand at Tin Mal. Vastly outnumbered, the last of the Almohads were finally defeated in 1276, and the original fortress town completely destroyed. The desecration of the Almohad tombs was a further blow.

The Tiz N'Test road finally reaches an end as it meets the Souss Plain, a few kilometers from the market town of Oulad Birhil. The town once had a sizeable *mellah*. The rabbis of Oulad Birhil also served the spiritual needs of the Jews living in the cluster of settlements in the immediate area.

Continuing south in the direction of Taroudant, the next stop of interest to Jews is the cemetery complex near Aghzou (Arrzoo). Within the complex lie the bodies of Rabbi David Barroukh

Cohen Azogh and his son, Benyamin Cohen Azogh. In fact, both are together under the same shrine canopy. There are also several unmarked tombs and a synagogue within the cemetery, and, around the sides, a large number of rooms to accommodate the visiting pilgrims, who come from as far away as the United States and Canada. The annual pilgrimage is held in December, but visits to the shrine can be made at any time of the year.

Another *tzadik* known as Baba Dudu or David Barroukh Ha-Qatan (the Younger) is interned within the cemetery in Taroudant. His great-grandfather and father had the same name. The three generations of the family were renowned throughout the region for their skills as healers and predictors of the future. Their services were sought by both Jews and Muslims. As a matter of fact, the local Berbers used the word *hazzan* to describe a Jewish healer. The descendents of the Barroukh family currently own a working synagogue of the same name in Casablanca.

Environs of Marrakech (East)

This region includes the lands between Marrakech and the town of Demnate. Predominately agricultural, the region originally supported the lives of thousands of Jews, who lived in the towns and several small villages. Jewish habitation can be traced as far back as the twelfth century, to the time of the Almoravids. Centuries later, it was part of the vast territories controlled by the Glaoui family. The caravans carried goods from Marrakech through this region and on to Fes in the north. It was also the route taken by successive sultans travelling between Marrakech and Fes.

Ait Ourir

On leaving Marrakech, and going eastwards, the first town associated with the Jews is Ait Ourir, named after the local Berber tribe of the same name. On the approaches to Ait Ourir, there is a fine view of part of the High Atlas Mountain range, looming spectacularly in the distance

The small town on the Marrakech plain was once part of the caravan route that travelled north from the Sahara, through the Draa Valley and over the High Atlas Mountains to Marrakech. The once opulent Glaoui *kasbah* is now in ruins. It was the former residence of *Caid* Mohammed El Glaoui, one of the sons of T'hami El Glaoui. Apparently, he lived a lavish life-style from taxes collected from all merchandise passing through to Marrakech or in the opposite direction. He lost his position and privileges at the point of Morocco's independence in 1956. These days the town looks more like a sleepy village surrounded by vast swathes of agricultural land, ideal for the internationally-known rock stars reputed to have luxury villas in the vicinity.

Close by is the small village of Douar Chems, where the shrine of Rabbi Habib El Mizrahi is located. The shrine is within a large building and is well maintained. Apart from the annual pilgrimage at the beginning of March, it can be visited almost at any other time of the year.

Sidi Rahal

The market town of Sidi Rahal takes its name from a Muslim holy man who lived in the fifteenth century. He has been credited with performing a long list of miracles and extraordinary deeds. His shrine or *marabout* is the venue for a week-long celebration that takes place every summer. Some Jews also revered this Muslim holy man.

It is thought the local Glaoui *kasbah* was constructed on the site of a sixteenth century village, formally known as Anmahi. Some proof could be derived from the fact that in the locality, a short distance upstream from the *marabout*, there is the shrine of a rabbi, who goes by the name of Moulay Anmahi, not his original name, which is unknown.

Giving unknown *tzadiks* the name of the local town or village was a common practice in the past. Again, the shrine of this particular *tzadik* is visited by both Jews and Muslims. Another of Sidi Rahal's Jewish *tzadiks* is Rabbi Yacoub Nahamais, also known as Mul L'Ma (L'Ma - Arabic for water). He is thought to have found a source of badly needed water.

Tazerte
The village of Tazerte was the seat of Madani El Glaoui, the elder brother of T'hami El Glaoui, the former Pasha of Marrakech. Madani collected a tax from all goods passing through his domain en route to Fes or Marrakech. Madani most certainly played a significant role in Morocco's history from 1893 until his death in 1918. He is particularly remembered for the support he gave in ousting the rightful sultan, Moulay Abd el-Aziz, in favor of the sultan's younger brother, Moulay Hafid. Madani was duly rewarded with the prestigious position of Grand Vizier.

In 1914, during the first years of the French Protectorate, Madani swore the allegiance of his family to France, and, on behalf of the French, took part in the subjugation of the south of the country. Further information on the political intrigues of the Glaoui family can be obtained from Gavin Maxwell's informative work *The Lords of the Atlas*.

In 2007, an interview was conducted with a former Jewish resident from the region of Demnate. The man interviewed praised the memory of Madani El Glaoui by declaring that he had heard stories passed down through generations that Madani had behaved well toward the Jews under his jurisdiction.

Today, all that physically remains in the village of Tazerte as a reminder of the former power held by the Glaoui family are four dilapidated *kasbahs*, the oldest one being Madani's.

Demnate
The largest town in the region, Demnate is built onto a mountainside and enclosed within a wall. Local sources say it began as a small settlement inhabited by a Berber tribe called Ait Yahya and only grew to a substantial size when Muslims settled

there in the tenth century. The town became a stop over for Muslim pilgrims making the long journey to Mecca.

In the twelfth century, the founders of the Almohad dynasty stayed in the town before setting out to take control of Marrakech from the Almoravids. Moulay er-Rachid, the first Alaouite sultan, did the same in the middle of the seventeenth century when he fought against the remnants of the Saadians in Marrakech.

Demnate's former Jewish community can be traced back to the fourteenth century; the original site of the *mellah* took up the entire town center, and, in time, grew larger until it came to be identified as a predominantly Jewish town. The *Alliance Israélite Universelle* opened a school in the town in1932, one of only two in the region that existed before World War II. The other was established in Midelt, a town at the eastern end of the Middle Atlas Mountains. Prior to the exodus to Israel in 1965, 10,000 Jews lived in Demnate and several hundreds more inhabited the thirty or so villages in the immediate proximity of the town.

The Jews in the town and around the region were cultivators and traders of olives and grapes, which provided an income from winemaking. Other men were employed as saddle makers and tailors. At one time in the past, Jews worked the few salt mines in the locality. Jewish women busied themselves with dressmaking, embroidery and the distilling of *mahiya*. In addition, a few women served as midwives to both the Jewish and Muslim communities.

Like many towns in Morocco's past, the Jews had a monopoly on commerce and a tax was paid to the local *caid*. During the latter part of the nineteenth century and up to Morocco's independence in 1956, the *caid* of Demnate was a member of Madani El Glaoui's family. Reportedly, Madani's family treated the Jews with respect and were well liked. The memory and reputation of one of Madani's sons, Omar by name, is still held in high regard by former Jewish residents of Demnate.

At the top end of the town a track leads about six and one-half kilometers to *Imi-n-Ifri,* a natural bridge spanning a gorge, where, nearby in a grotto, Jews and Muslims still sometimes come to perform the ritual sacrifice of animals.

In 2008, one elderly Jewish lady was all that remained of the Jewish community. At one time, the town had ten privately owned synagogues; however, all were subsequently sold. Currently, only one cemetery remains whereas previously there had been three. The local *tzadiks* include Rabbi Aaron Acohen, Rabbi Mdin and Rabbi Moulin Bou Halou. The most visited is, Rabbi David El-Draa Halevy, whose annual *hiloula* (celebration of his life and work) follows the festival *Shavouot*.

The village of Aghri (Arrri) lies a short distance from Demnate, where the shrine of the *tzadik*, Rabbi Braham Cohin, is venerated by Jews and Muslims.

Berbers of the High Atlas
Good Neighbors

Many books have been written about the coexistence of Jews living among the Berbers in the regions of the High Atlas Mountains. One thing they have in common is the symbiotic relationship once firmly embedded within the two communities made up of two distinctly different religions and, in some respects, cultures. This symbiosis played an integral part in the economic and everyday survival of the rural communities. In the region immediately to the southeast of Demnate, several thousands of Jews lived in close proximity to their Berber neighbors (Muslims) for many generations.

The Jews are said to have been drawn to the area due to its isolation from the instability of the so-called governed lands, the *Bled Makhzen*, further to the north of the country. Here, in the ungoverned lands, the *Bled es-Siba*, they found acceptance among the Berber tribes and the protection of the tribal chiefs, who invited the Jews into the region, so they and the local Berber population could benefit from their skills as merchants, farmers and craftsmen.

A reoccurring theme, which helps to explain the longevity of the close relationship, was the necessity for interdependence, supported by mutual respect, tolerance, even-handedness and deep bonds of personal friendship. Mutual dependence fell into many categories of daily life. To begin, the wealthier Jews bought land from the Berbers or put up the capital to create partnerships with their Berber neighbors. Some Jews, on the other hand, owned large flocks of sheep. When they were grazed on the land of a Muslim, they would make an agreement to share the lambs. Sheep farming could be a very profitable and lucrative business, particularly during the period leading up to the Islamic feast of *L'Eid Kebir*; every Muslim household in the entire country endeavours to purchase at least one sheep for the celebrations.

Wealthy Jews had a high standing within the local district, giving them great respect. The Muslims would call on them to intervene or give advice when problems arose with the local tribal chief or a Muslim neighbor. On the other hand, Berbers could play the role of witnesses and arbitrators in disputes between Jewish residents or traders.

In terms of trade and earning a living, the Berbers depended on the Jewish merchants to buy their agricultural produce for sale outside the district or region. Jewish merchants also brought in the daily necessities like sugar, salt, cooking oil and household items. Poor Jews worked for the wealthier members of either the Jewish or Muslim communities. Jewish craftsmen served both Jews and Muslims. Trades included shoemakers, especially embroidered women's shoes, which Jewish and Muslim women decorated. Other skills included carpentry, candle-making, metal-working and blacksmithing, which was important because the main mode of transport in the past was by mule.

Several Jews rented their houses from Berbers, sometimes with a small plot of land, which they themselves cultivated to supplement their incomes. The wealthier Jews, however, owned their own property, usually agricultural, and provided jobs for both Jews and Muslims.

***Dhimmi* status**. This refers to the special position that Jews and Christians (people of the book, i.e. Bible) have occupied historically in Muslim countries. They paid a special tax but otherwise were allowed to participate in most normal activities in society.

182   The full panoply of *Dhimmi* regulations was rarely enforced at any time in Morocco's long history. Sultans and *Caids* were well aware of how easy it would be for the sophisticated businessmen among the Jews to move elsewhere if they were dissatisfied with regulations. Not all was a bed of roses. Poor Jews like poor Muslims were not treated well in some parts of the country. Few sultans could remain in power for any length of time without the financial support, be it in taxes or other forms of revenue, paid by their Jewish subjects. This was one of the fundamental reasons why Jews, for the most part, had the protection of the sultans.

The same reasons applied out in the *Bled es-Siba*, where Jews relied on the protection of the tribal and district chiefs. Corrupt local officials and tribal chiefs abused their power on both the Jewish and Muslim underprivileged, and some required bribes to turn a blind eye to a minor infraction or to be granted a favor. Wealthier Jews and Muslims, however, had the sense not to flaunt their real wealth and often hid their money whenever a visit was made by someone in authority. In some respects the practice continues today. Many of the older generation of Berber businessmen, reluctant to show their true wealth, dress in a manner designed to give the impression they do not have two pennies to rub together. This is a carryover from the days before Morocco's independence, when the local *caid* made his rounds of the villages and farms to collect taxes.

Years of coexistence taught the Berbers and the Jews to respect each other's religious beliefs. Assistance with the preparation of the *Shabbat* meals by Berber neighbors is one indication of that collaboration. The exchange of customs and traditions periodically took place; the Jews adopted the Berber custom of decorating the hands of a bride with henna before the occasion of her wedding. The veneration of holy men had long been practiced by the Berbers before it became a Jewish custom.

Childhood friendships continued through adulthood, building trust and fair play in matters of business and trade. Moreover, Berbers truly believed that having Jews in their midst brought *baraka*, a divine blessing. There is even some evidence the Berbers thought it sinful or shameful to harm a Jew. Moroccan Jewish immigrants living in Israel, who had formally lived among the Berbers of the High Atlas Mountains, speak fondly of their former neighbors. By all accounts, relations were harmonious and bidding farewell when the time came to leave for Israel was a painful experience for all concerned.

183

Hebrew Inscription in the abandoned Synagogue in Khemis Arazane
Photo by Yehuda and Nurit Patt

15

Souss Region

Agadir
Taroudant
Khemis Arazane
Ighil N'Ogho
Aoulouz
Taliouine
Assads

✿ T he region of the Souss consists of the vast flatland or plain, which stretches from the Atlantic Ocean in the west and between the High Atlas Mountains to the north and the Anti-Atlas to the south. The majority of the inhabitants are made up of several indigenous Berber tribes and former African slaves that come under the collective name of Soussi Berbers.

The Souss Plain sustained the lives of thousands of Berber Jews, who, for centuries, lived and made a living in hundreds of small settlements and the few towns scattered around the region. Their mother tongue was the local Berber language, with males supplementing Arabic for the purposes of trading. Originally, the only source of education, provided by the local rabbis and their assistants, was Talmudic, often with the exclusion of girls, who, incidentally, spoke very little Arabic. Formal education for children of both genders only came into existence during the period of the French Protectorate, when schools were opened by the *Alliance Israélite Universelle*, the French-based organization.

After the expulsion of the Jews from Spain in 1492, several thousand Spanish speaking Jews, who refused to convert to Catholicism, arrived in the area in order to work alongside the Portuguese occupiers and representatives of other European powers that made good use of their linguistic skills. They were called the *Megorashim*, the banished ones, by the long settled Jews, the *Toshavim*. The knowledge of international trade by the *Megorashim* was appreciated by the sultans of the Saadian dynasty, who, in the sixteenth century, subsequently brought the region back under Moroccan rule and made it an agricultural success.

The nineteenth century ended with a long period of drought, causing hardship and suffering throughout the region. Many Jews, especially the young, abandoned their settlements and moved to the larger towns, mostly north of the High Atlas

Mountains. These days, the Souss Plain is one of Morocco's most productive regions in the cultivation of varieties of fruit.

Agadir

Agadir is the most developed and most popular of Morocco's beach resorts, due to its climatic position. It has more than 300 days per year of warm sunshine and attracts tourists all year round, especially German and Scandinavian people. The long, fine sandy beach, in a sheltered bay, is well protected from the dangerous undercurrents of the Atlantic Ocean, making it perfectly safe for swimmers and water sport enthusiasts.

Details on the town's ancient beginnings are extremely vague. There is, however, mention of a Carthaginian port somewhere in the vicinity. The Portuguese were definitely present a little way north of the area at the beginning the sixteenth century. After having built a fortress and subdued the local population, they developed the surrounding countryside, opened a small port and were involved in commercial activities. A large community of Jewish traders and intermediaries were on hand to support business transactions between Spanish, French and Italian merchants, who were obliged to pay duties to the Portuguese authorities.

In 1531, the Saadian sultan, Mohammed ech-Sheikh, decided the Portuguese were a serious obstacle to his plans for complete control of the country. The other motive for the removal of the occupying foreigners was that the Portuguese had developed large areas of valuable sugar plantations and other agricultural crops. In addition to that, the port was proving to be very successful.

A Moroccan military garrison (on the site of the *Kasbah* above the port) was established a few kilometers from the Portuguese fortress and, after several attempts made over a period of many years, the fortress finally fell in 1541 to Sudanese and Turkish mercenaries led by another Saadian sultan, Mohammed ibn Abd er-Rahman. Under the Saadians, the port was developed even further, as were huge swathes of land in the Souss. The shipment of goods from sub-

Saharan Africa, especially the Sudan, grew to enormous proportions. Agadir's Jewish merchants reaped the benefits from the exportation of sugar cane, beeswax, dates, gold and animal hides.

Agadir's success came to an end in 1760 when the Alaouite sultan, Mohammed ben Abdallah, created the new town of Essaouira, improved its port facilities and, to entice international trade, declared European merchants exempt from paying certain customs duties. The sultan's decision to move all trading activities away from the region was partly influenced by the fact that the people of Agadir showed little or no respect for his authority. On the other hand, he called for the local Jewish community to take his advice and take up residence in Essaouira, to which more than two thousand responded positively.

187

The town's name, Agadir, a Berber word for a communal granary, came into use around 1572. A European traveller, who visited Agadir in 1819, wrote in his journal that the town had hardly any buildings still standing.

At the turn of the twentieth century, the European powers, mainly France, Spain, Germany and Britain, were in discussion about how they would go about carving up parts of North Africa. Britain acknowledged France as having the main sphere of influence in Morocco, provoking a very negative German reaction. In 1911, Germany sent a gunboat, the *Panther*, to do sabre rattling off the coast of Agadir, an act that almost started a war.

During the years of the French Protectorate, the town received investment in the construction of small hotels, holiday villas and administrative buildings. The French also invested in the off-shore fishing industry and built a port. By the 1930s, the town was back to normal economic activity. The presence of the French had encouraged Jews to return to the town in quite considerable numbers. Many set up wholesale businesses in the selling of textiles and clothing, serving the territory of the Souss and beyond to the regions of the Anti-Atlas.

On February 29, 1960, the town was hit by a powerful earthquake, killing more than 15,000 inhabitants and destroying the port and virtually the entire town. The Jewish community alone suffered the loss of 1,200 people, which included several young children. The devastation to buildings was such that it was impossible to unearth the dead from beneath the rubble.

Fearing the spread of disease, the decision was taken to bury the deceased, Christian, Muslim and Jews, together under a massive mound. Despite the complications, several of the victims from the Jewish community were able to receive proper burial in the Jewish cemetery.

As would be expected, many of the earthquake survivors not only lost their homes but also their livelihoods. As a result, the Muslim and Jewish communities came together to form an association to collect funds to ease the hardship of the families of the victims. Many of the remaining Jewish community that had been struggling with the dilemma of whether or not to follow friends and family who had already left for Israel during the 1950s felt that the devastation caused by the earthquake had made the decision for them.

Prior to the 1950s, there were approximately 10,000 Jews living in Agadir, not all in the Jewish quarter, which incidentally was next to the *kasbah*, before being destroyed by the earthquake of 1960. By the end of the 1960s, only a few dozen Jews were left in Agadir. In 2007 there were seventy Jews. The town has one remaining synagogue and a kosher restaurant. The cemetery, mostly given over to the graves of the victims of the earthquake, is on the outskirts of the town on the old road to Taroudant.

Today's Agadir has very few traces of the 1960s earthquake disaster. The port has become one of Morocco's most successful international fishing ports, with fishing vessels calling in from as far away as Korea and Japan. Every year sees the expansion of holiday homes for both foreign tourists and Moroccan nationals. The town also plays host to international golf tournaments and other sporting events. Served by charter flights from all corners of Europe, Agadir has become a favorite and extremely well-liked destination.

Taroudant (and the environs)

Once known as the Forbidden City (Christians were barred from entering) the town of Taroudant is located on the vast Souss Plain between the High Atlas Mountains and the popular beach resort of Agadir. Local folklore tells a very interesting story about how the town got its name; long ago, a distraught mother of two Berber children came running into what was then a small town. "*Tarwa dant, Tarwa dant,*" she screamed hysterically in the local Berber dialect. (*Tarwa*, pronounced *Terwa*, is Berber for children, and *dant* means gone). Apparently, her children were swimming in the nearby Oued Souss, when they were swept away by the strong currents and drowned. Over the years, the two words, *Tarwa* and *dant*, were joined together and became Taroudant.

189

Taroudant played a very important commercial and political role in the history of Morocco. The town more or less had an independent status at the time the Almoravids captured it in 1056. Under the Almohad Dynasty, independence was revoked. However, during the fourteenth century, it was reinstated although the town did acknowledge the Merinids' right to rule.

In the sixteenth century, Mohammed ibn Abd er-Rahman, of the Saadian dynasty, chose the location and built a fortress with the town placed within. It was from here that he made plans to dislodge the Portuguese, who had already established themselves in nearby Agadir from the start of the sixteenth century.

Taroudant became an important trading post on the caravan routes from Akka and Guelmime in the southwest. Many Jews were drawn to the town, and for a few years in the sixteenth century it had a Golden Age.

The Saadians had by this time made Marrakech their capital, but despite this, the town flourished and even had its own coinage, made by Jews. Records show the principal forms of income were indigo and cotton, rice, sugar-cane and several types of fruit. What is more, Taroudant's reputation for fine silverware produced by Jewish craftsmen was second to none.

The residents of Taroudant paid a high price during the first few years under the Alaouite ruler, Moulay Ismail. The town's people had made the wrong choice in supporting his nephew's attempts to rule. In 1687, Moulay Ismail took his revenge by occupying the town and killing many of the inhabitants. Later in the nineteenth century, due to the development of direct shipping routes from Africa to Europe, Taroudant was by-passed and fell into decline.

190   At the beginning of the twentieth century, the Jewish community was 10 percent of the town's inhabitants, and they experienced chronic unemployment and acute poverty. Matters were made worse by the hundreds of young Jews drifting into town from the *mellahs* and small settlements in the surrounding countryside; drought and a lack of employment opportunities had forced them to abandon their homes.

Before the years of the French Protectorate, there were around 10,000 Jews in Taroundant's small *mellah*. Sickness and decease were rife and alcoholism was a serious problem. After 1912, with the news that the French were heavily involved in developing the large cities, the young and able-bodied moved away to Casablanca and Marrakech. They and their descendants later joined the mass exodus to Israel when the time came. The period of the 1950s saw 40 percent of the Jewish population of the town receiving some form of charitable assistance either from the local community or the American Jewish Joint Distribution Committee (JDC).

Today there is very little evidence of a Jewish community ever having lived in Taroudant for hundreds of years. The *mellah* was cleared out, and later partly demolished, after the last Jews left for Israel in 1967. The local Jewish cemetery is all that can be seen and visited today. It is the final resting place of Rabbi David Barroukh or Baba Dudu - from the renowned Barroukh family. The family served several local communities in the region of Taroudant. The cemetery has a Muslim caretaker and is well maintained.

Within easy reach of Taroudant, only a few kilometers, there are a few former Jewish settlements, namely Agadir L-Borg, Tiout and Freij. Agadir L-Borg, close to the town of Oulad Birhil, has an old *mellah*, presently inhabited by Muslims. The buildings and narrow lanes look just the same as they did before the Jews abandoned them so many years ago.

In the village of Tiout, there is a shrine to a rabbi, who, because his name was unknown, was given the title, Rabbi Tiout. He is buried next to the former Glaoui *kasbah*, which is perched on a hill overlooking the ruins of the ancient *mellah* and the picturesque oasis of the present Berber village. Unfortunately, nothing remains of the former Jewish community of Freij. It was originally located on a small hilltop next to a *kasbah*, now completely in ruins, on the east bank of the Oued Souss, and only a short distance from Tiout.

Kasbahs of the South

Up until the time of Morocco's independence in 1956, the region of Taroudant had its fair share of local tribal chiefs or the sultan's representatives, known as *Caids*, today's Governors or Administrators. The *caids* were very rich and politically powerful men. As they very often governed in isolated places and were open to attack by roving bandits or political rivals, they built massive, sprawling strongholds, which the Moroccans call *kasbahs*.

These kasbahs became the focus for trading and small settlements or villages began to develop around them. Many of the inhabitants were Jews, who were basically given the monopoly on all commerce to ensure the payment or collection of taxes. Sooner or later, the Jews created their own Jewish quarter. The alternative was for the *caids* to build their *kasbah* near to an already existing settlement, which Jews were drawn to in order to carry out their respective trades and, at the same time, benefit from the protection of the local *caid*.

This model seems to have been repeated all over the south of the country, from the environs of Marrakech and throughout the High Atlas Mountains and all the way down to the edge of the Sahara. Moreover, the majority of kasbahs mark the old caravan routes, a shrewd move by the business-minded *caids*.

Khemis Arazane

At a distance of twenty-eight kilometers from Taroudant lies the village of Khemis Arazane. Here the former Jewish community appears to have been more independent, seeing that there is no *kasbah* in the vicinity. However, the village is situated on one of the ancient caravan routes that came up from Tata in the south and continued westward to Taroudant. It was a twist of fate that the ancient synagogue in Arazane came to light at all.

Anxious to find and preserve as much as possible of Morocco's Jewish heritage, the Foundation for the History and Culture of Moroccan Jews, based at the Jewish Museum in Casablanca, sent the author, Raphael Elmaleh, to scout the villages in the south of the country to see what remained of their former Jewish inhabitants.

As he came to Khemis Arazane, he interviewed local Berber Muslims on whether there was anything remaining of the former Jewish community. Documented evidence confirms that Jews had lived in the village and the site had been in existence for more than 850 years. Other evidence demonstrates that many settlements along the caravan routes were first established by Berber Jews.

Some local men escorted him to the home of a local elder named Harim, who, on discovering the reason for coming to the village, asked why he had taken forty-three years to show up.

Harim then produced a large wooden key, a length of wood with pegs very similar to those used in the Middle East many hundreds of years before. The lock, too, is made of wood. According to Harim, who was seventeen-years-old at the time, he was given the key by the last Jew to leave the village for Israel during the 1960s. The Jew told him to give the key to any Jew who happened to turn up.

The *slat*, the Berber Jews never used the word synagogue, was built with packed mud, called *pisé*, and had in recent years been used for storing hay. Removal of the hay revealed the Ark with the original wooden doors decorated in typical Berber style. There was great excitement when some Hebrew script was also found written on the interior walls. The roof was in need of repair and the *mikvi* filled with dried mud and sludge, but, fortunately, the interior and outer walls were quite sound. The building was subsequently restored.

Harim, a Muslim, is now the guardian of the building and responsible for keeping an eye out for any signs of damage by the torrential rains that fall each rainy season. It is clear from the way he talks that he feels it a great honor to be in such a position. With his knowledge Harim could be considered as an unofficial historian of the Khemis Arazane's Jewish past. By the way, *Khemis* means Thursday in Arabic. The tag was added to the village name because the local market or souk always took place every Thursday. The Jews never worked on a Saturday, consequently, until fairly recently, there were no towns or villages with the tag *Sebt*, which means seven or the seventh day.

193

Harim opening the abandoned synagogue in Khemis Arazane
Photo by Yehuda and Nurit Patt

Arazane was home to between sixty to eighty Jewish families, who spoke Berber and Arabic. Working with leather to make saddles and sandals was one source of employment, and other tradesmen did tailoring with manually-operated sewing machines. Silver was brought from Marrakech, worked on, and then the finished articles were taken back to Marrakech to be sold. Additionally, a few families with land grew crops.

Poorer families were given food and clothing by the JDC, which made frequent visits to the area. According to Harim, the Berber Muslims and Berber Jews lived in harmony and all doors remained open for anyone to enter. Harim, as a young boy, was always in the company of Jewish children and adolescents, so much so that he can still recite verses in Hebrew from the Torah. Many tourists and visitors who have had the experience of meeting Harim are left flabbergasted.

He can remember the oven was changed each Passover and the exchange of invitations to feasts and weddings. Both communities ate the same food, of course, with the exception of non-kosher meat. *Mahiya* was always available and drank by the Jews at any excuse for a celebration.

Jewish children were schooled by the local rabbi. Later, young girls took a husband and the young men started working. The older women in the Jewish community looked after the children and kept home. Some created the designs for carpets and afterwards got the Berber women to help with the actual weaving. Head scarves were worn by the older women, but not in the way of the Islamic hijab. In contrast, younger women braided their hair to show off their beauty.

Jews started leaving Khemis Arazane in the 1940s, and the exodus continued until the 1960s. They left all their property to the local Berbers, who did not have the means to purchase it any way. Although it was never mentioned, local residents believe their final destination was Israel. No former Jewish inhabitant has ever returned, not even for a visit. The cemetery is completely overgrown after years of neglect and is beyond saving.

Ighil N'Ogho

Still in the region of Taroudant and situated a few kilometers along the narrow, winding road to Askoun (Region of Taliouine) is the village of Ighil N'Ogho. Some people shorten the name and say Ighil (pronounced Irril). N'Ogho is pronounced No-rro.

The Foundation and Jewish Museum already knew a former Jewish community had lived here for 600 or 700 years. When the author Raphael Elmaleh arrived at the village, he found the *slat* (Berber name for synagogue) in a state of dereliction. Part of the roof had fallen in and the entrance was blocked by a pile of dried mud and rubble.

A clean-up operation was put into action with assistance from the local Muslims. Once inside, two chambers were found where the floors were covered in dried mud. The sighting of arches and stone benches within the larger chamber confirmed beyond doubt the building was a *slat*. Further evidence came to light when the floor was cleared of mud and an underground cellar (*ganizan*) was discovered. From his experience of other sites, the author was aware that before the Jews had abandoned their villages and settlements they had placed or buried an assortment of documents and other items under the floor of the *slats*.

Throughout the initial clearing up, a small crowd of local inhabitants looked on, and when the time came to open up the cellar, an old lady warned him about a curse. Apparently, before the local rabbi left the village he had told the Muslim inhabitants that if anyone entered the cellar, they would be bitten by a scorpion and would die instantly. Assuming that the rabbi had made the threat to safeguard the documents, the author entered the cellar and removed the contents. Several crates were brought out, which later were found to contain scrolls, various books, schoolbooks and manuscripts.

With the task of emptying the cellar complete, he left the *slat*. People were surprised to see he was unharmed. There followed a moment of mutterings and whispers before a woman spoke in a clear voice saying the author had been left unharmed because he was a Jew.

Eventually, the restoration of the *slat* was carried out by local Muslim men, supervised by the author. Fortunately, most of the original beams were reusable, and three weeks later it was back to how it had looked the day the Jewish community had departed for a new life in Israel more than sixty years before.

196   When the contents of the crates taken from Ighil were given closer inspection in Casablanca, an extremely rare *meguillah* written in Hebrew and Arabic was discovered. The contents provided evidence that T'hami El Glaoui, ex-Pasha of Marrakech, who was a Berber chieftain, was an accomplice in the French Government plan to hand over the Moroccan Jews to the Nazis for extermination. Another document revealed that Ighil was a center for training young men to become synagogue teachers and assistants. In addition, they learned the laws of slaughtering.

Presently, the *slat* is regularly cleaned and maintained by a Muslim family. The local Muslim women are overjoyed to have a *slat* once again in the village. They say that when they are troubled they come and place a hand on the exterior wall before putting it to their lips with a kiss. The hope is that the Jewish presence will bring good fortune, *baraka*.

After the Jews had left for Israel in the late 1940s, the local Muslim inhabitants (Berbers) of Ighil made good use of the empty properties by moving in. The rabbi's house, which was bigger than most, is still occupied by a Berber family today and appears to be reasonably well maintained. The Jewish cemetery is on the outskirts of the village. The oldest part of the cemetery seems to have suffered from years of natural erosion and neglect, making it difficult to separate former tombstones from the surrounding natural rocks. Moreover, it appears from the piles of discarded female clothing that local Muslim women still perform the ritual of purification, previously carried out by Jewish women.

An elderly lady, who had gone blind and had lived in the village all her life, remembered there was a sizeable Jewish community in the village. In actual fact, several buses turned up to transport the first batch of Jewish residents to the port of Agadir for transit to

Israel. She often witnessed the procession of the Torah from the rabbi's house on the short walk to the *slat* and the return journey after the religious services were over. The chanting and singing, she said, was heavenly. As it was with so many Jews in the region, and now with the Berbers, the cultivation of crocus flowers for saffron was very popular.

Two other towns in the region of Taroudant, at one time, supported a large number of Moroccan Jews: Aoulouz (Land of Almonds) and Taliouine, which are both conveniently situated on the main road that runs across country from Taroudant in the west to Ouarzazate further to the east.

Aoulouz

Aoulouz and its surrounds had a concentration of approximately 6,000 Jews. They were responsible for starting the cultivation of a variety of fruit, almonds and saffron, which the local Berbers still continue to today. Sheep farming and its associated by-products; for instance, wool for heavy winter *djallabas* were additional occupations.

The entire Jewish community abandoned their properties and left for Israel in the late 1940s. These days nothing remains of the former Jewish quarter. The cemetery, after years of neglect, is in a sorry state, with every gravestone shattered into small fragments.

Taliouine

A little further on from Aoulouz stands the market town of Taliouine. The former *caid's kasbah*, although partly in ruins, still dominates the small town. It was built for Abdallah El Glaoui, a son of T'hami El Glaoui. Abdallah turned out to be the last Khalifa (deputy) of the region of Taliouine right up to his death and Morocco's independence in 1956.

Close by, and very visible on the crest of a hill, is what looks like a Greek monument, but in fact, once served as the local slave market and the *caid's* grain store (*agadir*). The breeding and trading of African slaves from the sub-Sahara was common among sultans, tribal chiefs and *caids* throughout the country. They were recruited into the private armies of their masters and, in addition, put to work in the domain of crop cultivation. Anyone who could afford them had slaves, including successful Jews.

Taliouine is virtually on the intersection between Ouarzazate, to the east, and Taroudant, to the west, and also at the start of the steep climb over the High Atlas Mountains, northwards, to Marrakech. Its position once played a central role on the caravan routes; therefore, it is logical to assume that there was a Jewish presence here. In reality, there were several thousand Berber Jews. Some lived within the limits of the town, close to the *souk* or market. Others chose to make their homes and livelihoods in the surrounding countryside or hills, where they relied on the cultivation of fruit, almonds and saffron.

The exodus of the entire Jewish population started in the late 1940s. Their last sighting of Morocco was the port of Agadir. Their ultimate destination was to be Israel.

Every year, in the month of February, the Festival of Fruit takes place. It coincides with the very popular pilgrimage to the shrine of Rabbi Ruben Wiesman, who died more than 500 years ago. The shrine is on the outskirts of Taliouine, in the direction of Ouarzazate, and sits on the slope of a medium-sized foothill above a small hamlet. Today, the Berbers of the region celebrate their festive occasions with dance and music adopted from their former Jewish neighbors.

Assads, A blessing from the Jews
Assads, a small settlement twenty-two kilometers southeast of Taroudant, was once inhabited primarily by Berber Jews. The exact number is not certain, but local sources remembered two to three dozen Jewish families. Their principal occupation was the cultivation of a citrus fruit known to the locals as *citren* (etrog), a close cousin to the lemon. Apparently, the original trees were imported as shrubs hundreds of years ago from present day Israel. When the day came for the Jewish families to depart for Israel in the 1940s, they left their land and homes to the small community of local Berbers.

Assads is the only location in the whole of Morocco where the *citren* is able to grow and mature successfully. Its success has been credited to the number of days of annual sunshine and the type and quality of the local soil. Harvesting the fruit takes place during the months of August and September. Many Jews then converge on Assads from all parts of the world to select and buy the best quality. One rabbi, in particular, makes the journey from London every year.

The fruit is used in hundreds of synagogues around the world during *Sukkot* (Feast of the Tabernacle). Its other use is the making of jam. The *citren* is also found growing in Israel, Italy, Greece and Yemen. However, there is a difference; the Israeli *citren,* as well as the Moroccan, has a crown or a hat whereas the Italian fruit has none. The latter is used solely by one group of Jews, the Lubavitch. The Moroccan *citron* is non-acidic, and some research done a few years ago found that the fruit-bearing trees were non-grafted.

Today, it is young Berbers who take care of every aspect of the production and sale of the *citrens.* The fact that when dealing with Jewish buyers they use Hebrew and Yiddish words is astonishing when heard for the first time during the selection process. The only possible explanation is that it has been passed down through the generations from earlier times when the original Jewish settlers worked with the fruit.

The quality of the fruit is decided by categories. In Hebrew, *zoug alef* is Category 1 and *zoug bet* comes out as Category 2. In Yiddish, for the European Jews, *git* is decided when the quality is good. And should the quality be considered under par, *nich git*, meaning not good, is said. The young Berbers of Assads work almost exclusively with the *citren*, only growing other crops mostly for their everyday needs. They declare that they are deeply grateful to the former Jewish community for their *Baraka* – blessing.

Getting from Taroudant to the place where the *citren* grows requires a guide with some knowledge of the region.

16
Anti Atlas Mountains

Tiznit
Iligh
Tafraoute
Ifrane
Foum el-Hassan
Akka
Tata
Goulimine

T he most southerly of Morocco's mountain ranges, the Anti-Atlas Mountains divide the vast Souss plain from the region of the pre-Sahara. The region is, for the most part, arid and semi-desert, interspersed at intervals, with lush green oases strung out like strings of pearls along partially dried up river beds and wide valleys. Its inhabitants are an interesting melange of various Berber tribes who speak the Berber dialect Tachelhite and Arabic. Judeo-Berber (Tamazight interspersed with Hebrew) was in wide use among the Jewish communities.

Due to the lack of sufficient annual rainfall, water cisterns and irrigation systems ensure human habitation and cultivation of crops that require a minimum of water: such as olives, almonds and figs. Storage of foodstuffs and other necessities are kept safe in collective granaries called *agadirs.*

The most common tree is the argan, which produces a fruit from which edible oil is extracted and then eaten with bread or added to tagines. Argan oil, low in cholesterol, can be purchased in most upmarket delicatessens in the major cities of many countries.

Prehistoric rock-drawings give proof of human life in the region of the Anti-Atlas in the distant past. Around 800 B.C.E. there is evidence of Jewish presence in the coastal regions of Morocco with trading links between the Sudan and other countries south of the Sahara into which the settlements in the region of the Anti-Atlas were certainly incorporated.

In order to escape wars, political instability and religious persecution, the Jews of the Maghreb countries migrated deeper and deeper into the interior, often into mountainous terrain and desert oases. For some of the Jewish communities of Morocco, the region of the Anti-Atlas and the pre-Sahara was considered safe territory; the local inhabitants, the indigenous Berber tribes, were known to have similar moral and ethical standards of behavior.

Raphael Elmaleh & George Ricketts

The Jews subsequently settled and set about trading on the caravan routes that ran through Algeria and Mauritania, and beyond: gold, ostrich feathers, animal skins and leather, ivory, copper and, very lucrative for many, the trade in African slaves. Relations with the local Berbers proved to be very successful, so much so that many of the Berber tribes converted to Judaism.

The region was one of the last to come under the influence of Islam and its forced conversions. However, there still remained several Jewish communities in the twelfth century. As with most regions in the south, the Jews of the Anti-Atlas followed the rules and rituals of *Toshavim*. By the nineteenth century, the bulk of transportation of sub-Saharan trade had switched to passage by sea, ending the dependence on the ancient caravan routes. The latter part of the same century brought drought and famine to the region. As a result, young people of the region were forced to seek employment in the larger towns and cities in the north, and other family members inevitably followed.

The region suffered from famine and drought during the years of World War II, and the plight of the inhabitants was further exacerbated due to the lack of transportation in bringing food supplies from Agadir. Throughout the 1950s and 1960s, the entire Jewish community in the region, after almost 2,000 years, left their homes for ever and moved to Israel.

Tiznit

The last large town before striking the region of the pre-Sahara, Tiznit, named after a local woman, Lalla Tiznit, a healer and sorcerer, lies in the middle of a plain often deprived of adequate rainfall. This makes most forms of crop cultivation completely impossible. Confirmation of this fact is backed up by the sparsely populated, arid landscape and the absence of trees in the surrounding countryside.

The town of Tiznit was founded in 1882 by the Alaouite sultan, Moulay el-Hassan (1873-1894). His principal motivation for building the town was the subjugation of the independent

Berber tribes in the region of the Souss and the areas of the Anti-Atlas. Later historical events suggest his efforts were not entirely successful.

A strong defensive wall was constructed around the original site, which consisted of a cluster of *ksour* (fortified settlements) and a *souk*. Other buildings and streets were then added within. One *ksar* (singular of *ksour*) was inhabited by a small number of Jewish families, who had their own rabbi and synagogue. The town very quickly became the regional center for trade and commerce, drawing a large contingent of Jewish settlers and their families.

203

Many of the Jews were expert silversmiths and jewelers and their finished products were of the highest quality and standard, so much so that they were in great demand both within the country and abroad. The Jews of Tiznit also benefited from producing goods made from copper, which was mined in the region around the Anti-Atlas from as far back as the eleventh century and exported to sub-Saharan Africa and Europe.

On May 12, 1912, Ahmed El-Hiba, originally from Mauritania and a leader of the Toureg tribe, known as the Blue People, proclaimed himself sultan of Morocco in Tiznit. His action was in retaliation for the fact that the rightful sultan, Moulay Hafid, had very recently signed the Treaty of Fes, practically giving up control of the country to the French and the Spanish, or, as the Moroccan Muslims expressed most vehemently, the Christian infidels.

El-Hiba had no difficulty in rallying the tribes of the Souss and the Anti-Atlas to march against the French. The field of battle was on the plains just north of Marrakech, but the old muskets and hand-daggers of the tribes were outmatched by the superior modern weapons of the French.

Defeated, El-Hiba fled back south over the Tiz N'Test Pass and returned to Tiznit, only to be dislodged by the French. The

French occupied the town in 1917 and remained until Moroccan independence in 1956. El-Hiba died in Taroudant in 1919.

Prior to the 1960s and the movement of the Jewish population to Israel, Tiznit had three synagogues. Two were subsequently converted into houses by their Muslim owners. The other synagogue, which is very ancient and in danger of collapse, had its doorway bricked up and is abandoned.

The town's former Jewish community stood at around 10,000, which required two *mellahs* to accommodate them, namely Ouzzane and Ait Oufrane. During the French Protectorate, most children attended the local *Alliance Israélite Universelle* school, where they studied Hebrew and French. In addition, many families were employed in the trades associated with the craft of producing jewelry and other precious objects from silver and gold.

Other trades included grocers and greengrocers, kosher butchers, dealers in textiles and distillers of *mahiya*. Several small traders travelled around the countryside, peddling copperware and other household essentials, returning home in time to spend *Shabbat* with their families.

The role of Tiznit as a center of commerce and administration for the region has remained the same since the day of its original construction. These days, it is the predominately Berber inhabitants that carry on the trades of silversmiths and goldsmiths, having learned the special skills and knowledge from their former Jewish compatriots.

Presently, the town has a look of prosperity due to the many former Muslim inhabitants returning from several years of working as migrant workers in Europe. They have built large homes and invested their savings in local commerce. The Moroccan Government has also done its bit by spending large sums of money on cleaning up the town and landscaping the principle thoroughfares.

Iligh

A relatively short distance from Tiznit is the town of Iligh (pron - Ilirr), in the region of Tazeroualt. The region, from the sixteenth to nineteenth century, was under the control of Idrissid *marabouts*, an Islamic religious sect, that governed independently of the central power. The area under their authority extended from the tributary of the Oued Massa, and included a large part of the Souss region and the pre-Sahara region between the Oued Souss and the Oued Draa. Iligh served as the capital of the region during the sixteenth and seventeenth centuries.

The Alaouite ruler, Moulay Ismail, destroyed the town around 1670 and brought the region into the sphere of the *Bled Makhzen*. The destruction of the town led to the Jewish community abandoning the area. The Idrissid *marabouts* re-established control of the region and rebuilt the town in 1745. This encouraged the Jewish community to return. By 1869, the Jewish community was estimated to be about 500.

In 1882, Moulay el-Hassan, an Alaouite, succeeded in subjugating parts of the region. To maintain his authority, he ordered the construction of a *kasbah*, and manned it with a small garrison. At this juncture, the Jewish community had decreased to 300, very likely due to the fighting and instability around this time.

The local Jews are known to have specialized in the trading of animal skins and pelts, plus copper and silver. However, years of drought and famine during the latter part of the nineteenth century forced a large section of the Jewish community to move to the town of Tiznit. Despite this fact, a small number of Jews (around 250) were still living in the town in the early 1950s when the *Alliance Israélite Universelle* opened a school. Less than a decade later the community uprooted and left to Israel. The only evidence of a former thriving Jewish presence today is the ruined *mellah* and two badly neglected cemeteries.

The region of Tazeroualt is famous for its acrobats; some can be seen performing on the Place Djemaa el-Fna in Marrakech and others perform on the circuit of international circuses.

Tafraoute

The Ameln valley, enchanting and tranquil as it is picturesque, is home to several mixed Berber tribes, who seem to have inhabited the valley for several generations. The valley is peppered with pretty villages and hamlets in a setting of green oases and encircled by spectacular and extraordinary shaped, pink-coloured mountains. At the heart of all this beauty is the town of Tafraoute, the administrative center and focal point for the region of the same name. Most visitors use the town as a base from where they set out to explore the surrounding region.

The women of the region, following the local interpretations for Islamic dress, are fully covered, Middle Eastern-style, in black cloth with only one eye on view. The lack of sufficient annual rainfall prevents any serious cultivation of crops; preventing any real means of making a decent living. The men are then forced to seek employment in the larger cities around the country and, even, abroad mainly in France, Belgium and Holland.

Berbers from the region of Tafraoute, known as Tafraoutis, are known for their business acumen; many run the small corner-shops around Morocco and in some European countries. They moved with ease into the economic void left when Jews migrated to Israel between the 1950s and 1960s. Thousands of Berbers return to their villages, or *bleds*, for one month every summer and, as a statement of their achievements, and with retirement in mind, many have built palatial houses there.

Although most former Jewish settlements around the region, several by all accounts, have all but disappeared with the ravages of time, local Berbers still recount with much respect and fondness about the time when they lived among Jewish neighbors. An elderly Berber woman from Askoun (region of Tafraoute), who was ten years old in 1947, remembered there was a large community of Berber Jews in a village called T'lin, a short distance from the regional town of Adai.

According to her testimony, the young Jewish women were extremely beautiful. She mentioned a Jewish man by the name of Hanna, who visited Askoun on a regular basis to sell small household items from door to door. Relations between the Jewish community and the Muslims (Berbers) could not have been better. For instance, the Muslim neighbors understood that the Jews were prohibited from lighting a fire on *Shabbat*. As confirmation of the closeness of the two communities, the Muslims helped in the preparation of the *Shabbat* meals.

The same elderly Berber woman added that nearby was another village known as Ait Shimon (Tribe of Simon), a community that was reported to have converted to Islam in the distant past. She said that since the majority of Jews were poor, there was no hesitation when the time came to immigrate to Israel in the late 40s and early 50s, especially with the promise of a better life. The Jews abandoned everything, including their homes, which are in ruins today after more than half a century.

Grapes, almonds, argon oil and olives were among the agricultural products produced on their land. The leaves from the argon trees were used as fodder for the goats, thought to enhance the taste of their meat, a practice that lasted for centuries and is still done today. Jobs or trades included coppersmiths, tailors who made the *guandoura* (Berber-type overall) and *djallabas*. Some were shoemakers, who used camel skin to make *idoukane* (Berber footwear). After the invention of rubber tires, Jews cobblers had the idea of cutting up discarded ones and using the pieces to make soles for shoes.

An old Berber man, living in the village of Agigal, near Tafraoute, mentioned that he worked alongside Jews in the open and underground mines in the hills just above his village. Zinc, lead, copper and uranium were extracted from the site. The elderly man spoke about how the Muslims prepared the accommodation and dug wells for the Jews. The Jews lived and worked onsite, but returned to their family homes in Tahala, some kilometers away, at the end of each week, in time for Shabbat.

Another side to this story came from a young man, a Berber businessman, living in Casablanca. His family originally hail from Tahala, which had a large concentration of Jews as well as descendents of Jews who had converted to Islam. The town had been the main center of administration for the region, before the French took over control from the local *Caid* or *Sheikh* (local leader) and moved it to Tafraoute.

The young man remembers his grandfather talking about when, as a baby in the 1920s, he was wet nursed by a Jewish woman from the neighborhood. Later, the young man's father, born in the late 1940s, confirmed that he, too, had been wet nursed by a Jewish woman. This only goes to underscore the strong bond between the Berber Jews and the Berber Muslims in the regions throughout the south of the country.

Tahala has a medium-sized Jewish cemetery, which includes a section with three or four large tombs, probably the burial sites of important rabbis. The other graves are mostly covered by simple piles of rocks. The cemetery can be found at the top of the town in an area opposite the school called Madrasa Ighi Tahala. The former *mellah* is located close to the center of town. Like most *mellahs* in the region, the buildings are crumbling fast and are totally abandoned.

Ifrane, Anti Atlas

The oasis town of Ifrane, known as Oufrane by the Jews and local Berbers, was in existence before the destruction of Jerusalem by the Babylonian ruler, Nebuchadnezzar in the sixth century B.C.E. The original small settlement in the valley of the Oued Ifrane was a principal stop-over on the ancient caravan routes, bringing valuable commodities up from the sub-Saharan countries. It was to this settlement and others in the surrounding region that several of the first Jewish migrants settled, eventually, becoming successful traders. As they married local Berber women, the number of Berber Jews grew.

On the other hand, people say that local Berber tribes, on witnessing the success of Jewish traders and the way they conducted their religion, thought it was a divine gift from the Almighty and converted to Judaism, also becoming known as Berber Jews.

Ifrane's Jewish community left for Israel around 1958. The abandoned and very much ruined *mellah* is on the edge of town in a place called Souk Oufula (The Upper Souk). However, there remains a small whitewashed *slat* (synagogue) which was restored a few years ago.

The Jewish cemetery is found further up on the right side of the river bed, with the graves marked out by a series of large stones. It is believed the ashes of fifty Jewish martyrs are buried somewhere in the area. During the reign of Moulay al-Yazid (1790–1792), these devout Jews chose to perish in a fire rather than convert to Islam.

The town, as seen today, is made up of several hamlets and villages spread out among the many oases that run along the valley of the Oued Ifrane. Visitors who make the effort to travel so far south will find the oases to be the most attractive and tranquil in the southern regions of the country.

Foum el-Hassan

Situated on the boundary of the pre-Sahara, Foum el-Hassan (foum – Arabic for mouth) was once one of the principal gateways on the ancient caravan routes between Morocco and the sub-Sahara. Locals around the region call the place Lahssan, which is a shortened version. Unfortunately, very little, if any, evidence remains of the former Jewish community. However, elderly locals vouch for the fact that Jews had lived in the area.

From here there was a direct route, across the *Hamada du Draa*, to Tindouf, now base of the Polisario, in Southern Algeria, beyond which lies the Sahara Desert. Jewish traders and their camel trains would have certainly passed this way en route to Mauritania. The discovery of sites with prehistoric rock-engravings in the area of the town is testament to the presence of human habitation long before the arrival of the Jews.

To the southwest of Foum el-Hassan, near the small oasis of Assa, a rabbi by the name of Mordecai ben Sourour reported seeing two groups of rock-drawings, and a European traveller, Oskar Lenz, mentions visiting them in 1880.

Akka

Northeast of Foum el-Hassan is the oasis town of Akka, formally one of the key pre-Sahara desert ports. From this location the Jewish traders set out for lands far beyond the sub-Sahara, bringing back camel trains laden with valuable merchandise, including black slaves. The merchandise was then forwarded on to the region of Guelmime to the west or Tata to the east. As with elsewhere in the region, the lucrative trading along the caravan routes collapsed with the arrival of transportation by sea.

The story has been told of how some hundreds of years ago a rabbi arrived from the land of Israel and told the Jews of Akka to build a wall around their settlement, effectively, creating an enclosed *mellah* or Jewish quarter. The same rabbi is said to have struck a stone with a stick, and water came gushing from the ground. When the rabbi died, he was buried near Akka. His shrine is five or six kilometers on the approach road to Akka, coming from the direction of Goulimine. With the passing of time, his real name became forgotten, so pilgrims to his shrine adopted the name Rabbi Baa L'Maayan, which means "Father of the water source" or "Creator of the spring". Pilgrims, Jewish and Muslim, still come to pray at his grave and drink from the source today.

Before leaving for Israel, the former Jewish community was comprised of 250 families, and the largest extended family had the name of Assaraf. Some family members were local elders looking after the affairs of the community. The Assaraf family were also experts in the distilling of *mahiya*. Remnants of this family presently (2007) live in Inezgane, near Agadir, and one man and his wife run an off-license business in Goulimine further south, but often return to Inezgane to observe *shabbat*.

The designing and manufacture of gold and silver jewelry was a major occupation, with clients or customers coming from as far away as the north of the country to place orders. Fruit cultivation was another common source of income: figs, dates, peaches, grapes, pomegranates, quince and nuts.

The majority of Jewish families left for Israel in the 1960s. Their desire to live in a Jewish state was expressed as the principal reason for leaving, even though, Akka provided for most of their needs.

Coming from the direction of Goulimine, the former Jewish quarter, known as Tagadirt, lies on the left just before the entrance to the town proper. There were originally two *slats* in Akka, but only one remains. It is in reasonable condition, but not in use. The former 1950's *Alliance Israélite Universelle* school is in total ruin. The graves in the cemetery are marked with piles of stones, and the local *tzadik* is Rabbi Ed Hrara.

Akka today has a sizeable population made up of Berbers and sub-Saharan Africans, very likely the descendents of former slaves brought from the interior of Africa. Traditional and colourful Saraoui clothing is worn by most women. There are *ksour* scattered among the palm groves. Viewed from a high point, the entire scene looks most impressive and tranquil.

Tata

Situated on the pre-Saharan plain on the south side of the Anti-Atlas, Tata was one of the main oasis settlements on the caravan routes, particularly for goods going through the Souss settlement of Irherm to the north, and then on to Taroudant.

The main Jewish settlement was actually in an oasis on the fringes of the town. These days, however, there is very little remaining of the former *mellah*, originally built mostly from mud. The two cemeteries have all but disappeared. The Jews of Tata are known to have specialized in the trading of camels and their skins and the production of saddles, footwear and the dying of leather.

The local population today is a mixture of Berber and sub-Saharan Africans. Traditional Saraoui dress is worn by both men and women.

Goulimine, The Western route to the Sahara

Today the small town of Goulimine is touted by various guidebooks as the "Gateway to the Sahara". This might be true for modern times, but it certainly could not claim this title in the days of the ancient caravan routes. Knowledgeable people place the gateway in the region between Ifrane (Anti-Atlas) and Akka. A map of Morocco indicating the locations of Jewish populations in the sixteenth century has a small settlement called Taghaoust, just northwest of Goulimine, as a transit point for the ancient caravan routes. It appears that Goulimine did not exist at this time.

In the eleventh century, all lands south of Goulimine from the Atlantic coast and into Mauritania were the area of a nomadic Berber tribe called the Lemtouna, the men of the *litam* or veil. Elements of the tribe later ruled Morocco as the Almoravid dynasty.

Evidently, in the nineteenth century, there was some limited trade and communication with Cap Juby, a small island near the southern port city of Tan Tan. The island was owned by a British trader and later sold to the sultan, Moulay Hassan.

Maps for 1950 and 1971 show the existence of a Jewish community still present in Taghaoust. However, with investigations conducted in the area in 1995, no trace of the former Jewish presence was found. As of 2007, only one Jewish man and his wife were residents in Goulimine. The man, family name Assaraf, was brought up in Akka. He is known to sell the high quality *mahiya*.

Today, the town lies almost deserted except for Saturday mornings, when a multitude of tourists, bused down from Agadir, with cameras at the ready, arrive to what is presented as a traditional camel market, located just outside the town. The Touareg, generally known as the "Blue Men", in their traditional

Saraoui blue robes sell souvenir trinkets at inflated prices. Anyone interested in buying fabric (L'Hafa), the kind worn by local women, can find some interesting pieces but will have to bargain for them.

Ksar or Fortified Settlement
Ait Ben Haddou near Ouarzazate
Photo by Yehuda and Nurit Patt

17

Deep South

Tidili
Telouet
Amerzgane
Ait Ben Haddou
Tazenakht
Ouarzazate
Skoura
Dades Valley
Kal'at M'Gouna
Boulmane Dades
Tenerhir

Ziz Valley
Rich
Er-Rachidia

Tafilalt Region
Erfoud
Rissani

Draa Valley
Agdz
Zagora
Amzrou
Tagounite
M'hamid

❀ T he vast area of Ouarzazate and the Deep South has the most diversified landscapes and scenery in the whole of Morocco: snow–capped mountains, rugged and mountainous terrain, which reminds the onlooker of Western movies. Medieval style fortifications, desert oases and date *palmeraies* that continue endlessly for many kilometers. The south also has a number of spectacular and dramatic gorges, carved out by fast-flowing rivers and a lake that has become a habitat for hundreds of pink flamingos.

Many people consider the south to be most picturesque and beautiful. The "Real Morocco" someone once said, with a joyful sigh. In many ways, it is also the least developed, which allows the curious and interested to have a closer look at certain aspects of the daily routine of the inhabitants and particular customs that have survived hundreds of years. The locals are, in the main, Berbers and sub-Saharan Africans whose common language is Tamazight.

Over the High Atlas Mountains

To get to the Deep South from Marrakech, the visitor or, to be more accurate, the adventurer must first experience the nail-biting climb up the Tizi N'Tichka Pass (completed by the French in 1936), where the road literally clings to the side of the mountains as it spirals up and over the High Atlas Mountains. The winding road and hairpin bends literally take you above the soaring peaks and into the clouds.

The approaches to the Tichka Pass are peppered with small Berber villages, some defying gravity as they sit precariously on the top of mountains. Others look quaint and tranquil, nestled hundreds of feet below in deep valleys formed by the will of nature over millions of years. In winter, the mountain peaks are decorated with deep snow, adding another dimension to an already spectacular and magnificent scene.

Some of the villages on this route were home to Berber Jews who came to find sanctuary and a life of peace without fear of persecution. The villages of Tidili, Tazlida, L'Arba Tighedouine and Ighi (pronounced - Irri) had fairly large communities whose livelihood was mainly farming. Aside from the grazing of sheep and goats, the Jews also cultivated crops such as almonds and hazelnuts. Some of the harvest was put into store for human consumption during the winter months and the rest was transported to the *souks* of Marrakech.

Tidili

This town had a religious training center for young Jewish men to prepare them for synagogue and community life. Many Jews in the south spoke Judeo-Berber, which was used to explain religious texts, and sometimes written with the use of Hebrew characters. The shrine of the much venerated Jewish *tzadik*, Rabbi David Ou Moshi, is within a large white complex en route to Tidili. It includes a cemetery and synagogue. The shrine has been restored and receives countless international pilgrims at *Lag Baomer*, after Passover. The complex and the region once had a Jewish community numbering 2,000. All were transported to Israel in the late 1940s.

Telouet

A few kilometers after the road begins to descend on the south side of the Tizi N'Tichka Pass is a signpost giving directions to the village and *Kasbah* of Telouet (Teloowet). This was the original home and base of the Glaoui family, one of Morocco's most powerful and notorious families, responsible for much of the upheaval and turmoil in Morocco's history at the end of the nineteenth century and first half of the twentieth century. They made their initial fortune by owning a salt mine on their extensive land holdings.

Gavin Maxwell's book *Lords of the Atlas*, which tells the story of the Glaoui family, will enthrall the reader and give some very interesting historical facts about Morocco from the dying years of the nineteenth century to the year of Moroccan independence in 1956.

A visit to the *kasbah* is certainly worth the time it takes to get there (2 ½ hours drive from Marrakech).

A small Jewish community of around forty families once existed in Telouet. Their expertise was called upon to work the salt mine and market the end product. Records show there was a prominent Jewish family living locally that went by the name of Ait Robin (Ait means tribe in Berber). Apart from the shrine of Rabbi Yehouda Abuhatzira in the Jewish cemetery, very little else survives of the former Jewish community.

Rabbi Abuhatzira (derived from *hasira*, the Arabic for straw mat) came from an eminent family of educators or teachers of Jewish subjects such as the Torah, and taught in Telouet for many years until his death. His father, Rabbi Yacoub, originated from the land of Israel and settled in the oasis town of Rissani, not so far from the southern town of Erfoud.

When they were ready, he sent his children out as teachers or educators to various towns and settlements throughout the south. Some went to the area of Rich, Er-Rachidia (formally Ksar-es-Souk) and Gourrama, where they subsequently died and lie buried in the Jewish cemeteries of the forementioned towns. Yacoub, the father, travelled to Egypt, where he continued his teaching, and was finally buried there. His subsequent *tzadik* status began a long line of family *tzadiks*.

The River El Mellah (River of Salt), so called because it actually contains salt from its source within the mountains, runs through what was once part of the huge Glaoui estates.

Furthermore, part of the original caravan route from the south followed the course of the river. Among today's inhabitants in the village of Telouet are dark-skinned Berbers or sub-Saharan Africans, descendents of the former slaves of the Glaoui family.

On the south side of the High Atlas Mountains the terrain flattens out and the countryside becomes rugged and almost uninhabited. But look closer at the frequent number of tracks that veer off the main road; they lead to villages that were once inhabited by Jews and where there is a sizeable concentration of shrines to Jewish *tzadiks*.

Amerzgane

This was called Imerzgane by the former Jewish inhabitants, and it is one of the villages with such shrines. Most Jews were farmers with small holdings where they grew crops and kept and bred livestock, later to be sold at the weekly *souk*.

Local Berbers recall the story passed down through previous generations about how the first Jews to arrive in the locality took cuttings from a single tree and, from that one tree, grew thirty more. Acts like these were considered to be a gift or blessing given to the Jews by God. As a direct consequence, the local Berber tribes converted to Judaism. The surrounding area also includes a few *kasbahs* and fortified settlements attributed to the Glaoui family, who set themselves up as *caids* to administer the region.

Ait Ben Haddou

Around thirty kilometers before reaching Ouarzazate a signpost points left to Ait Ben Haddou, another former Glaoui controlled fortified settlement or *ksar*. This historical and ancient settlement, thought to be founded in the eleventh century, was a very important trading-post along the caravan routes coming up from the desert town of Zagora and beyond as far as Timbuktu and Mali. Jews took full advantage and settled here, and they once lived in a separate section of the *ksar*.

The Jewish community departed from Ait Ben Haddou in the late1940s to the new state of Israel. The last inhabitants, Berber Muslims, moved out to more modern housing in the 1970s. The location of Ait ben Haddou has become a popular tourist attraction and is registered as an UNESCO World Heritage site. The large and impressive fortified settlement has also played a starring role in many of films, including *Lawrence of Arabia* and *Gladiator*.

Tazenakht

On the same road as Taliouine, Tazenakht, a small semi-desert town, is so far east that it is on the periphery of the region of Ouarzazate. The Jewish community that previously lived here specialized in the wool trade, specifically, wool dyeing and the weaving of carpets and rugs. They hired local Berber women to assist with the actual weaving.

The Galerie Athar in Casablanca, sell and hold auctions of nineteenth century and early twentieth century carpets and rugs made by Berber Jews in the region of Tazenakht. The open land around the region was used for agriculture, producing: olives and olive oil, almonds, vegetable crops and, like so many other small holdings in the foothills of the High Atlas Mountains, the cultivation of saffron was extensive.

The town was more of a watering hole and a place to rest up before traders and travellers on the ancient caravan route moved on to either Ouarzazate in one direction or Taliouine in the other. The Jewish inhabitants left in the late 1940s, leaving everything to their Berber neighbors, who to this day carry on carpet production, where the Jews left off.

The region around Tazenakht is well-known for its co-operatives, specializing in the weaving of carpets and rugs.

Ouarzazate

Claimed by most guide books to be the "Gateway to the Deep South", the town of Ouarzazate is where things really start to play on your senses: the sandy-coloured buildings, the sudden change in the dress-style of the locals, and the most obvious, the scent of the desert air. It is claimed that Berber Jews were responsible for establishing a settlement and trading-post in this location. The town is strategically placed on a central plain and sits conveniently on the former caravan routes that came up from the sub-Sahara through Zagora and Tafilalt.

Jews had lucrative businesses in the buying and selling of dates as well as camel and mule hides for the making of saddles etc. The design and production of silver jewelry and trays for special occasions such as weddings was a popular occupation.

Later in its history, the central focus of the settlement was the enormous Taourirt Kasbah, the residence of the local *caid*, a member of the Glaoui family. Parts of the structure have recently undergone restoration.

The town's *mellah* was very close to the *kasbah*, which suggests the *Caids* gave the Jews some degree of protection. The synagogue was sold some years ago and is now in use as a center for the production and sale of blankets. However, the Jewish cemetery is in good condition and is regularly maintained. The French took over control of the town's administration in the 1920s, and developed the small settlement into a town, with the addition of a military garrison.

After the discriminatory laws passed by the Nazi-controlled, French Vichy Government came into effect in 1941, the Jews in the region of Ouarzazate were required to dress exclusively in black garments along with certain other restrictions. As the main power base around the region was still in the hands of Glaoui family, the enforcement of these policies could have only been carried out on the orders of the head of the family, T'hami El-Glaoui.

The last Jewish resident, named Meyer, left Ouarzazate in 2001 to live in Casablanca. Today, the town relies mainly on tourism and is used as a base from which tourists go out on sightseeing excursions to the places of interest around the region. In recent years, King Mohammed VI, has designated the development of tourism as a top priority, and large-scale investment is underway.

Skoura

East of Ouarzazate is the oasis town of Skoura. Here the surrounding landscape is abundant with *palmeraies* and *ksour*. The fact that the area is affectionately known as the "Valley of a Thousand *Kasbahs*" is something of a misnomer. The correct terminology is simple to explain; a *ksar* (pl. *ksour*) is a fortified settlement with ramparts and towers. They were constructed out of necessity to keep the inhabitants safe from attack. A *kasbah* is a fortified stronghold, built to protect and house a local chief, *Caid* or Pasha and his family. That having been said, most Moroccans do not often distinguish between the two. If they say it is a *kasbah*, then a *kasbah* it is.

Most *ksour* were abandoned long ago and left to the mercy of the elements; the last Berber family moved out in 1975. One *ksar*, in particular, was solely inhabited by Berber Jews, who worked as craftsmen and traders of dates. As was with every Jewish settlement and small town around Morocco, the young people left their *bleds* between the 1940s and 1960s to seek work and a better life in the larger towns and cities. Eventually, more and more people followed suit, and ultimately, when the time came, they went in droves to Israel.

These days the only real evidence of an earlier Jewish community is the restored shrine of a Jewish *tzadik*, Moulay Bah, which draws pilgrims to the site once a year.

Dades Valley

The Dades Valley, named after the river that in the past sustained the life of every human, plant or animal that lived or travelled along this stretch of the ancient caravan routes. The landscape and scenery in this region are stunningly attractive and varied from semi-arid deserts and medieval *kasbahs* to surreal rock formations created by the natural elements over millions of years. What captivates the imagination most are the lush green oases that follow the course of the river as it threads its way along the valley floor.

Kal'at M'Gouna

The small town of Kal'at M'Gouna, once the area of the Berber tribe, the M'Goun, started out as an oasis, later becoming a trading-post settlement. Today, it is famous for rose cultivation and its by-products like creams, soap and, of course, rose water. The origin of where the first roses came from is something of a mystery. However, the Berber Jews are known to have been involved in their cultivation and used them during the ceremony of circumcision.

Jews were also engaged in the manufacture of everyday items such as metal utensils for cooking, blankets, carpet weaving and associated wool trades and silver jewelry. A few cultivated the land by growing vegetables and fruit and also kept livestock. All the results of their labor were either sold at the local *souk* or transported by mule or camel to other towns and regions. M'Gouna had a center which trained young men in the practical skills connected with the synagogue and communal life.

If further proof were needed of how important and lucrative the town was in long distance trade, the visitor need only look toward the huge fortified *kasbah* constructed by the Glaoui family, who, as *caids*, controlled the entire region of the Deep South.

Close by is the village of Tiliit, which the Spanish Jewish family Perez controlled from the latter part of the fifteenth century until the reign of Moulay Ismail in the seventeenth century. The village also has a pilgrimage site with the shrine of Rabbi Abraham Cohen Bou-Douaya.

Boulmane Dades

The town of Boulmane Dades was originally a settlement built on a small hilltop. Limited for space as the town expanded, further construction spread to the flatter ground below.

Jews created small industries in blacksmithing, metalwork, and the production of jewelry. Wool and its by-products along with leather goods and saddle making were also sources of earning a living. In fact, many Jews could turn their hands to anything that fed and clothed their families.

The weekly market, which still exists, served the needs of the inhabitants living in the villages in the surrounding area. Here they could buy and sell livestock, especially goats, which are more suited to the mountainous and semi-arid terrain found only a few kilometers away in the *Gorges du Dades*.

The French colonists designated Boulmane as the center of administration for the Dades Valley. These days, the town has very little to hold the visitor except, perhaps, the petrol station where it may be necessary to fill up the tank of the 4-wheel-drive before setting out to explore the nearby Dades Gorge.

Tenerhir

Fifty-four kilometers east of Boulmane Dades, through semi-arid country, you arrive in the small mining town of Tenerhir. It was the French colonists who first took advantage of the mineral deposits in the area around the town. They also began the construction of the new town. The original old town has a *kasbah* and did have a *mellah* close by, at least up until the 1940s. It is now inhabited by Muslims.

The Jews worked in the *souk*, selling items of hardware, herbs and spices, textiles and produce from the land. Others made a living from working with leather and various metals, and the main language spoken was Judeo-Berber. Like elsewhere in the region, the Jews moved away because of various personal insecurities, real or feared. All eventually ended up in Israel.

The Ziz Valley

Located along the southeast border of Morocco, the Ziz Valley runs from north to south from the small town of Rich and disappears at Rissani in the region of Tafilalt on the edge of the Sahara Desert.

Most of the valley, which follows the river of the same name, is full of spectacular scenery with a large scattering of fortified *ksour* and abundant green palm groves in romantic desert oases. Visitors will witness a region where time seems to have stood still and the pace of daily life is unhurried.

The inhabitants of the region of Tafilalt are a blend of Berbers and sub-Saharan Africans with Arabic speaking Saraoui (natives of the Sahara). Dress for women is, in the main, traditional. A person from the region of Tafilalt is known as a Filali, just as someone from Meknes is called a Meknesi, and from Fes, a Fassi (Fessi).

Jews had lived in this region long before the destruction of the second temple in Jerusalem. They were traders on the caravan routes, which extended from the countries of the sub-Sahara to the Mediterranean coast and throughout the lands of North Africa.

Relations with local Berber and Bedouin tribes flourished due to the admiration of the various skills and religious practices of the Jewish population. Additionally, the Jews were perceived as possessing what would later be known in the Arabic language as *Baraka*, a special blessing. As a consequence, whole tribes converted to Judaism, becoming what is now termed as Berber Jews. The region offered the Jews a life of relative peace far from the political instability and uncertainties of the regions in the north of the country.

Prior to the arrival of Islam, the region was an independent state under the control of a branch of the Meknassa, a Berber tribe, whose capital is thought to have been a small trading settlement on or near the site of Sijiilmassa, in the region of Tafilalt.

Rich

The name of the town of Rich is thought to have been derived from the Arabic word for feather, and it is located at the northern end of the Ziz Valley near the routes used to bring ostrich feathers from sub-Sahara Africa. The town was a virtual crossroads of caravan routes serving the north and south of the country and those transporting goods to Figuig to the east on the Algerian frontier.

Evidently, Jews not only inhabited the town but also some small settlements in the region; for instance, Gourrama, a little to the east on the direct route to Figuig. Members of the renowned Abuhatzira family, originally from Rissani at the southern end of the Ziz valley, came to the area as educators in religious studies and remained until they died. Their bodies lie buried in the Jewish cemeteries of Rich, Gourrama, and Er-Rachidia, which in their day was known as Ksar-es-Souk.

Three Jews were known to still be living in Rich in 2008. The synagogue is only in operation in December or January for the period of the pilgrimage by the descendents and followers of Rabbi Israel Abuhatzira, buried in Gourrama. In 2008, 3,000 Jews, mainly Moroccan Jews from Israel, attended the services and celebrations.

The route south between Rich and the next large town, Er-Rachidia, is stunningly beautiful and represents most people's impressions of a desert paradise. Small *ksour*, fortified villages, with their distinct regional architecture can be seen in among the abundant palm groves, and, added to that, the magnificent Ziz Gorges are a favorite with tourists who love scenic photos.

Er-Rachidia

Until 1979, Er-Rachidia was known as Ksar-es-Souk. The name was officially changed to honor the first Alaouite sultan, Moulay er-Rachid. The town sits at an important crossroad or main junction connecting traffic moving north to south or east to west to different parts of the country, a fact which has existed for centuries.

Originally consisting of a cluster of *ksour*, it was occupied by the French during the Protectorate, rebuilt as a modern garrison town and made the administrative center for the region.

In 1997, a local Jewish woman, Lalla Yacout, was interviewed with her husband, Youssef, on video, which is deposited in the archives at the Jewish Museum, Casablanca. The couple, both in their 70s, gave a lively and most informative interview. Lalla's parents came from Goulmima and Rich, and gave birth to her in Er-Rachidia. She had no formal education, but her mother made some attempt to educate her at home.

Youssef's parents, on the other hand, were natives of the town, as were three generations before. His father was a local businessman selling everyday items. Lalla and Youssef were born in the *mellah* when the town was known as Ksar-es-Souk. Lalla's family left the *mellah* for the French-built new town when she was two years old in 1930, and her husband's family left in 1934.

The French told the Jews to leave the Jewish quarter, after deciding it was too old and a health hazard. As a result, the Jews were the first to construct homes in the new part of town and, at one point, they were the only residents. However, with the passing of time, Muslims, mainly Berber, took up residence and, as there was no *mellah*, the two communities coexisted side by side. Regretfully, both were unable to give any information about life in the former *mellah* as they were too young to remember.

Several Jewish men took advantage of the changes and set themselves up as builders. The first houses built had no running water or electricity; light was provided by oil lamps, and water either came from a well or from the nearby river.

Some men were employed as metal workers and shoemakers. The very poor eked out a living by repairing broken plates, while the better off were involved in the trading of dates and almonds. Most Jewish women were housewives involved in taking care of the children and keeping house. Carpet weaving by some was a way of earning extra income.

Mothers giving birth had the assistance of the local midwife, a Jewish woman, who made no distinction between

226

the two religious communities. Celebrations lasted for up to seven days whenever a boy was born and went on throughout the night. For girls, the period of rejoicing was three days. The local rabbi attended the celebrations and conducted the ceremony in naming the baby.

Medical services for the very poor Jews were paid for by the community, and volunteers sat at the bedside of the sick and dying. The Joint Distribution Committee, an American Jewish charitable organization, periodically, brought money and clothing and distributed them among those in the greatest need.

Fear and anxiety spread through the Jewish community in 1944. With rumors that a German delegation was coming to Er-Rachidia to register the Jews in the community, many of them fled. However, the situation was soon resolved when the sultan, Mohammed V, made a declaration that all Moroccan Jews were his subjects and, therefore, he was personally responsible for their protection.

Lalla and Youssef had an arranged marriage in 1943, very much the custom at that time, and later started a family. In 1948, Youssef began work as a tailor's apprentice with one of the tailors in the town, also Jewish. The tailor was fortunate enough to have some French army officers among his clientele and, therefore, needed the extra help. Lalla was trained as a dressmaker by a French woman who had a small shop serving French women, the wives of the men serving in the local garrison. The couple eventually ended up with six children, five girls and one boy, who all attended the local *Alliance Israélite Universelle* school, where Hebrew, French and Arabic were among the subjects taught.

Reluctant to disrupt the children's education, the couple decided to stay on in Morocco when the first wave of Jewish emigrants left for Israel. The resulting break up of the close-knit community left both feeling very sad.

A local rabbi promised to remain until the last Jew had left the town, but later changed his mind on account of having five unmarried daughters, who without protection and very few prospects of a future marriage, caused him great concern.

Lalla and Youssef's only son now lives in Switzerland and never fails to help his parents with financial assistance. The daughters are all married and dispersed between France and Israel. Lalla and Youssef are grateful to their children for the opportunity to make regular visits to their respective homes.

Lalla Yacout, like countless Moroccan Jews, has great respect and reverence for certain deceased rabbis, who, when alive, are said to have led pious and virtuous lives. Many are also credited with performing miracles before and after their deaths. Lalla mentioned regular visits by the former Jewish community to an old and isolated cemetery on the outskirts of Er-Rachidia, where the shrines of three Jewish *tzadiks* are located.

As the cemetery was some distance from the town, they carried all the necessities required to stay overnight, sometimes longer. Fires were lit and oil lamps provided lighting. Washing their clothes to get rid of evil spirits (*djnoun*) was one of the rituals performed besides placing scores of candles on the shrines.

On a recent visit to the area, three old and isolated cemeteries were identified about ten kilometers north of the Er-Rachidia (in the direction of Rich) where three Jewish *tzadiks* are still venerated by local Muslims, and the occasional Jewish pilgrim. The *tzadiks* are said to have died several years ago. The original names of two were unknown, so following Moroccan customs, were given identifiable names by the former Jewish community.

The story goes that Jewish pilgrims were attending a *hiloula* for the well-known Rabbi Yahia Lahlou, when a bright light descended from the heavens and shone on an unmarked grave. The pilgrims interpreted this as sign there was a *tzadik* buried in the grave. From that day he has been known as Mul Tria, a derivative of the Moroccan word for a chandelier.

The other unknown *tzadik* was given the name Mul Sidra, after the tree that grows over the site of his grave. *Sidra* is the Berber name given to the tree that bears small red berries. This particular tree is not native to this semi-desert and arid region and appears to be the only one of its kind. There is an air of mystery as to how it actually survives and remains healthy and green.

The berries are picked from the tree and mashed to a paste-like substance by local Muslim women, who inherited the idea from Jews. It is then spread on sprained wrists and ankles and covered with a bandage. It is claimed the injury is completely healed within two days.

229

Other practices Muslim women have inherited from the Jews are the ritual washing of clothing worn to the cemetery and ablutions carried out over the grave of this particular *tzadik*. The rituals are done to divest their clothes and bodies of evil spirits. On the same recent visit the *Sidra* tree was found to be covered in discarded clothing and the surrounding area littered with water carrying vessels.

Er-Rachidia's Jewish cemetery is in the town. Burial procedures followed the *Toshavim* custom of interring men in a separate section of the cemetery from the women. The site is enclosed and in reasonable condition.

The town originally had three synagogues, but today only one survives. Closed for years and located in the heart of town, it is amazing to find that the only damage to the adobe building has been caused through lack of regular maintenance.

In 2007, restoration began with funds donated by foreign benefactors, which has allowed for the hiring of specialist craftsmen and the use of original materials. A decision was also made to leave the collection of school and religious books on the premises. Hebrew lettering is visible above the arch framing the steel doors at the entrance.

Tafilalt Region

Erfoud

The small, administrative town of Erfoud is in the region of Tafilalt, the last region before the vast Hammada du Guir, part of the Sahara Desert (*hammada* means barren). Erfoud had the largest population of Jews in the region of Tafilalt. Many were traders specializing in the buying and selling of dates; others made a good living as artisans in jewelry and leather goods. Tafilalt was also the center for the transportation of animal hides to Fes. Further still, several Jewish communities lived outside the town in a series of *ksour* scattered along the course of the Oued Ziz.

On a visit to the region in the first quarter of the nineteenth century, the French writer and traveller, René Caillié, reported a sharp contrast between rich and poor Jews. He saw the poorer members of the Jewish communities bare-footed and in rags, dirty, and insulted by the local Arabs in contrast to the wealthy Jews who were respected and had luxurious life-styles.

Walter Harris, who lived in Tangier and was a correspondent for a London newspaper, travelled around the Tafilalt in the late 1890s. He reported that the Jews were protected and treated well by the local Berbers. Indeed, it was the custom to severely punish anyone who abused a Jew, which was dealt with in such a way as though harm had been done to a member of their own family.

The Jewish cemetery is covered with sand; otherwise, the large tombstones are intact and well-preserved. Evidently, some former Jewish residents now living in Israel return periodically with their families to visit the cemetery and carry out maintenance; for instance, adding a fresh coat of whitewash to the tombstones.

Rabbi Shemouel Abuhatzira, a member of the Abuhatzira family of religious educators, was laid to rest here. His tomb is housed in a room within a small building on one side of the cemetery. It was built by fervent and devout followers. The room is simple in design, with the *tzadik's* picture hung on the wall. Until their exit from Morocco to Israel in the early 1960s, the Jews had lived in the region for centuries.

At Ksar Gourlian, between Erfoud and Rissani, there is a restored synagogue.

Rissani

Set at the point where the Oued Ziz is swallowed up by the encroaching desert, is the town of Rissani, which at one time was the capital of the Tafilalt region. The town is the ancestral home, or *bled*, of the Alaouite dynasty, which has sat on the Moroccan throne since the seventeenth century.

231

The Alaouites originated from a town called Yanbo in what was then Arabia, and, after coming to Morocco, settled in the region of Tafilalt at the start of the thirteenth century. Their relationship to the Prophet Mohammed's family afforded them some standing and status around the region. However, it was only in the seventeenth century that they made their mark nationally.

The region had for years been in turmoil due to insurrections against unpopular local *marabouts* (religious fraternities). Under the leadership of the Alaouite, Mohammed ech-*Charif* (pronounced – shereef), the inhabitants ultimately defeated the detested *marabouts*.

The first Alaouite to make an attempt to take control of the country, Moulay Mohammed, son of ech-Charif, was defeated on the outskirts of Fes and withdrew to the region of Tafilalt. His brother, Moulay er Rachid, on the other hand, was eventually able to exert his authority over a large portion of the country, an achievement which could be said made him the real founder of the Alaouite dynasty.

Successive Alaouite rulers continued their connections with Rissani by building a series of palaces and *ksour*, mostly inhabited by the wives and families of dead sultans, or unruly sons and nephews. Moulay Ismail, for instance, had a *ksar* constructed as a residence for members of his family whom he strongly desired to be kept at arms length, far away from the business of the royal courts.

In the 1890s, Rissani was still receiving caravan shipments of gold and slaves, and the precious commodities were later sold by auction. The majority of bidders are said to have been Jewish traders. Later, under the French Protectorate, the trade in human cargo was strictly prohibited.

Rissani's Jewish community was one of the first to move to Israel. The most famous of the town's Jewish sons, Rabbi Israel Abuhatzira, also called Baba Sale, another descendant of the family of educators, left to Israel in 1963, where he later died. Every year, a large *hiloula* (pilgrimage) is held at his shrine in Netivot, Israel. Most of the pilgrims are Jews of Moroccan descent.

Baba Sale is considered by many Moroccan Jews to be the patron *tzadik* of travellers, and prayers are said in his name before setting out on a journey. A key ring engraved with his likeness on the front side and a prayer for the road on the reverse has been produced.

A house, once the home of a member of the Abuhatzira family, still exists in the former *mellah* today. The enclosed Jewish cemetery is near the walls of the town.

The Draa Valley

The Draa valley, which follows the natural course of the Oued Draa, runs in a southeasterly direction from the town of Ouarzazate to the desert, just beyond Zagora. The valley merits the claim of being one of the most attractive regions of Morocco; old, abandoned *kasbahs* and great stretches of *palmeraie* that run like gigantic green serpents, slithering through the landscape. The clay constructed Berber villages and *ksour* are a reminder of very ancient times. It is a region where most women still go about their daily chores dressed in traditional clothing, and where some methods of cultivation have survived for centuries; irrigation systems that have ensured the survival of the palm groves is only one example. Henna, dates, almonds and a variety of exotic fruit are the main agricultural produce.

The bulk of the population are Berbers and Haratine, and they speak Tachelhite (a dialect of the Berber language), as well as Arabic. The Haratine are descendents of the original inhabitants of the region and former slaves, originally from Mauritania, Sudan and Ethiopia. Haratine comes from the Arabic word for farmer, *harrath*.

Although some *ksour* are inhabited by people of Arab descent, years of mixed marriages have produced a wide range of skin colouring and physical types. Cultural assimilation has blurred differences between Berbers, Haratine and Arabs, so that anyone originating from the Draa is called simply a Draaoui.

The most southern end of the Draa valley is claimed to have had one of the oldest Jewish communities in Morocco. The fact that ancient chronicles mention the Draa as being inhabited by Jewish traders long before the fall of the temples might give the statement some credibility. The Oued Draa was certainly known to the Romans; it was listed as *Dara* on the first world map in history created by Ptolemy (90-168 C.E.) .

The coming of Islam and forced conversions in the eighth century caused Jews living in the north of the country to take refuge in the Draa valley, where, along with the regional Berber tribes, they were able to sustain some degree of independence from the sultans.

The final years of the ninth century witnessed a three-way struggle between Kairouan in Tunisia, Fes and the Draa for the Jewish intellectual and religious leadership of western countries of North Africa. The Karaite doctrine, or heresy, was eventually adopted in Fes in the eleventh century, and later accepted in the Draa; Karaite Jews did not accept the rabbinic Oral Laws or the Talmud.

The Karaites' hold on Jewish practice and thought remained dominant for the next few centuries, however, with the arrival of the more educated Talmudists who took flight from Spain in the latter part of the fifteenth century, the Karaite influence evaporated.

In the middle of the eleventh century, the Almoravids conquered the entire region of the south, including the Draa, before moving on to take control of the North of Morocco. Disruption to the peaceful valley came in the thirteenth century with the invasion of the region by the M'qil Arabs, recently arrived in North Africa. Their presence caused many of the farming Jews and Berbers to leave the area.

The M'qil dominated the region until halfway through the fourteenth century, after which a large majority among them migrated northwards. Their absence enabled several Jews and Berbers to return. However, in the fifteenth century, the region continued to experience skirmishes between those Arabs who had stayed on and the local Berbers.

The Draa, in the sixteenth century, reappeared in the history of Morocco with the emergence of the Saadian dynasty, whose roots were at Tagmadert, then, a small village at the south end of the valley between Zagora and Tamegroute. Tagmadert served as the Saadian capital of the Draa. Under the Saadians, the region played a dominant role in the wealth of the country; gold shipments from the Sudan increased substantially, which made many Jewish traders involved with the caravan trade very wealthy. Jews were also given the monopoly on striking the gold into coins, later transported to Marrakech. Despite the success, the Draa valley later fell back into decline, particularly, following the death of the best-known Saadian sultan, Abu el-Abbas (*el-Mansour* – The Victorious).

The first of the Alaouites, Moulay er-Rachid, conquered the Draa in the seventeenth century and, to reinforce his authority, built a series of *ksour* at strategic points. He also moved the capital to D'Aghlan, about twenty kilometers north of Zagora; however, the governor had his *kasbah* in Amzrou.

Moulay Ismail, Moulay er-Rachid's successor, assigned one of his many sons to Tamegroute to supervise the arrival and distribution of the valuable commodities coming up from the sub-Sahara, a task dependent on the commercial skills of Jewish traders.

The next two centuries were full of turbulent times as nomadic tribes fought for dominance in the region by attacking the sedentary population and almost ignoring the authority of local *caids* and tribal chiefs.

It was customary for the nomadic tribes to offer protection to the local population in exchange for a section of their land. The Jews, however, were always under the protection of the *caids*, who were aware of their important role within the local economy and whom they depended upon for the collection of tax revenues.

235

The years following the collapse of the lucrative caravan routes exerted a heavy toll on the *mellahs* of the Draa. With the departure of the unemployed and discontented youth to the large cities in the north, the Jewish communities suffered.

With the advent of the French Protectorate in the early years of the twentieth century, the region went through a period of pacification, in which the French were assisted by the armies of T'hami el-Glaoui, the Pasha of Marrakech. Over the next few years, the French brought to an end the nomadic tribes' influence by introducing policies that completely changed the social structures of the region. The French also set up Tagounit as the administrative center of the southern region of the Draa valley.

Relief for the Draa's Jewish communities came with the formation of Israel, and between 1948 and 1958 the entire Jewish population was moved to there.

Agdz

A small, but pleasant oasis town, Agdz is the main administrative center for the region of Mezguita, in the Draa valley. It also serves as a way station for transport and people travelling between Zagora and Ouarzazate, a role it has been playing for centuries.

Up until the 1950s, Jewish traders and artisans lived in a large *mellah*, and sold their goods at the local *souk*. The town's Jewish cemetery lies neglected and forgotten. The center of activity is along the main street, lined with bazaars selling all types of tourist paraphernalia. Many bazaars sell a wide assortment of carpets. The most attractive and sought after are those of the Glaouia pattern; blue and white with decorated and indented rectangular shapes. Also very prominent is a fine selection of brightly coloured carpets produced at cooperatives in and around the region of Ouarzazate.

From the town of Agdz, the mother of all *palmeraies* meanders for almost one hundred kilometers, following the course of the Oued Draa. It is also the starting point for those interested in visiting the many *ksour* that dot the landscape.

About four kilometers beyond Agdz, a road goes off to the left, leading to Tamnougalt, which in ancient times was the capital of Mezguita region. Here, there is a concentration of excellent examples of the finest *ksour*. The construction of those on view today took place in the nineteenth century.

The first one on the road is El Hara, once exclusively inhabited by the Jewish community. The huge structure, which includes traces of the former synagogue, is deserted and slowly crumbling. Nearby is the *kasbah* of the much despised *Caid* Ali, who administered the region on behalf of the French before the years of Morocco's independence.

Tamnougalt looks out onto an area of *palmeraie*, where Jews once toiled in the cultivation of dates. The Draa produces *boufeggou* dates, highly regarded for their deliciously sweet taste. The Alaouite sultan, Moulay Hassan, at the end of the nineteenth century, appointed a *caid* as his representative in the region, and the *caid's* sons held sway over the area during the French period.

In 1924, as part of the French campaign for total pacification of the south, an army of 5,000 men led by Hammou El Glaoui, a cousin of T'hami El Glaoui, laid a two-week siege on Tamnougalt. The tactic forced the residing *caid* to raise the flag of surrender and agree to a pact.

About twenty kilometers south of Agdz, at Ait Hammou-ou-Said, a road goes off to the left, which leads to Tazzarine, and Timesla, a large fortified village. Timesla's former *mellah*, originally made from clay, was mostly demolished years after it was abandoned in the 1950s. The site was later reclaimed to provide housing for local Muslims, the majority being Haratine. The synagogue, though, remains in fairly good condition and awaits the collection of sufficient funds to carry out some restoration work.

Zagora

Everyone visiting the Draa valley eventually makes for Zagora, the largest town in the region. The town takes its name from the nearby mountain, Jebel Zagora. From a historical point of view, the town is relatively modern. It was built by French colonists as an administrative center, with the real intention of exploiting the area's abundant date production.

The regional population is predominately of sub-Saharan African origins. They have a reputation for honesty, virtues that qualify them to take up jobs in the larger cities as guardians within the homes of the well-to-do. There are also small groupings of Arabs who have lived in the area for centuries.

Perhaps of more interest to Jewish visitors is the knowledge that the region south of Zagora was where many Jewish communities first settled and flourished around two thousand years ago. In the past, the region had countless *ksour* inhabited solely by Jews. However, periods of drought, economic decline, political insecurities and incidences of forced conversions forced much of the Jewish population to migrate to other parts of the country in search of a better and more peaceful way of life.

Centuries of survival in this region were sustained by commerce and trades associated with the sub-Saharan caravan routes. In addition, every community cultivated the essential crops needed to feed their families, with the extra produce sold at the local souks.

Although most of the former *mellahs* have long disappeared, a small number, now inhabited by Muslims, still exist today.

Amzrou

Formally a *ksour* village, Amzrou had a thriving Jewish community that had existed from the seventeenth century, until departure to Israel between 1948 and 1958. Much of the *mellah*, or, *La Kasbah des Juifs*, now occupied by Muslims, can still be seen today. The synagogue is closed, but reported to be in fairly good condition despite the passing years. The narrow lanes and high walls of the town are a throw-back to ancient times, when the villages in the region were vulnerable to attacks by hostile nomadic tribes. Jews entered by the gate on the west side, while Muslims used the gate facing east.

The Jews had the monopoly on the silver trade and were expert blacksmiths. Before leaving for Israel, they passed on their skills to the local Berbers, who now continue to turn out silver jewelry and metalwork based on the models created by the Jews.

Amzrou is thought to have been constructed on the site of Tagmadert, a small town that existed in the sixteenth century. The town had strong associations with the rise of the Saadian dynasty. The most heroic and celebrated Saadian sultan, Abou el-Abbas, *el-Mansour* (The Victorious), mustered a huge army at Tagmadert, before setting out in 1591 to conquer Timbuktu, in the Sudan. Having accomplished control of the caravan routes, he returned triumphantly with huge shipments of valuable commodities, which included gold and silver, bales of ostrich feathers and thousands of slaves.

Tagmadert may have been completely obliterated during the reign of Moulay Ismail. After all, it is well documented that he went to great lengths to wipe out much of the physical evidence of the Saadian's former existence.

Tagounite

The last but one sizeable town before the sands of the Sahara, Tagounite was founded around the time of the first Arab invasion of the Draa region in the seventh century. Arabs settled in the region and made Tagounite their capital. In the thirteenth century, another wave of Arabs, the M'qil, arrived. Their crude and undisciplined behavior so upset the balance of peace and tranquillity that many Berber residents left the area.

Later, in the fourteenth century, when a large portion of the Arabs had moved out of the region, the Berbers started returning. Still, down through the centuries, the area was frequently under attack from hostile nomadic tribes. It was only during the period of the French Protectorate (1912-1956) that stability was finally achieved.

As little as one kilometer beyond the southern end of town, a road goes to the left, leading to the *ksour* of Beni Sbih (approximately five kilometers). Beni Sbih can be traced back as far as the seventh century. From that time, the settlement had a Jewish community up until 1948. The ruins of the former *mellah* can still be seen today. It consists of a *ksar* honeycombed with covered passageways, with each of the dwellings having an open courtyard at its core.

Another five kilometers further on from Beni Sbih, and you come to the *ksour* of Beni Hayoune, another settlement known to have existed in the seventh century. Here, too, there was once a Jewish community until the emigration to Israel. The Jewish inhabitants of both settlements ran the souk in Tagounite. Although both *ksour* now have electricity, the overall impression is that both look like very little has changed since ancient times.

In the same region, between Tagounite and M'hamid, there is the small oasis of Ighir N'Tidri, named after a tribe of the same name. Tidri lies 68 kilometers out in the desert northwest of Tagounite and is famous for its "Golden Palm Grove".

The oasis is said to have had the oldest Jewish community in Morocco. The local Jews venerated the tomb of a rabbi named Isaac Akkouim, claimed to be the founder of Tidri. Muslims, today, revere the Jewish *tzadik*, but call him Sidi Moussa, which may be derived from the name Moses.

The ancient necropolis, Foum Larjam, the largest in North Africa, is on the approaches to Tidri. The site consists of thousands of rock-mounds, thought to be the final resting place of Jews massacred by the Almohads in the twelfth century. However, this theory is yet to be confirmed.

M'hamid

The end of the line for most visitors to the Draa valley comes at the oasis town of M'hamid el-Ghizlane, to give it its full name (*ghizlane* is Arabic for gazelle). Apparently, there used to be numerous herds of gazelles roaming in the surrounding desert. After years of hunting them down for their skins and meat, they became extinct.

M'hamid is also the point where the Oued Draa changes direction and makes a sharp turn to the west for about 750 kilometers, eventually meeting up with the Atlantic Ocean some distance south of Goulimine. In actual fact, it is only in the years of exceptional flooding that the waters pass M'hamid and reach the Atlantic; and then only for up to a week. The rest of the time the westward section of riverbed is completely dry with little or no vegetation.

The existence of human life around the region of M'hamid goes back thousands of years; the discovery of numerous rock drawings in the surrounding desert offers convincing evidence. The regions importance as a desert port on the ancient trans-Saharan caravan routes was known by the Phoenicians, the Carthaginians and the Romans, and the latter had the area indicated on a map made by Ptolemy (90–168 C.E.).

This region has been the source of many stories and legends concerning the 2,000-year-old history of the Moroccan Jews. Definitely no legend is the actual presence of a 150 meter-stretch of sand dunes about ten kilometers northwest of M'hamid called

L'Erg L'Yehoud (Dunes of the Jews). Some locals use a more precise Arabic expression, translated as "Root of the Jews".

They also say it was the first place the Jews came to when they arrived in the area in ancient times. The Jews lived in Bedouin-type tents, supported by poles with an emblem of the Star of David on top. The Jewish Museum, in Casablanca, has a more recent example in its collection.

Formally a Touareg Berber settlement with a few *ksour*, it is difficult to find information on exactly when the town was given the Arabic name, M'hamid. However, M'hamid is what it was called in the sixteenth century, when the Saadians built El Aaouj (The Fort of the European Legion). As the name implies, it housed some of the Christian mercenaries that marched with el-Mansour (The Victorious) to conquer Timbuktu in 1591.

The *ksar* also served as a customs house for the powdered gold arriving from the Sudan. It was here that the Jews had the job of striking the gold into coins, before transportation to the Saadian capital, Marrakech.

The ruins of El Aaouj can be located in the old part of M'hamid between the Ksar Bounou and Ksar Tahla. Moulay Ismail, at the latter part of the seventeenth century, sent a military expedition to M'hamid to put down a rebellion involving the local desert tribes. The troops were led by Thomas Pellow, an Englishman, who stayed twenty-three years in Morocco.

During the 1960s and the 1970s the desert regions beyond M'hamid were considered unsafe for foreign tourists when Morocco and Algeria were in conflict over water resources. Now the region is tranquil and safe.

Section Three
Jewish Culture in Morocco

Synagogue at the Shrine of *tzadik*
Rabbi Amram Ben Diwan in Ouezzane
Photo by Ron Joseph

18

Culture of Venerating *Tzadiks*

*T*zaddik veneration has roots in history and culture and can be associated with ancient popular legends. Without the cultural background outsiders can find difficulty in understanding the depth of devotion paid by devout believers. The veneration of *tzadiks* among Moroccan Jews is a part of religious practice, regardless of rank or social standing. The word most extensively expressed for a *tzadik* by Moroccan Jews is *tsaddiq* or *saddiq*, meaning a virtuous or holy person. *Saddiqim* is the plural form.

Being accepted as a *tzadik* can be determined in different ways. The following are some examples: Most *tzadiks* are deceased rabbis, said to have led charitable and pious lives or worked miracles during their lives or posthumously. Several died hundreds of years ago. Others have supposedly been interred since the arrival of the Jews following the destruction of the first and second temple.

According to oral tradition many came to Morocco to collect funds for religious schools in the land of Israel. The phenomenon of the inclusion of actual living *tzadiks* is rare but also possible. The stories of a deceased rabbi becoming a *tzadik* after appearing in someone's dreams and asking to be made a *tzadik* are a common occurrence.

Moreover, a number of *tzadiks* are claimed to have succumbed to martyrdom. There are also a few deceased women *tzadiks* who were the wives of rabbis or did exceptional deeds in helping the needy.

Another group falls into the category of *tzadiks* and their descendants. This grouping almost takes on a dynastic dimension. There are two good examples. First, the family and descendants of Rabbi Haim Pinto, the highly revered *tzadik* buried in one of the two cemeteries in Essaouira. His son, grandson and some of his subsequent male descendants became *tzadiks*.

A descendant of the Pintos lives in France, and he comes to Morocco to lead the annual pilgrimages to the shrine of his venerated ancestor. He is highly respected personally and is mentioned as a possible future *tzadik*.

Secondly, there is the Abuhatzira family, with origins in Rissani, a town in the Tafilalt region. Most male descendants of the first *tzadik*, Yacoub Abuhatzira, including nephews with the same name, were shown great respect and reverence while still alive. Their name alone almost automatically qualified them for *tzadik* status after burial. In actual fact, the same reverence continues in Israel today where the present members of the family now live.

The believers, followers, or disciples have a deep spiritual and emotional relationship with the *tzadiks*. At times the *tzadiks* are placed in the role of intermediaries between the disciples and God. As an example, requests and appeals for some urgent assistance are made through the *tzadiks*, who are perceived as having been chosen by the Almighty and, thus, there is little chance of a refusal.

Sometimes a family will adopt a particular *tzadik* and have a likeness or picture hanging or an object that has touched the grave or tomb of the *tzadik*. Prayers are offered in front of the picture or the object, which might be caressed and kissed during prayers.

Many disciples desire to continue their close relationship with the *tzadik* after death and might request to be buried next to that *tzadik*. For those disciples fortunate enough to be living close to shrines of *tzadik*, regular Friday visits are made in order to have a closer or more emotional relationship.

At the grave shrine the ritual of lighting candles is followed by prayers, after which the disciples may take the opportunity to unburden their personal problems. Requests might be made for concerns as diverse as a solution to a domestic concern, business problems, or the need for rain during a drought.

The *tzadik* may be asked to heal or cure a sick member of the family. In one instance an elderly man laid down on his back on top of a *tzadik's* tombstone and began rubbing his back against the stone begging the *tzadik* to cure his extremely painful backache.

A person with mental health problems can sometimes be assumed to have been possessed by a *djnoun* or *jinn* (bad spirit). In that case the person is made to lie down on the *tzadik's* grave, and water is poured down through the cracks. The hope is the spirit of the *tzadik* will rise to the surface and cure the mentally disturbed person. Many people are careful not to upset a *tzadik* for fear that something unfortunate might happen to them.

Any negative comments made about the *tzadiks* are seen as blasphemous. Doubting or discrediting their power is strictly prohibited and subject to some kind of punishment by the offended *tzadik*.

One young man who had scorned another's claim that his sister had been cured of an illness she had since childhood was haunted in his dreams for several nights, and on each occasion severely scolded by the *tzadik*. The offender's nightmares only stopped after he had visited the graveside of the *tzadik* and begged forgiveness.

A serious transgression could result in the offender paying the ultimate price. An elderly Jewish man from a mountain village remembered one night in his youth when he was with some friends, secretly drinking *mahiya* close to the local Jewish cemetery. One youth became very intoxicated and needed to urinate. Having staggered a few meters, he relieved himself under a tree used by pilgrims to hang tokens of worship to the local *tzadik*. The next day the transgressor went missing. His decomposing body was eventually found by a shepherd's dog some distance from the village. The elderly man firmly believes his friend had been punished, after provoking the wrath of the local *tzadik*.

The accounts of miracles performed by the *tzadiks* are endless. Not only do they happen within the confines or the vicinity of the shrines but also in everyday life. There is the belief that a whole community living in the Middle Atlas Mountains was cured of an epidemic. Also, young women thought to be infertile produce children after appealing to the *tzadiks*. There are accounts of the terminally ill inexplicably making a complete recovery, said to be attributed to the intervention of a particular *tzadik*.

Some *tzadiks* are known for their speciality. They might, for example, specialize in finding prospective brides or bridegrooms to link up in marriage, or assist a desperate mother whose daughter is beyond what would be considered a suitable age limit for marriage.

People suffering from mental illnesses may have the choice of visiting or appealing to two or three *tzadiks* known to specialize in this particular field.

The belief in *baraka,* blessing or luck, also plays a very important part in Moroccan Jewish culture. In this case, the name of a certain *tzadik* may be invoked in the hope that good fortune will strike just when and where it is required. The faithful also believe some *tzadiks* have the power to make the blind see and the deaf hear.

Stories about how *tzadiks* have control over the forces of nature are countless. These include the miraculous creation of springs, *aïn*, and the ability to make rain during periods of drought. There are even tales suggesting some *tzadiks* have the power to move boulders at the site of their tombs.

Daily or weekly worship of the *tzadiks* in no way compares to the grand scale of the annual pilgrimage, the *hiloula (hiloulot –*

plural). Normally held in May (Lag Baomer) and in September, the *hiloulot* draw a substantial amount of pilgrims.

It should be mentioned that since the years of mass emigration to Israel, especially between the 1950s and the 1970s, the number of well attended and regular *hiloulot* have been significantly reduced, particularly those of the hundreds of *tzadiks* located in the far-off and remote regions. However, the reduction has made it more advantageous for the committees responsible for the organization and planning involved in making a successful *hiloula*.

Recent years have seen the development of infrastructure at the sites of the more famous *tzadiks*; the construction of more accommodations for pilgrims and the improvement of access roads, for instance. The reduced number of sites has also made it possible for Muslim dignitaries, as representatives of the king, to put in an appearance. The occasion is used to reaffirm the strong bond between the king and his Jewish subjects.

Unlike the regular daily or weekly visits to the grave or shrine of a *tzadik*, the *hiloula* includes the ritual slaughter of several animals, with the intention of sharing the meat with as many of the pilgrims as possible. It might also consist of a public auction of candles and drinking glasses, with a certain amount of prestige and honor bestowed upon the highest bidders. The sale and distribution of *mahiya*, the drink distilled from figs or dates, also takes place at most pilgrimages. All monies collected go toward the expenses of holding the *hiloula* and the annual upkeep of the shrine and cemetery, which includes salaries paid to the small staff responsible for the maintenance and security of the cemetery, in most cases, local Muslims.

Celebrations get underway with the ritual lighting of candles and prayer, followed by joyful, uninhibited dancing and singing. At one point the meat of the slaughtered animals is served and *mahiya* is served after which the atmosphere can reach an ecstatic phase. The pilgrims may look for signs that the spirit of the *tzadik* is in their midst or that he has even made a personal appearance, an animal or bird passing through the cemetery or close to the shrine is received with great excitement. Many disciples believe the *tzadiks* are able to manifest themselves in the form of animals.

248   The *tzadik* may also speak through someone present at the *hiloula*; a woman who lived a long distance from the site of a pilgrimage, and therefore knew very few of the people present, passed on a message from a *tzadik* to a male disciple, that his wife, who had remained at home, would give birth to a baby boy two days hence. Sure enough, two days later, when the man returned home, his wife brought a healthy baby boy into the world. The child was subsequently given the name of the *tzadik*, and the occasion was celebrated as a miracle.

The conclusion of the *hiloula* leaves the disciples feeling they have been infused with the power and spirit of the *tzadik* and been gifted with a new lease on life.

The social aspect of the pilgrimage allows relatives who may have spent a number of years separated by distance to spend time together. These days, pilgrims with ties to Morocco arrive from as far as Canada, the United States and Israel. However, recent years have witnessed a trend in visitors from the United States with no former ties. Their first reaction is one of awe, caused by the open way Moroccan Jews practice their religion and traditions in a predominately Islamic country. They may also be unaware of the connection between Moroccan Jews and their Muslim counterparts in the veneration of *tzadiks*.

Both Moroccan Jews and Muslims venerate people with special spiritual powers after they have died. Moroccan Muslims also practice *moussem*, a pilgrimage to a *siyyed* (Moroccan Muslim holy man) and also the Jewish *tzadik* shrines. In comparison a *hiloula* and a *moussem* bear similar elements: prayer, the ritual lighting of candles and slaughtering of animals, dancing and singing, visitation of dignitaries, opportunities for socializing, and celebrations lasting up to seven days.

Centuries of coexistence between Moroccan Jews and Moroccan Muslims have led to sharing of beliefs, such as the exorcism of spirits, to the veneration of one another's holy men. However, Muslims are known to visit the shrines of Jewish *tzadiks* more frequently than the small number of Jews visiting the *marabouts* of Muslim equivalents. A *marabout*, or *siyyed* as Moroccan Muslims call it, is normally a white doomed structure housing the tomb of a Muslim holy man, also known as a *siyyed*. There are many located throughout Morocco.

A Jewish person would only visit a Muslim holy man's sanctuary, for example, if he were known to cure some illness, or if a particularly well known mystic or fortune teller worked at the site. Fortune tellers and people with mystical powers commonly huddle around the exterior of *marabouts*.

Poor Muslims might sit at the gate of a Jewish cemetery, hoping to receive alms or the offer of some food from Jews on a visit to a *tzadik*. When there is no success in solving a problem or curing an illness from a Muslim holy man, a Muslim may decide to turn to a Jewish *tzadik,* who they believe can perform miracles.

There was a case some years ago where a young Muslim woman in Casablanca complained of an acute respiratory problem that caused her difficulty in breathing normally. After a thorough examination by three doctors, no physical reason for her condition was found. The third doctor, however, recommended the young woman visit the shrine of a particular *tzadik*, which she did. While at the shrine, the young woman gradually began to feel much better, and, within the next few days, she had made a complete recovery.

Perhaps, the doctor had realized the source of the young woman's problem was psychosomatic, but for the young woman and her family, it was seen as a miracle performed by the *tzadik*.

Muslims are always on hand to assist in the supply and distribution of food at a *hiloula*. They also rent lodgings to pilgrims to supplement their income. Usually Muslim men do the actual construction of the shrine and adjoining buildings, including the synagogue, at the site of the pilgrimage. Wealthy or influential Muslims are known to make generous contributions in honor of Jewish *tzadiks*.

Muslims have great respect for abandoned Jewish cemeteries; a recent survey of more than 150 in the region around Marrakech found no sign of vandalism or any unlawful misappropriation of the land for construction or agriculture. The Jewish cemetery at Arba-Tighedouine, fifty-three kilometers south of Marrakech, could be held up as a good example. It was abandoned by the local Jewish inhabitants when they left for Israel in the 1960s. A small stone-built building houses the shrine of Rabbi Sabag. Local Berber women are known to carry out ritual ablutions at this site to improve their fertility.

The respect shown to rabbis and Jewish *tzadiks* by the Muslim community is notable. In addition to Muslims visiting the shrines of tzadiks in various parts of the country, the Alouite kings have honored leading rabbis. The late King Mohammed V, took part in the funeral cortège of one of Casablanca's most respected rabbis, Rabbi Elyahou, who even before his death was considered to be a living *tzadik* by both communities. In 2009, the current king, Mohammed VI bestowed the Wissam Al Arch, Knight of the Order of the Throne of the Kingdom of Morocco on the Chief Rabbi of Morocco, Rabbi Aaron Monsonego.

Important *Tzadikim* by Location

In addition to annual pilgrimages, most shrines can be visited at almost any other time of the year, except Passover.

North of Morocco

Ouezzane. Rabbi Amram Ben Diwan. This much venerated *tzadik* is buried near the village of Azjen, nine kilometers outside of Ouezzane. The cemetery is enclosed behind whitewashed walls and has some accommodation for pilgrims. His grave is simple, being covered only with a mound of several large stones. There are two annual pilgrimages; May (Lag Baomer) and the first week in September.

Meknes. Rabbis Haim Messas, David Boussidan and Raphael Berdugo. Meknes' old cemetery is the only place in Morocco where some of the *tzadiks'* tombs were placed within the walls.

Fes. Lalla Solica Hachwelle – A young woman martyr who was condemned to death in 1834. She strongly denied claims made by one of the sultan's sons of having converted to Islam, which would have allowed him to marry her.

Sefrou. At different times during the year there are pilgrimages to the burial sites of Rabbis Eliahou Harraoch, David Arazil and Moshe Elbaz. Sefrou is thirty kilometers southeast of Fes.

Debdou (Northeast). Rabbis Mardoche Ben Moche Cohen, Jacob Cohen, Ishak Ben Moshe Cohen and Moche Ben Sultan. Pilgrimages are scheduled at separate times during the year for each, and they are attended by national and international visitors.

Ksar El Kebir (near Larache). Rabbi Yehuda Jabali. The shrine is within a large walled enclosure with a tower.

Central Morocco

Rabat. King Mohammed V. The King Mohammed V Mausoleum is situated next to the Tour Hassan. Although he was a Muslim, he is venerated by Moroccan Jews for saving them from the threat of being transported to the Nazi concentration camps in Europe. Every year, a delegation of prominent Jews lays a memorial wreath at the foot of his tomb.

Salé. Rabbi Raphael Encaoua. The town of Salé is practically a suburb of Rabat. The *tzadik's* shrine is in the form of a small mausoleum on a raised platform. The tomb is highly decorated with moulded engravings and Hebrew wording.

Casablanca. Rabbi Elyahou, the Jewish patron *tzadik* of Casablanca, is buried in the Ben M'sick cemetery, in a suburb of the same name. His shrine is in the form of a grand mausoleum, which dominates the cemetery.

Ben Ahmed. Rabbi Yahia El Khdar, known to Muslims as L'Hashra, after the rock at the site of the shrine. Ben Ahmed is in the region of Settat, just southeast of Casablanca. The site consists of a large complex and offers accommodation to pilgrims.

Berrechid. (Dad) Rabbi Abraham Aouriouer is one of the group of *tzadiks* buried here, known as Moulin Dad (Masters of Dad). The town of Dad is situated forty kilometers south of Berrechid, a short distance from Casablanca. The site offers pilgrims rooms to let. Any money collected goes toward the maintenance of the shrine. The main pilgrimage is held in Lag Baomer (May).

Azemmour. Rabbi Ibraham Moul Niss. His shrine is inside the walls of the old medina, and his pilgrimage is held in May (Lag Baomer). The ancient walled town of Azemmour is on the coast, approximately eighty kilometers south of Casablanca.

Middle Atlas

Gourrama. Rabbi Shemouel Abuhatzira. He is related to the Abuhatzira family of Talmudic teachers that served in the regions around the southeast of Morocco. As there is no synagogue in Gourrama, the normally closed synagogue in the town of Rich is opened up to enable the 3,000 or so pilgrims to attend religious services. Pilgrimage held in December or January.

Er Rachidia. Rabbi Yahia Lahlou. His simple shrine is located in a cemetery about ten kilometers north of the town in semi-desert countryside. The cemetery is said to be nearly 2,000 years old. Er Rachidia is in the southeast, on the main road running from Fes, in the north, to Erfoud, in the south.

Demnate. Rabbi David El-Draa Halevy. A large pilgrimage takes place in the days following Shavuot. Demnate is to the east of Marrakech on the road to Azilal.

252

The South of Morocco

Marrakech. Rabbi Hanania Cohen is buried in the Jewish cemetery in Marrakech. The tomb lies within a small whitewashed mausoleum. It is possible to visit the shrine at any time throughout the year - with the exception of Passover.

Ouirika Valley. Rabbi Salomon Bel-Hench is said to have died more than 500 years ago. His shrine can be found at Aghbalou, in the Ouirika Valley. The interior walls and floor of the sanctuary are covered with decorative tiles, and the actual tomb is topped with marble. Visitors are welcome to pay their respects most days of the year. The Ouirika valley is only a matter of forty kilometers south of Marrakech.

253

Anrhaz (Route Tiz N'Test). Rabbi Haim Ben Diwan is the son of Amram Ben Diwan, buried near Ouezzane. Located in a stunning and peaceful site, the sanctuary was rebuilt or modernized by his descendents in the 1980s. Despite the work done, the accommodation within the complex is badly in need of attention; the toilets and hammams were in a shocking state of disrepair when visited in 2008.

Aghzou (The Souss Plain between Oulad Birhil and Taroudant). Rabbi David Barroukh Cohen Azogh. He was famous as a *hazzan*, the Berber word for a healer. The cemetery and shrine complex has several rooms to accommodate the large number of followers who attend his pilgrimage in December.

Route Marrakech – Ouarzazate

Ait Ourir, Rabbi Abraham El Mizrahi. The actual shrine complex is in a nearby small village called Douar Chems. The village is off to the right en route to the Tizi N'Tichka Pass from Marrakech. There is a large pilgrimage for *Lag Baomer*, on the thirty-third day of the Omer following Passover.

L'Arba Tighedouine. Rabbi Sabag. Located fifty-three kilometers south of Marrakech. There is also a former *mellah* nearby. The local Berber women practice ritual of ablution and discarding underwear on this site with the hope that the *tzadik* will grant them fertility.

Tidili (Region of Agouim). After the Tizi N'Tichka Pass from Marrakech. Rabbi David Ou Moshi. It is claimed he does not like music being played during the pilgrimages. The pilgrims only slaughter goats, after which the meat is shared among the poor.

This is a region where local Berber women still wear their hair in braids, something they inherited from the Jews. The period of pilgrimage is eight days after the Feast of the Tabernacle.

Ighi. Rabbi Moulay Ighi (pronounced – *irri*). Near the village of Zerktoun, on the road to the Tizi N'Tichka Pass from Marrakech. Rabbi Ighi died approximately 300 years ago. As his real name was unknown, he was named after the village. His followers were reluctant to leave when the call came to move to Israel. It is said the *tzadik* appeared to each individual in a dream, telling them to go. The pilgrimage takes place eight days after *Sukkot*, Feast of the Tabernacle.

Atlantic Coast (South)

Safi. Rabbi Brahim Ben Zmirou and his seven sons, better known as Ouled Zmirou. The sanctuary is in a separate location from the Jewish cemetery, and has to be one of the largest and most impressive in the country. The external architecture in many ways follows the concepts of a nineteenth century European grand pavilion. The tombs of the *tzadiks* are lined up along the walls of an inner chamber and covered in marble. The month of July sees hundreds of pilgrims from around the world attending the pilgrimage.

Essaouira. Rabbi Haim Pinto is one of the most visited and venerated of Morocco's Jewish *tzadiks*. His mausoleum, though quite small, towers above the hundreds of gravestones in the older of the two cemeteries outside the walls of the old town. Many pilgrims turn up for his main pilgrimage held in September, however, many visitors visit the cemetery and shrine throughout the year.

Raphael Elmaleh, author
with documents in old synagogue
Photo by Yehuda and Nurit Patt

19

Beliefs, Feasts and Food

✾M oroccan Jews and Muslims commonly believe
in the power of the supernatural, including good spirits such as
angels, and evil demons, widely known as *jenoun* (*djnoun*) in the
plural and *jinn* (*djinn*) in the singular.

Beliefs

As an example, Moroccan children are taught never to pour
hot water into a toilet because it will anger the *djnoun*, which
parents continually remind them inhabit the plumbing system
in a house. Both Moroccan communities also have a strong
belief in the evil eye, *Al Ein* (*al ayn*).

Such beliefs and the practice of sorcery are said to have
their roots in the ancient culture of the indigenous Berbers,
from whom it was adopted by Moroccan Jews centuries ago.
Protection is provided by wearing amulets or by consulting a
particular person considered to be an expert in such matters,
a *sahir* (*sehir*) in the case of Muslims or certain rabbis for Jews.

The *sahir*, for a fee, is also called upon to cast a spell on
an unsuspecting *masshour*, victim. It is understood that several
Moroccan sultans had at least one *sahir* permanently on call
within the royal palace. It should be pointed out that because the
word *sahir* has negative connotations, most Moroccan Muslims
prefer instead to quote the word *fquih* (*fekey*), the same name
given to the person who leads the prayers in a mosque. In rural
areas it is often an elderly woman who takes on the role, and she
is called a *shara* (*sehara*).

The most common protective amulet is the *Khmassa*
(*khmessa*) in the form of a hand, representing the lucky number
five. According to information at Casablanca's Jewish Museum,

the *Khmassa* is of Carthaginian origin. The thumb on the Moroccan Jewish version depicts the head of a bird. The amulet is worn to give protection against harmful spirits and illnesses. The *Khmassa* is displayed in many Jewish Moroccan households and sometimes worn as a personal ornament.

Jewish craftsmen once had the monopoly on making metal *Khmassa* objects, frequently in silver. As for the more expensive ones, the quality was so good that they were often seen as works of art in themselves, being that they were so highly decorated. The trade is still carried on in the lower part of the Draa valley by Muslims today. However, most items are produced to satisfy the growing demand by tourists. The *Khmassa* in the form of a doorknocker is the most popular choice.

Shour (Sehore) falls into the category of sorcery and witchcraft. The belief in its power is shared equally between Moroccan Jews and Muslims. In the minds of the believers it is a form of evil that can be anywhere at any time: in a rock or stone, in everyday objects; for instance, clothing or the henna used to dye a woman's hair. It can also be in natural surroundings like forests and rivers.

It can be hidden in any object or room by spirits bent on getting revenge or wantonly bringing harm to someone. Food and drinks are very often used to hide or conceal substances containing *shour*. People thought to be affected by *shour* are those who act in a bizarre manner, or, in reality, suffer from a wide range of chronic physical and mental disturbances.

Believers think *shour* is the cause of many medical conditions. In the case of one young man who had lost his appetite and refused to eat regularly, leading to rapid weight loss and bizarre behavior, his family put the blame on a local girl to whom he was attracted. They accused her of visiting a *sahir* to ask him to put a spell on the young man so she could have his hand in marriage. It later became known that the young man was addicted to hashish.

Prior to modern medicine discovering what is thought to be the causes of diabetes, the symptoms were attributed to the practice of *shour*. The suspicion was that it had been placed in food or drink. Diabetes is a common hereditary factor in many Moroccan Jewish and Muslim families. Furthermore, countless individuals suffer from the disease through bad dietary habits and a lack of physical exercise.

259

An example of the use of *shour* was a disgruntled mother who disapproved of her son's choice of a woman to marry. After visiting a *sahir*, she went to her son's home and placed *shour*. During the following months, the son and his wife continually bickered and, at times, had heated arguments; something they had never done before. Eventually, on the advice of another family member, they called in the *fquih*, the imam or prayer leader from the local mosque. The *fquih* did a search of the couple's living room and found a *jedouel* (*jidwel*), a piece of paper with writing comprising of a spell. Another *jedouel* was immediately written by the *fquih* to break or counter the spell.

Later, working together, the couple came to the conclusion the spell had been placed by the mother, and, very soon, the peaceful and loving relationship between them was re-established.

The Jewish version of a *jedouel* is sometimes in the form a small piece of paper on which the Star of David is first drawn. Hebrew inscriptions are then written into the various triangles and the center. The inscriptions may also include names.

Some Moroccan Muslim versions contain a grid of squares, into which a series of crosses, Arabic inscriptions and some names might be written. In both cases the blood of an animal, usually a chicken, is sprinkled onto the paper.

A common way to deliver a spell is to leave it under the door of the intended victim, which instills fear and apprehension. With superstition and the fervent belief in *shour* and the evil eye so deeply entrenched within Moroccan culture, the desired effects can cause great anxiety and stress within the household of the *masshour*.

Feasts

Mimouna

The festival of Mimouna is celebrated on the last day of Passover and celebrates the regeneration of agriculture. The Moroccan Jews who left for Israel and elsewhere continue the custom each year and have passed it on to a new generation born outside of Morocco. It is a day when Jewish families visit each other's homes, bringing wishes for prosperity by citing the name of *Lalla Mimouna*, the *tzadik* recognized by both Moroccan Jews and Muslims as the distributor of wealth.

Casablanca's Jewish homes are decorated with sheaves of wheat and bunches of wild celery, sold on the streets by young Moroccan Muslims. Tables are laden with food specially prepared for the festival: milk, honey and several varieties of cakes. The evening meal is set aside to welcome the "new bread", prepared these days by Muslim women.

Tahdid

The Tahdid or the ritual of the sword is still practiced today with newly born Jewish boys. The ceremony ensures the new born child protection against the evil eye and the *djnoun* (spirits), until he has been circumcised, after which time he will have the protection of the Almighty. The mother also needs to be protected as she may be vulnerable and become depressed.

Immediately after the birth the midwife traces a magic sign, the *Khemousa,* on the baby's forehead with black smoke and ties a bag filled with herbs and grains to keep away the *djnoun*. A knife and salt are also placed under the baby's mattress for the same reason.

Each of the seven evenings before the circumcision takes place, parents, neighbors and friends gather at the home of the newly born. The evenings begin with singing, eating, drinking *mahiya*, leading to much merry making. At midnight, when the spirits are about, the all male ceremony of Tahdid commences. A man takes a sword and brandishes it along the walls, windows and doors while the others who are present sing psalms. When the guests have gone home, an older woman usually stays the night with the mother and child to chase away unwelcomed spirits.

The exact origins of the Tahdid are somewhat blurred, but the belief in the *djnoun* and the evil eye appears to have its roots in the Berber culture. Some Moroccan Jewish sources say the Tahdid originates from the *Song of Songs,* which mentions that King Solomon slept surrounded by sixty soldiers, each of whom held a sword. With 2,000 years of Jewish and Berber coexistence, the two cultures are so intertwined that a final conclusion about the origins of this ritual is difficult to reach.

261

Purim

The festival of Purim takes place sometime during the month of March. It is a joyous occasion when Moroccan Jewish children dress in costumes and attend the synagogue to listen to a reading of the scroll, or *megilla,* of Esther. The children also exchange presents, usually food. A special kind of Purim bread is baked and decorated with one or two boiled eggs, sometimes three, representing eyes. Purim commemorates the deliverance of the Jewish people living in Persia from Haman's plot to annihilate them.

Food

Anyone with doubts about the close links between the Moroccan Jewish culture and the Moroccan Muslim culture need only look at the way food is prepared and cooked. Apart from the fact that Jewish cooking is always kosher, there is little difference.

Moroccan mixed salads with the freshest of ingredients are a popular entrée in both Jewish and Muslim homes. Couscous is synonymous with Morocco. Both Jews and Muslims regularly have it on the table. The couscous is served and topped with portions of beef or lamb and a variety of seasonal vegetables. Pumpkin is always a particular favorite vegetable.

The Muslims living in the region of the Doukkala (south of Casablanca) have followed the Jewish custom of serving seven vegetables with couscous on special occasions such as wedding feasts. The Jewish meal served on *Shabbat*, known as *Davina*, has been adopted by some Muslim communities in the region around Talioune. It was very common among mixed communities around the country for the Muslim neighbors to assist in the preparation of the *Shabbat* meal.

The more exotic and richer dishes were introduced into Morocco by the Sephardic Jews, those expelled from Spain in 1492, and either adopted or adapted by the Moroccan population as a whole. One good example would be roast chicken cooked with prunes, which looks great and adds a very distinctive rich taste.

Another is *pastilla*, which is formed to look like small parcels, made of pastry and packed with either chicken or seafood. The chicken version is covered with a light sprinkling of powered sugar and cinnamon. The result is a very interesting, sweet and savoury dish.

Next are the much renowned Moroccan *gateaux,* a fine selection of pastries and cakes, first introduced by the Sephardic Jews in Fes centuries ago. These have become a firm favorite of Morocco's Muslims, reserved for very special occasions.

Both the Jewish and Muslim communities have a fondness for fish cooked in a variety of different ways. In the past, those Jews fortunate enough to be living close to the larger rivers like the *Oum ou Rbia* ate fish most Fridays. Coincidently, the fish is called *L'Hut L'Oued*, fish from the river. (*L'Hut* – pronounced L'Hoot).

Espadon (swordfish) is eaten by the Jews in the north, regardless of being caught with or without scales. Those in the south, however, only eat the fish if the scales are still present, as stipulated by Jewish dietary laws.

A favorite drink for Jewish men is the alcoholic drink, *mahiya,* which is normally made from figs and anise, but it can also be made from dates and anise or cherry and anise.

It is also used for medicinal purposes, especially for head and chest colds; pour four or five ounces, into a glass, and drink in one gulp. Allow the liquid to soothe away your discomfort in a matter of a few minutes. In the past, *mahiya* was more of a home brew, made by specialists. The modern equivalent is now produced by large commercial brewers but lacks the kick or punch of the original.

The region of Meknes is famous for its vineyards and wines. Stories told through the grapevine claim that the first vines were planted by Jews. The Gueroune brand of wine, guaranteed kosher, is the one preferred by Moroccan Jews, but today kosher wine for the Shabbat table can come from Israel to California.

The three things most offered as a welcoming snack when visiting a Moroccan home are a *berrad* (teapot) of Moroccan mint tea, argan oil and amlou. Argan oil comes from the fruit of the argan tree. The tree is indigenous to the regions in the south-west of Morocco, taking in the Anti-Atlas and the Souss. It is particularly evident when passing through the region of Haha, south of Essaouira.

The amber coloured oil is extracted from the kernel by grinding and pressing. It is served as a dip with freshly baked bread. Argan oil is also added to salads as a dressing and a variety of culinary dishes such as tagines. Companies and cooperatives involved in its production and sales have a lucrative market exporting the oil to Moroccan Jews in Israel, Canada, France and the United States, who it seems can not get enough of it.

Amlou is made by mixing argan oil with ground almonds and honey. Its paste-like substance is similar to peanut butter in texture and taste. It is normally spread on freshly baked bread.

One of the most popular Moroccan recipes requested by tourists is *harira*, a thick soup, served in all Moroccan Muslim households, especially during the holy month of Ramadan. Anyone coming to Morocco will at some time be introduced to the Berber dishes known as chicken *tagine* and lamb *tagine*, so called after the special cone shaped earthenware dish known as a tagine. It is used in the slow process of cooking these delicious, mouth-watering dishes, a complete meal.

20
Maariv

🌸 Morocco has a Jewish history and presence like none other. In this Muslim land, Jews are recognized along with Berbers and Arabs as one of the founding populations, and Jews have an uninterrupted history since the time of the Phoenicians. Jews have lived in Morocco longer than Western civilization has existed.

Reaching the close of this book and perhaps the beginning of your experience in Jewish Morocco, we recall the experience that Ron Hart narrates from Tangier. While sitting in synagogue one Shabbat after Minhah service waiting for sundown and the Maariv service to begin, he heard one man ask another, "Have you heard it yet?" It was a question about the hour and if it were time to start Maariv. He thought the question referred perhaps to a clock chiming. Not long afterwards he heard the *muezzin* calling across the streets of the city for the beginning of the Muslim evening prayer. The synagogue goers ended their conversations, moved back to their seats, picked up siddurs, and began the Maariv service. The call of the *muezzin* for evening prayer advised the Jewish worshippers that night had arrived.

In Morocco, Muslims have cooked Jewish foods and cared for synagogues and cemeteries while Jews have added richness to the cultural and spiritual life of this nation for more than two thousand years. Jews and Muslims have lived together, sometimes with strife but also with respect.

Morocco is a land to remember.

Glossary

Bled el Makhzen -- Historically referred to the territory under the control of the central government in Morocco.

Bled es-Siba -- Territory not under the control of the central government.

Caid -- Leader of a region or locality.

Hiloula -- An annual celebration of the life of a respected Jewish scholar and religious leader.

Kasbah -- A fortified stronghold, built to protect and house a local chief, *Caid* or Pasha and his family.

Ksar (pl. *ksour*) -- a fortified settlement with ramparts and towers.

Mahiya -- A distilled liquor drink made from figs.

Marabout -- White domed structure housing the tomb of a Muslim *siyyed* or holy man.

Medina -- An old walled town with narrow streets.

Megorashim -- Jewish newcomers to Morocco after the Expulsion from Spain.

Mellah -- The traditional name for the Jewish area in a Moroccan town or city.

Moshavim -- One of the main settlement movements in Israel with cooperative villages.

Palmeraie -- A palm tree grove.

Sephardim -- Jews from Spain.

Souk -- The market.

Tzadik -- A religious person recognized as having extraordinary spiritual qualities.

Toshavim -- Jews who were long settled in Morocco before the arrival of the Sephardim after 1492.

Zaouia -- Islamic religious fraternity.

Recommended Readings

- Ben-Ami, Issaachar. 1998. *Saint Veneration among the Jews of Morocco*. Detroit: Wayne State University Press.
- Bidwell, Margaret and Robin. 2005. *Morocco: The Traveller's Companion*. London: Tauris Parke Paperbacks.
- Deshen, Shlomo. 1989. *The Mellah Society: Jewish Community Life in Sherifian, Morocco*. Chicago: University of Chicago Press.
- Gottreich, Emily. 2007. *The Mellah of Marrakesh: Jewish and Muslim Space in Morocco's Red City*. Bloomington: Indiana University Press.
- Graham, R.B. Cunninghame. 1923 (Reprinted 2010). *Mogreb-el-Acksa: A Journey in Morocco*. Charleston: Nabu Press associated with Bibliolabs.
- Hart, Ron D. 2011. *Islam and Muslims: Religion, History and Ethnicity*. Santa Fe: Gaon Books.
- Jalfón de Bentolila, Estrella. 2011. *Haketía: A Memoir of Judeo-Spanish Language and Culture from Morocco*. Santa Fe: Gaon Books.
- Laskier, Michael M. 1997. *North African Jewry in the Twentieth Century: The Jews of Morocco, Tunisia and Algeria*. New York: New York University Press.
- Mann, Vivian B. 2000. *Morocco: Jews and Art in a Muslim Land*. New York: Merrell Publishers.
- Maxwell, Gavin. 1966. *Lords of the Atlas: The Rise and Fall of the House of Glaoua 1893-1956*. New York: E.P. Dutton & Co.
- Paloma, Vanessa. 2010. *The Mountain, the Desert and the Pomegranate: Stories from Morocco and Beyond*. Santa Fe: Gaon Books.
- Porch, Douglas. 1987. *The Conquest of Morocco*. London: Papermac (Macmillan).
- Stillman, Norman A. 1991. *The Jews of Arab Lands in Modern Times*. Philadelphia: The Jewish Publication Society.
- 1988. *The Language and Culture of the Jews of Sefrou, Morocco: An Ethnoliguistic Study*. Oxford: Journal of Semitic Studies.
- Zafrani, Haim. 2005. *Two Thousand Years of Jewish Life in Morocco*. New York: Sephardic House.
- Weich-Shahak, Susana. 2012. *Sephardic Romances from Morocco*. Santa Fe: Gaon Books.

Index

J

Jewish Cemeteries 126, 134
Jewish cemetery 67, 75, 79, 85, 87, 117, 120, 123, 126, 142, 143,
    147, 164, 168, 169, 173, 188, 190, 196, 208, 209, 217, 220,
    229, 230, 232, 235, 245, 249, 250, 253, 254
Jewish Joint Distribution Committee 35, 51, 115, 190
Jewish museum 8, 43, 49
Jinn 245, 257

K

Kal'at M'Gouna 214, 222
Karaite 233
Karaite Jews 233
Kasbah 83, 97, 104, 105, 152, 159, 171, 174, 177, 188, 191, 192,
    197, 205, 217, 220, 221, 222, 223, 234, 236
Khemis Arazane 184, 192, 193, 194
King Hassan II 7, 18, 28, 39, 107, 108, 163
King Mohammed V 18, 37, 250, 251
King Mohammed VI 18, 40, 221
kosher butcher 56
Kosher butcher 56
Ksar El Kebir 17, 91, 251
Ksour 156, 157, 203, 211, 221, 224, 225, 230, 231, 232, 233, 234,
    236, 237, 238, 239, 241, 266

L

Lag Baomer 88, 174, 216, 247, 251, 252, 253
Lalla Solica 142, 143, 251
Lalla Solica Hachwelle 142, 251
Larache 49, 90, 91, 93, 96, 97, 98, 99, 100, 251
La Sinagoga Nahom. *See also* Tangier
La Sinagoga Nahon 67

M

Madani El Glaoui 178, 179
Mahiya 35, 49, 53, 56, 99, 155, 179, 204, 210, 212, 245, 247, 260,
    262, 263
Marabouts 83, 138, 205, 231, 249

O

273

Gaon Books
Sephardic Traditions

1. Paloma, Vanessa. 2007. *Mystic Siren: Woman's Voice in the Balance of Creation*. ISBN: 978-0-9777514-5-7 (Paper).

2. Hamui Sutton, Silvia. 2008. *Cantos judeo-españoles: simbología poética y visión del mundo*. (Judeo-Spanish Songs: Poetic Symbolism and World View). ISBN: 978-0-9820657-0-9 (Cloth); 978-0-9820657-1-6 (Paper).

3. Toro, Sandra. 2010. *By Fire Possessed: Doña Gracia Nasi*. ISBN: 978-1-935604-06-8.

4. Paloma, Vanessa. 2010. *The Mountain, the Desert and the Pomegranate: Stories from Morocco and Beyond*. ISBN: 978-1-935604-03-7.

5. Toro, Sandra. 2011. *Princes, Popes and Pirates*. ISBN: 978-1-935604-11-2.

6. Jalfón de Bentolila, Estrella. 2011. *Haketía: A Memoir of Judeo-Spanish Language and Culture from Morocco*. ISBN: 978-1-935604-09-9.

7. Raphael David Elmaleh and George Ricketts. 2012. *Jews under Moroccan Skies: Two Thousand Years of Jewish Life*. ISBN: 978-1-935604-19-8.

8. Weich-Shahak, Susana. 2013. *Sephardic Romances from Morocco*. ISBN: 978-1-935604-10-5.

With the collaboration of:

Gaon Institute

A 501 c 3 organization that supports
tolerance and diversity
www.gaoninstitute.org

Gloria Abella Ballen
Ron Hart
Vanessa Paloma
Yehuda and Nurit Patt
and
Mordekhai Perez and Isaac Ohayon
for photographs of Morocco

Nurit Patt
for copy-editing assistance

CPSIA information can be obtained
at www.ICGtesting.com
Printed in the USA
BVHW072256161221
624066BV00002B/73

9 781935 604242